French or Foe?

French or Foe?

Getting the Most out of Visiting,
Living and Working in France

Polly Platt

First published in March, 1994 by Culture Crossings, Ltd., in London
reprinted in September 1994 and January 1995

First American edition published in June 1995
reprinted in January 1996
updated and reprinted in September 1996
reprinted in 1997

Second American edition published in January 1998
reprinted in 1999, 2000
11th reprinting, updated, in February 2002

ISBN 0-9646684-0-8

Printed in Canada by Groupe Beauchemin, Laval Canada

Distributed in the UK by Plymbridge Distributors
Estover, Plymouth, Devon, England
tel: 44 1752 202 301
fax: 44 1752 202 330

Distributed in the US by Distribooks
8120 N. Ridgeway Avenue
Skokie, Ill. 60076
e-mail: info@distribooks.com

To contact the author:
http://www.pollyplatt.com
e-mail: polly@pollyplatt.com

Cover design by Ian Heard
Illustrations by Ande Grchich
Layout by Marta Lyon

To Ande, who introduced me to the French

and to Andrea, who loved her French friends so much

FRANCE

AND THE FORMER FRENCH PROVINCES

Dunkerque
Calais
BELGIUM
ENGLISH CHANNEL
FLANDRES
PICARDY
Compiègne
ILE DE FRANCE
Reims
CHAMPAGNE
Verdun
LORRAINE
NORMANDY
Paris
ALSACE
MAINE
Chartres
BRITTANY
Rennes
Orléans
ANJOU
Angers
TOURAINE
Tours
BERRY
Bourges
Dijon
FRANCHE
BURGUNDY
Nantes
POITOU
Poitiers
SWITZERLAND
La Rochelle
-COMTÉ
AQUITAINE
AUVERGNE
Lyon
Grenoble
ITALY
Bordeaux
DAUPHINÉ
GASCONY
Cahors
Avignon
Toulouse
LANGUEDOC
Nîmes
PROVENCE
BÉARN
Pau
Carcassonne
Marseille
NAVARRE
ROUSSILLON
Perpignan
PYRÉNÉES
SPAIN
MEDITERRANEAN SEA

Acknowledgements

Books like this, full of real people, their ideas and emotions, don't happen alone. If it hadn't been for the enthusiasm of the working and "trailing" spouses, and the singles, transferred to France, I'd never have had the material, much less the idea, for a book. I'm grateful to all of the people who participated in Culture Crossings seminars for giving me the insights that led to it. Special thanks go to Marina Eloy, senior vice-president of human resources, European management, at J. P. Morgan, my first corporate client; to David Guia, a J. P. Morgan vice-president, and his wife Cathie, the very first participants, who assured me that this budding enterprise was important for English-speaking corporate transfers; and to Emily Borel, my assistant for years, who not only helped me with her business expertise in launching Culture Crossings, but also immeasurably with preparing material for this book.

I would like to thank especially those "alumni" who gave generously of their time for interviews and discussions: Mark Adamczyk, Charlotte and Kirk Coyne, Jeff Dore, Lola and Robert Elliott, Brigid and Henry Haley, Ron Issen, Ron Locklin, Cathie Lowney, Greg McNevin, Bruce MacDonald, Lou Martin, Robert Pingeon, Steve Skoczylas, Gail and Dixon Thayer, Larry Waisanen, Amanda and Nigel Waskett, and Julie and David Winn.

For observations on French management and the Franco-American cultural context, I am especially grateful to several leading French executives: Michel Barba, Claude Bébéar, Nicholas Bussière, Bertrand Collomb, Claude Courteaux, Philippe Eloy, Michel François-Poncet, Jean-Claude Guez, Georges Hervet, Didier Pineau-Valencienne, Philippe Quennouëlle and Elie de Rothschild.

Without the eagle eyes, patience and professional editorial competence of Marta Lyon, Julie Winn and Judson Gooding, the book would never have gotten to the printer, nor without the counsel of Karen Minke and

Richard Hill. The support and professionalism of the late Colin Corder were as helpful as they were cheering. For their kindness in reading the manuscript and making suggestions, I would like to thank also Emmanuelle and Brani Dalyac, Robert Elliott, Andrew Mason, Mark Meigs, Davis Platt, Judith Oringer and Steve Skoczylas. A book needs a title ! I'm indebted to Lee Greve for "French or Foe ?"

In particular I want to thank Ambassador Walter J. P. Curley for his continuing efforts to promote and improve mutual understanding between French and American people, in which I have had a small but enthusiastic part. For his gracious foreword to this book I am endlessly grateful.

Finally, despite the tragic war in his country of origin, my husband, Ande Grchich, had the patience and humor and charm to urge and encourage me to finish the book – and also to make the drawings.

Contents

Part IV: Office Life

Part V: The Other Side of the Mirror

Coda: Marvels for 16 Headaches

- Line-jumpers
- Waiters
- Phoning
- Dog Dirt
- Customer Service
- Peeing in Public
- Banking
- Getting Information

- Neighbors
- Not Being Introduced in Public
- Driving
- Smoking
- Lice
- Doctors
- Taboos
- Making Friends

Foreword

I had always believed that a *soul* was invisible. I am not so sure about that now that I have seen Polly Platt in action, and have read the manuscript of her book, *French or Foe?*

Polly Platt has some secret means of seeing into a soul clearly – like through a glass darkly – and capturing its hidden essence. She has also the magic gift of making visible, along with souls, such intangibles as psyches and instincts.

I do not know how she does it–by hypnotism or mind-reading–but the Platt method has harvested an impressive crop of information about French and American attitudes towards each other, as well as the related biases, beliefs, fears, passions, superstitions, and all manner of psycho-quirks that heretofore have crouched concealed in the high grass of the Gallic and Yankee persona.

I was first exposed to the phenomenon of Polly Platt when, as the American Ambassador to Paris, I invited her to speak to a group of our senior Foreign Service Officers in the Embassy. She was a smash hit. Her lectures to American corporate couples, diplomats, doctors, lawyers, military personnel – and, in fact, any Americans who have come to live in France, and also to French people of all kinds who have dealings with Americans – have become extremely popular events in the City of Light.

Polly Platt has identified and exorcised the devilish misconceptions that have fretted at the relationship between the French and the Americans. She has always spotted the eccentric – often hilarious – differences in our cultures which add a nice spice to the intercourse.

French or Foe? puts it all together: an extraordinarily useful, amusing and stunningly insightful analysis of all aspects of Franco-American communication. It is an elegant sort of "Everything-You-Ever-Wanted-to-Know-About-the-French-But-No-One-Knew-How-Tell-You." This book is an important contribution to a better understanding of the crucial but prickly partnership between two great countries who are historical allies.

Polly Platt not only knows how to probe and analyze; she knows how to write – with charm, wit, and craftsmanship. She uses a scalpel or a sledge hammer with equal skill and relish. You will have memorable pleasure and enduring reward in being exposed to Polly Platt's special insights. I envy you reading *French or Foe?* for the first time.

Walter J. P. Curley
U.S. Ambassador to France (1989-1993)
and to Ireland (1975-1977)

New York City
March, 1994

Introduction

On November 3, 1991, the London *Times*, which, unlike the hysterical London *Sun*, expects to be taken seriously, came out with a story that rocked France.

CITY OF LOVE DRIVES
FOREIGNERS TO DESPAIR

screamed the inch-high headline. Under it, the subhead, only slightly smaller, warned

Psychiatrist says Paris is
a mental health hazard

Parisians were shocked. Their beloved city – the only really livable capital in the world, the City of Love, the City of Light, the City of Thought, the City of Art and Beauty – was dangerous to mental health? It drove foreigners to despair? Really? Then why were there always such hordes of them around?

Well, foreigners are there because it's not only the most beautiful, elegant, glamorous and sexiest capital in the world, with the best restaurants, it's also the best managed and maintained. It offers clean, fast, reliable, comfortable public transportation, mail reaching French destinations overnight and delivered twice daily, clean streets washed down regularly, garbage collected daily, even Sundays and holidays, by Frenchmen in bright green uniforms dumping into brightly painted green trucks. Even the golden tops of the trash cans gleam with the fine shine of regular polishing. And its streets, subways and underground garages are *safe*.

The problem for the foreigners in the London *Times* story is that French people live there too.

And French people are different. Wonderfully different – and differently wonderful. The trick is in knowing what the differences are.

French or Foe? explores these differences, drawing on 25 years of living in Paris and eight years of experience in conducting cross-cultural seminars for over 1,000 English-speaking executives and managers – and their spouses – transferred to France. It's about their concrete problems and misunderstandings with each other and about what has helped in handling them: partly experience and knowledge of the codes, and partly being aware of the French "context", or what has formed "Frenchness." In a culture one or two thousand years old, depending on how you count, this is certainly presumptuous to try in a few pages. But we live in a century in a hurry: I've tried to do it anyway.

I had two objectives in writing it: the first was to publicize this live-witness information clearly, and as far as I know for the first time, for the benefit of other working newcomers and their spouses. Being prepared for something reduces the pain and anger level decisively.

The second is doing my part, I hope, in deflating the French-bashing parties around town. The title is the result of shock at the number of times I've heard Britons and Americans proclaim two things in a sort of hiss: "France is okay – but the French!" and "The French are rude, cold and arrogant." Despite the vituperation of Mark Twain and a few others beloved of Americans, the French are the U.S.'s oldest and only historically loyal ally. Like lots of friends, we have our differences from time to time. But Americans should remember that it was the French treasury, and experienced French naval and army leaders, that made the difference between the colonists' winning – or losing – their war against Great Britain. The French are generous, exhilarating friends to a great many of us. It behooves all of us to regard them as friends, and treat them as such. I hope this book will make its readers *want* to.

As for the British and the recurring friction between England and France, this rivalry goes back almost 1,000 years. Nevertheless, studies show that much of the anti-French feeling is the fault of the foreign-owned tabloid press and recurring phrases like "strutting, sex-obsessed frogs."

But let's get one thing straight right away. Whether tourist, business traveler or ex-pat executive, trying to function on any level in France with the same mechanisms as in other countries is like putting an Intel chip into a Motorola operating system. It simply doesn't work. French thinking, reactions, evaluations, approaches, procedures, behavior, attitudes, and rules are not what anglophones are used to, not to mention the Germans, Japanese and everybody else.

This doesn't matter so much if you just come to look at the paintings in the Louvre and enjoy the food, without bothering to interact with the people.

If you're living here for an extended length of time, it *does* matter. If your livelihood involves interacting with French people, it matters a lot. If you want to be able to really appreciate this unique country, it's crucial.

With Paris's location at a crossroads of Europe in a world becoming a "global village", more and more international managers have been moving here with their families. Lots of them, like the ones in the *Times* story, have a curious way of blaming the French for being French.

It's because the foreigners feel cheated. They don't find the France of their assumptions.

Talking about "the French," an American often sounds like a deceived husband. Same tone as in: "Dirty bitch! After all I did for her!" (Crossed the Atlantic during two world wars to save her, etc.) Or like a spurned lover – "How can she resist me? I'm the handsomest and the best – and who does she think she is, anyway?"

Others – most American and English executives and managers – feel distressed, surprised and bewildered.

Lou Martin, a surgeon and professor at Louisiana State University, spent a year in Paris on a sabbatical doing research on fat metabolism. He's one of a new generation of Americans confident of being able to take on a world they expect to be peopled by others very much like themselves, and who underestimate the effect of an unfamiliar environment on performance.

"I've always been used to dominating situations," he said, in his soft southern accent. "Or at the very least, coping with them. In Paris I was as helpless as a baby. It was deeply troubling."

Ron Issen, a Canadian with Williams and Stanford Business School degrees, had a similar shock when he came to Paris with the Indosuez Bank. "I speak French," he said, "so I thought working in France would be a matter of intelligence, common sense and good will. Unfortunately, that's not nearly enough."

"I was totally fed up and about to go back to England," said Louise Walker, a computer engineer with Honda in Paris. "Then I signed up for the Culture Crossings seminar and found out that what I perceived as nastiness and rudeness here isn't intended at all, but is just due to cultural difference."

"I've gotten to my present position by using my instincts," said the global head of human resources for a major pharmaceutical multinational. "In France, I've had to learn not to heed a single one, or get into terrible trouble."

"I thought France would be a piece of cake after Zaire, snakes in my bed and wood fires. But it was worse," said Joan Byrne, a former Peace Corps director.

"Five years in Japan did nothing to prepare me for France," said Robert Elliott, global director of systems information for Groupe Bull. "I had a much harder time."

From surprise and bewilderment it's a short leap to resentment, bitterness and animosity.

Judith Oringer, an American who is a French interpreter for the U.S. State Department, moved to France expecting smooth sailing all the way. After all, she knew the language and the culture, and had lots of French friends.

"I found myself getting furious at someone every day, ready to kill," she said.

What are the complaints?

In that London *Times* story, Anglo-Saxons, Scandinavians, Germans and Japanese reproached the French for being "hostile," "rude," "not helpful" and "cruel".

It's not true.

What is true is that French differentness is unexpected. The French image abroad is about as accurate a picture as you'd get if all you saw of a person was the back of his head. The Anglo-Saxon myth about the French is that they're luxuriating lotus-eaters, who are so busy making love and stuffing themselves with foie gras and champagne that they don't know the difference between a fax and a floppy disk. Lotus-eaters? Well, yes, everyone knows it's the land of the 4 F's – Food, Fashion, Fragrance and Frivolity.

While we're at it, the Anglo-Saxon mind runs on, seems to me there's a fifth F – Feminine. After all, what's their national symbol? A female in a Phrygian cap! So while the lotus-eaters of this rural, backward, feminine country are merrily reveling in their four F's, a savvy foreign yuppie will have no trouble closing a fast and easy deal... while he has a nice big helping of that foie gras and champagne himself, preferably while watching the naughty Folies Bergères. In other words, he'll be in heaven.

Thus, a Briton or an American, who wouldn't let a balance sheet leave his desk without being checked over several times by a team of experts, and if going to Japan, takes studies of the correct angle of various Japanese bows very seriously, sets off for France with little more than a list of good restaurants. When he runs into problems, his illusions are like dry tinder to the burning of his frustration... which flares into resentment and anger.

A minimum of research would have revealed the other and more significant symbol of France: the rooster, the cock of the walk, the male who controls the females, and crows from a summit even if it's the top of a dung heap.

He would then have been less traumatized discovering that, while indeed France abounds in the first three F's, which are about big bucks, the fourth and fifth are dangerous misconceptions. France is run by tough guys. I mean *men*. Even if the Prime Minister is a woman, she is given masculine gender: she is *Madame le Ministre** and her pronoun in news articles is *il* (he). In a group of thousands of women, the presence of one solitary man makes them collectively masculine – *ils*. The French are world masters of higher mathematics. Their telephone computer network, the Minitel, offering thousands of services for everything from airplane reservations to weather and financial information, is the first of its kind and is being bought up internationally. Their TGV, the fast train, goes at 300 kilometers an hour and more, and hasn't had a serious accident in 15 years of carrying 300 million people. Their nukes are second to none, except in numbers. Their Exocet missiles, sold to Argentina, almost lost the English the Falklands War. They drive their cars like lethal weapons and one of their most formidable army corps, the Foreign Legion, is made up of an awful lot of tough guys. Their three movie idols, Jean-Paul Belmondo, Alain Delon and Gérard Depardieu, are men who frequently play roles of very macho Robin Hood-type gangsters. Particularly ingenious criminals are treated like heroes by the media, provided they don't hurt anyone.

Above all, the French had two centuries of running the universe themselves, until not so very long ago.

Just how different the French are begins to come through when foreigners find out that a Frenchman spent the fall of 1991 rowing – rowing! – across the Pacific, alone, with just two oars between him and the vast deep; and that the results of a national vote in 1992 for the two most popular people in the country were two octogenarians – a priest, the Abbé Pierre, who thundered about helping the homeless poor, and a sailor, the late Commandant Cousteau, who thundered about protecting the oceans.

And what about this, that they pay 20 percent more taxes than Americans to provide child care, health insurance and higher education for everyone – and yet, though the recession is beginning to be felt at this writing in 1994, they are still the world's fourth largest economy.

The French would have to be different from everyone else to have lifted and provoked the human spirit so mightily for the last 1,000 years as artists, revolutionaries, explorers, writers, poets, philosophers, kings, emperors, architects; to have created an atmosphere where math is fun and where mathematicians and scientists, from Curie to Montagnier, discoverer of the AIDS virus, and writers, from Anatole France to Albert Camus, have carried off countless Nobel prizes.

* This practice has been somewhat modified lately

In fact, you need to go through Alice's Looking Glass and learn a new set of codes, values, beliefs and facial and body signals to trigger French kindness and generosity, and above all, their zest and humor. You have to learn to reason differently. You have to know *their* rules of good manners and behavior to understand that it is the foreigner, not the French person, who is being rude in their country.

Business people who don't catch onto their rules lose the deal. The deal is almost never the top priority for a French businessman. Managers dropped into France without preparation might as well be playing Blind Man's Bluff. They go around in circles, not knowing what they're bumping into or how to deal with what is going on around them, and are only marginally aware of the corns they're continually stepping on. All they do know is that they're helpless and miserable. Their spouses, unable to cope with the local scene, are depressed, if not having a nervous breakdown. They join the nearest group practicing the popular sport of French-bashing.

And often demand early repatriation. According to a survey by the Society for Human Resource Management and the Commerce Clearing House, 10 to 30 percent of American managers abroad are "expatriate retention failures." Other surveys have put the rate at 40 percent, a devastating loss to a company, which, when the manager has been moved with his family for three years, has invested up to a million dollars in the move.

On the plane for Paris, the savvy executive needs to remind himself:

- I won't take anything personally.
- I won't judge.
- The devastating soul of the Parisian, with its genius for creating delights for the senses and the spirit, as well as major scientific inventions, is hidden. It lies deep within an armored tank of strict procedures, protected from strangers by the heavy artillery of banter, criticism, aggressiveness and sarcasm.
- And if I really provoke him... arrogance and insults.
- I must acquire special weapons – knowledge, a change in perception, flexibility – to disarm the tank and discover and manage the treasures inside.
- I must keep my head, my confidence, my own values and my sense of humor. And consider it a thrilling adventure... into myself, as well as into France.

"I knew the language and the culture, but not the codes," said Judith Oringer, after taking the Culture Crossings seminar. "The codes are the most important thing for feeling well in France. That's when you find out how extraordinary and wonderful the French are."

There are other ways to find out, usually some kind of an emergency. John Gagnon, professor of sociology at the State University of New York, was quoted in the *International Herald Tribune* about what happened to him in Tours with a burst appendix in the middle of the night. A doctor came to see him immediately, arranged for him to be taken to a hospital, which, not having the necessary equipment, had him transferred to another hospital. The operation cost a sixth of what it would have in the U.S. "There is more to be learned from the French than lessons in culture and good food and drink," said Gagnon. "We Americans ought to learn how they deliver responsive, skilled, humane, and economical health care."

While *French or Foe?* can be dipped into at random according to chapter headings, it's designed to lead you gradually through the early steps involved in dealing effectively with French people in business and in daily life, first superficially and then more profoundly, until you know enough about the game to play it brilliantly and exuberantly yourself, for high stakes, in the workplace.

France is not only the crossroads but the linchpin of Europe, in the sense that it is in some ways like all the other countries, yet totally different. The French are Latins, but the Italians and Spanish often complain bitterly about them. They are also Franks, an ancient German tribe, but the Germans throw up their hands at them. And like the English, they're Celts (the Gaulois), but they've been fighting the "Hundred Years War" with the English since the Norman invasion in 1066.

The French have been called "the Chinese of Europe." Their paradoxes and contradictions, which they delight in, are such that the road to understanding them is as full of pitfalls as of exhilarating discoveries.

In other words, if you can make it in France, you can make it anywhere else afterwards, with much less effort.

French or Foe? is for foreign managers and executives and their spouses transferred to France, diplomats, professional people and anyone else who is interested in having an agreeable and successful stay in what former U.S. Ambassador to France, Walter J.P. Curley called this "marvelous, mysterious, elegant, enigmatic country."

As with the process of adapting to any foreign culture, but particularly to the culture of France, you find out an awful lot about your own culture, and your own "mental software" – and about who you really are.

The rewards are enormous.

A few notes to the reader...

• The use of the third person singular pronoun has become an issue of political correctness in American English, presenting authors with a quandary. Since the all-inclusive "one" sounds pompous to us, I don't know how it can be resolved. For reasons given earlier, it would be grotesque to use "she" as a generic for the human species in a book about the French. I've therefore used the Biblical "he" throughout, taking my cue from Webster (New Collegiate Dictionary 1973). Thus "he" is "used in the generic sense when the sex of the person is unspecified," while "she" is "used to refer to one regarded as feminine."

• I beg the reader's indulgence for generalizations and for lumping together all the citizens of various countries, neglecting the regional differences. The "French" refers to the citizens of mainland France, particularly those to be found around Paris; "English" and "Briton" to, above all, Londoners, and "Americans" to citizens of the USA of mostly northern European descent.

• Americans, Canadians, Britons, Australians and South African whites share many reactions to "the French", cross-culturally speaking. Alas for writers, there isn't a generic term for this general group of cultures. My non-solution for this is to refer to them sometimes, like General de Gaulle, as "the Anglo-Saxons," sometimes, like Churchill, as "the English-speaking peoples" and sometimes by their specific names.

• Finally, to French readers: rare are those who gladly suffer comments about their culture from an outsider, particularly when concerning the workplace. "The way things are done around here" feels right in one's own country. The point of the book is not who is right or who is wrong, because both cultures are right, according to their own "mental software." The goal instead is to make clear what precisely the perceptions of difference are that give trouble, and how Anglo-Saxons can understand them from the French point of view. If one thing is sure, it's that you don't understand another culture just by living in it; you need to find out the reasons behind different procedures and thought processes. After this comes recognition that other cultures do some things better than you do. Then comes the possibility of the richly creative intercultural synergy described by the Anglo-Saxon executive-veterans of the French workplace in Chapter 17.

I beg French people to take the sometimes belligerent comments of distressed, uncomprehending Anglo-Saxon managers in this spirit. In Part V of this new edition (page 237) French people express some opinions about life in the U.S.A.

If you have comments or travel anecdotes, please send them to me via fax (331 455 59186) or e-mail (platt@club-internet.fr).

Part I

Starting Off on the Right Foot

Chapter 1

Six Codes

Rudeness is in the Eye of the Beholder

Vivre en société est un jeu; il faut donc en connaître les règles et les servitudes. (Living in a community is a game; therefore one must know the rules and obligations.)

Duc de Brissac
Former director
Schneider-Westinghouse

Code 1: Don't Smile!

It begins at the airport.

The public French face is closed. The grim-looking passport control policeman probably ignores your "hi." The taxi driver and the hotel concierge may look stern or grumpy. That doesn't mean you look or talk funny, or that they hate Americans, or Britons or Asians, or that their mother has just died. Nor does it mean they'll cheat you. They're just being French.

"We just visited Brussels," said Denise Fiske, a pretty blond nurse who came to France from Chicago with her husband, Bret, a chemical engineer with Eli Lilly. "What a different world! People just keep smiling! They're friendly! You can touch the clothing in the store! The Parisians treat everybody as if they're worthless, and I take it personally. I'd hate to go home now and say I just don't like it here – I put a lot of pressure on myself to like this place – but, well, I'm pretty pessimistic right now."

"We're just back from Amsterdam," said Larry Waisanen, vice president and controller of Lafarge Coppée, the world's second largest cement producer. "It felt so good. We couldn't figure out why – and then realized that it was because everyone was so friendly. To each other. To us. Smiling. Paris certainly takes getting used to after St. Paul. And we've been here almost three years."

Europeans react to this in various ways.

The British shrug. "Bloody frogs don't know how to behave. But what can you expect? After all, we've won all the wars since 1598."

The Italians are disappointed, because they sent two Medicis north to be Queens of the French in 1540 and 1600, with forks and other niceties to teach them manners, and it obviously didn't click. Too bad.

The Germans, envious of the French reputation as models of civilized behavior, are secretly pleased.

But Americans are stung, deep inside the place where their self assurance lives. They take it personally.

No matter where they're from, no matter how powerful or underprivileged, whether strangers or acquaintances, Americans deal with each other and everyone else in the world in a manner known as "friendly."

The French don't. "Stranger" (*étranger*) means "danger" (*danger*). The two words rhyme in French too. Smiling at strangers is simply not part of French culture. There isn't even a word in the language meaning "friendly" with its resonance of spontaneous warmth toward everybody. *Amical*, the closest French word to "friendly", can only be defined in terms of what the person referred to is not: if a person is *amical*, all it means is that he's not hostile. So the first assumption to get rid of is that the world at large expects a smile, and owes you one in response. Just because you're there.

Nothing separates Americans and French people more than their smile codes. No French ways freeze Americans in Paris more, nothing reinforces the "rude arrogant cold" Frenchman label more. French people smile a lot, they have wonderful smiles. Nothing pleases them more than an event of some kind to smile at. It has been said of them, as of their ancestors the Romans, that you can keep them happy with *du pain et du cirque* – full bellies and a spectacle to laugh at. The thing to hold onto is that you can always get any Frenchman to smile eventually, even a stranger, if you know how.

However, they don't smile blandly as they walk down the street. They don't smile without a reason.

Philippe Labro, a well known French journalist and television figure, had a hard time learning the local rules during a summer workshop at the University of Virginia. In his book *L'Etudiant Etranger*, he tells of being summoned before the Student Council and reprimanded for not saying "Hi" as he passed by other students on campus. Summoned a second time, he said plaintively, "What's the trouble now? I always say 'Hi' when I run into people – strangers! – crossing the campus!" "Yes," said the chairman, "but you don't smile when you say it."

This sort of thing is very odd for French people. You're free to sweep your eyes over French people if you like the look of them, on a bus or at a party, but not to smile if your eyes meet, which is an American's automatic way of showing he means no harm. (If you want to start a flirtation, that's different, see Chapter 13.)

For strangers to smile at each other in Paris, there has to be some kind of incident involving them both, and not just stumbling into someone's stare. Smiles usually come if you bump into each other by mistake, and they come instantly if you're both caught in the same pickle (two cyclists pedaling down a one-way street the wrong way, suddenly confronted with advancing policemen), or if he rescued you from one... that is, if you weren't smiling beatifically to begin with. You have to be in sync, deadpan, as you navigate through Paris streets, if you want to play this game, and Parisians are playing games all day – but only with other deadpans. The key is that the face changes. If you were smiling to begin with, where is the fun? Where is the recognition of complicity?

I have finally perfected the French *mine d'enterrement* (funereal expression) and the quick swing to a *tête ludique* (jocose look) to such an extent that I now get smiles from strangers of both sexes and all ages all the time. A recent smile triumph came at the market as I was scooping up some lettuce leaves neglected by the cashier as she racked up the various vegetables from my shopping basket. My self-mocking smile at the Frenchman behind me brought an instant twinkle from him, as if saying, "Well, it does look a little silly, but I agree that it is terrible to waste things, even lowly lettuce leaves."

The same day, jamming my bike brakes loudly, because the car just in front of me had stalled, brought a wide grin from one of the female driver's daughters in the back seat: "You can see how it is, my mother still can't drive!"

Denise Fiske, the pretty blond nurse from Chicago, began loving Paris after about six months. She mastered the *mine d'enterrement* and reaped marvels of smiles.

De-smiling your public face is one thing. Even more excruciating is getting rid of the expectation of the reflection of your smile on the face of the person you're buying your *baguette* (bread) from, or that you're being introduced to, or introducing yourself to. Our cult of friendliness has made the reflection-smile seem like a fundamental right. You may not think so until it's happened to you, but smiling at someone who doesn't smile back can be catastrophic for Americans. None of us escapes a violent reaction of injury. We're inspired to strike back in various ways. Like blowing up the Eiffel Tower.

It's the first symptom of a disease American ex-pats are particularly susceptible to, known as the Battered Ego, or I'm no good, what happened?

Even now, after over 20 years in France, a no-smile deadpan can trigger panic in me in certain situations. When I was doing a story for the monthly *International Management* on what the French thought about the sudden German giant next door, after the fall of the Berlin Wall, I signed up for a Stanford Business School alumni luncheon as a good source of able French Yuppies to interview. I didn't happen to know any of them. When I spotted a likely target, I sidled up to him, smilingly, full charm ahead, and explained my mission. A dumbfounding scowl spread over his handsome young face. I contemplated flight. But – the story! Minutes went by, oh so slowly as I babbled on about the material I needed. After about six of them, the scowl gradually subsided. He invited me to join him at his table. Introduced me to the others. After about half an hour, he smiled! They all did! I got a super story. And incidentally, had a wonderful time.

"Smile! Look cheerful when you go out in public!" says the American mother to her toddler. So we grow up into automatic smilers. Our politicians have to be able to grin. Our Presidents usually have the crowning grin of all – except Nixon. And look what happened to him. Roosevelt, Truman, Eisenhower, Kennedy, Carter, Reagan, Bush and Clinton – great grinners all.

Not French politicians. François Mitterrand won two presidential elections looking remote and grim. Talk about a *mine d'enterrement!!* When I came across a news photo of him grinning – in Texas, sitting next to President Bush at the theatre – I showed it to a seminar of French managers going to the U.S. and, for a gag, asked them who it was. They didn't recognize him.

Agence France Presse – Photos A.F.P.

Smiling is not taught in French families, let alone grinning. French parental education, along with the school system, is about the most rigorous and demanding on the planet (see Chapter 9), but smiles are not included. You might say it's one of the few things they're not constantly nagged about.

The result is that even socially, when you're introduced, you're greeted with an empty stare. This is when the Battered Ego comes down with a Bomb the Tower fever.

I first discovered the Empty Stare when I was 24, free-lancing around Europe for a Philadelphia paper and having a whirl of fun in various capitals. I hit Paris with letters of introduction prompting invitations to glamorous parties. I went to six of them. At each one I was introduced to the same young people, and each time they looked at me with a blank face and eyes of ice. I searched the mirror for signs of leprosy or smallpox. At the seventh party, they smiled. Chatted. Were delightful. Invited me to other parties. Suggested I join a group of them going skiing.

For the French, this is perfectly normal.

"What is there to smile about, when you don't know someone?" says my French son-in-law, François-Xavier Deniau. "That person is a stranger until you know him. One must be on one's guard with strangers. *Méfiant..*"

Jenifer Armand de Lille, a Bostonian married to a Frenchman, says she was given two pieces of advice from her aristocratic mother-in-law after she got married: "She called me in for tea and a talk, and told me, 'If you want the French to respect you, never drive a flashy car. And don't smile until you've been here for 10 years.'"

My son-in-law is a charming young diplomat and the proud father of four sons, for whom he does not ration his smiles, nor for Sasha, my daughter. We talk about this.

"You Americans have banalized the smile," he says. "Americans smile all the time, always the same. For us there must be a reason. There is a different smile for a friend, for a joke, for a child, for love. For good luck – and for bad luck. And in between, no smiles."

He pauses a moment. "When I am introduced to another man, if he smiles, then I think to myself he is one of three things: he is making fun of me, he is hypocritical or he's very stupid." Then he adds, "If it's a woman I'm meeting for the first time and she smiles at me, there's a fourth possibility – she wants to flirt."

The dangers of smiles and laughs were tackled by the magazine *Ressources Humaines* in its July 1989 issue. It reported that smiling, or laughing, was taking a risk – the risk of being oneself, and of giving the other person opportunities to break taboos. Quoting the firm CREAPAC, the magazine offered this chart of 13 smiles:

SMILE TYPE	MEANING
Self-denial	Failure, fatalism
Self-mockery	Submissiveness, provocation
Ephemeral	Weakness, cowardice
Stopper	Effort at de-emphasis
Flattering	Effort at seduction
Courteous	Effort at communicating
Convivial	Shared pleasure
Expansive	Desire to inspire others
Possessive	Condescending, sign of ownership
Mocking	Effort to discredit the other
Aggressive	Effort to destabilize the other
Cynical	Show superiority
Sadistic	Show dominance

Listing the smiles in order of the least to the most involvement with the person one is smiling at, the magazine advised utmost caution with smiles received or given in the upper and lower boxes. The article went on to quote a long list of eminent executives on the subject of whether smiling and laughing is *sérieux* (serious, very serious) or not, and appropriate at work.

I mentioned the smile factor to the group of French managers being relocated to the U.S. I added that they really must make an effort to smile on meeting people over there.

Their faces took on expressions of utmost gloom.

"That is impossible," said Mark Toussaint, a handsome 45-year-old engineer who was going to head a General Motors plant in Ohio (a place the group referred to as Oeeo). "I cannot do that."

"Why not?" I asked. "You laugh at my jokes here, you have a wonderful smile."

"But that is different. To smile at someone I do not know, when I am introduced, that would be ... " he hesitated.

"That would be what?" I encouraged him.

"Ah, that would be hypocritical."

Hypocrites are particularly despised by Frenchmen. The word is automatically applied to the English, and on a par with the two worst French insults: *mal élevé* (bad mannered, not knowing how to behave, a shocker in France) and *pas professionnel* (not professional).

I only understood Mark Toussaint's reluctance to smile automatically when I read about the kind of French people who do, and that the language has a special contemptuous word for it. In court, being prosecuted for insider trading, a shady businessman was described as having a *sourire de circonstance* – a fake, or hypocritical smile demanded by the occasion.

But the label of hypocrisy is not the only indignity awaiting the complacent smiler.

Nicolas Bussière, the young boss of Desgrandchamps, a printing plant in Paris, came back from two years working in America full of smiles for his staff and workers. He soon heard that they were concerned for his mental health, pointing to their temples with a spiraling forefinger.

"They thought I'd gone nuts over there," he said. "So I had to stop. Personally, I like the smiling in the U.S., even if it is superficial. It's hard for Frenchmen to come back here. They often feel depressed."

I went around the plant with him to have a good look at non-smiling greetings. He shook hands with all of the workers and indeed, did not smile at them. But he looked far from stern. He wore the pleasant expression of an American alone in public.

Some Americans skip town because they don't want to measure their smile with a slide rule. They miss all the fun of the big day when you figure it out, and, like the mists of Avalon suddenly lifting, you're in sync with the French. You feel *bien dans votre peau* (well in your skin) – and – what's happening? They're smiling at you!

Besides, you've got the French to thank for being aware of the friendliness and spontaneity you took for granted in Peoria!

Meanwhile, don't give up on them – or yourself.

Code 2: Flirt!

The delight of French men and women in each other's company is expressed in a ballet which needs a whole chapter to celebrate (Chapter 13). For now, on arrival, just keep the delight in mind, and if you can't find your luggage at the airport, look for an official who is a member of the opposite sex to help you. Flirt! Don't smile – do it with your eyes. Your baggage will show up in a jiffy.

Ande, my Serbian husband, came to France at 18 and absorbed Frenchness into his bones. I watch him checking in at the airport when his luggage is at least 10 kilos overweight. He goes to the prettiest airline checker, works his eyes, puts his foot on the scales till they register 100 kilos overweight, and works his eyes again at the agent.

She bursts out laughing and waves him through without charging him a cent.

The caressing look of the French stranger of the opposite sex is a compliment, and, for a woman, without any of the sordid undertones of hard-hat catcalls in New York City. Picking up on it, basking in it as it washes over you, and looking back (no smiles!) is part of the French person's "secret garden". It gives a lift to the day to both of you, without sequel (unless you want one) and is much missed by French people in foreign countries.

The Look is often misunderstood as one more proof of French "rudeness" and has soured many a stay from the start. Basking in it doesn't come naturally to Britons or Americans or most northern Europeans.

That this can – and must – be considered a compliment, galvanized a pretty and well-groomed but rather pale, self-conscious young American redhead, a computer systems expert who intellectualizes everything: "I noticed the looks and was suffering. I thought they were critical – that I looked awful," she said. "Now I can enjoy them."

David Guia, a good-looking young vice president at J.P. Morgan, said he was bothered by being stared at. "I take the Métro," he said, "wearing a French suit and French shoes and walking as much like a Frenchman as I can, and still they stare at me!"

"Of course," I said. "Enjoy it. They're staring at you because you're so handsome. Otherwise, they'd ignore you. That's worse!"

Code 3: Use the Ten Magic Words!

If stranger means danger in French, there are plenty of good reasons for this, about 2,000 years of them.

Ferocious things have been happening to French people since they first started living in the six-sided geographical shape that French first-graders learn to call the Hexagon. Ruthless strangers invaded their earliest ancestors, the Celts, from all sides, starting with Julius Caesar. After about 300 years of Roman occupation, savage barbarians from the East began hundreds years of burning, pillaging and raping. The Goths, Visigoths,

Franks, Burgundians and most terrifying of all, the Huns, came in wave after terrifying wave, followed in the 8th and 9th centuries by the fearsome Vikings from the North. The Hexagon didn't fare much better from the English in the 14th century: the Hundred Years War meant nothing less than another century of raping, pillaging, burning. Three German invasions in 70 years, between 1870 and 1940, did not help to make the French foreigner-friendly.

The wars and invasions came on top of famines and floods. There were periodic outbreaks of the catastrophic Black Death, the Plague, which exterminated a third of the French population between 1340 and 1440. If you were a farmer in 1350 whose four sons had been killed off by a germ in a traveler's backpack, and only one son remained to help you plow the fields, chances are you wouldn't welcome the next human shapes looming up over the rise of the hill.

Communication between strangers in France has been honed over the centuries to a system of ratified codes. Foreigners are to be shunned, and as they give themselves away instantly by their ignorance of the codes, nothing is easier. Foreigners who know the codes, however, immediately shed most of their alarming foreignness.

I wonder if a lot of the "rude cold arrogant Frenchmen" complaints don't come from foreigners on the Champs Elysées – a place now avoided as much as possible by the French, swarming as it is with threatening-looking strangers – who accost a Parisian hurrying away from them with the equivalent in their language of, "Hey, Mister, where's the Eiffel Tower?"

The Frenchman, taken aback, feeling attacked, in shock, doesn't understand the foreign language, nor the mangled pronunciation of France's most famous monument. Eyebrows raised, eyes staring, expression of stone, he presents a blank mask disguising non-comprehension and fright, which the foreigner interprets as coldness and arrogance. The foreigner shrugs, says to himself, "Everyone told me they were like this," and asks someone else, the same way. Finally he goes back to Liverpool, or Denver, or Melbourne with numbing tales of French arrogance and rudeness.

The code guaranteed to avoid this kind of incident is the Five Magic Words. It is possibly the most important phrase in the whole French language:

"Excusez-moi de vous déranger, monsieur (or madame)..." ("Excuse me for disturbing you, Sir, or Madam...")

This is the charm that warms the hearts of impatient Parisians on the street, of inquisitorial telephone operators, and even of those most preposterously maddening of creatures, bureaucrats in post offices and Police Headquarters. The Five Magic Words click with Frenchmen like the responding smile with Americans.

Bombs may fall or the house catch fire, but French people will not shorten this formality by so much as a syllable. In an Yves Montand-Simone Signoret detective film called *Police Python 357*, a detective, having just discovered that Yves Montand, the monster they've been hunting, is about to blow up the city, rushes to a phone booth for orders from his boss, who's at home. When the boss's wife answers the phone, though the city is only seconds from destruction, the detective starts the conversation, *"Bonsoir, madame, excusez-moi de vous déranger...."*

Beretta in hand, a thief robbing a gas station in Paris, according to *Le Parisien* of September 24, 1993, began his holdup with this indispensable code: *"Excusez-moi de vous déranger, mais j'ai besoin de fric."* ("Excuse me for bothering you, but I need some dough.")

The new CEO takes over, using the Magic Words (Plantu, *Le Monde*)

Approached with this code, a Frenchman, right away reassured that the intruder knows how to behave (is *bien élevé*), is less *méfiant* (suspicious) and understands that this is a helpless, harmless brand of foreigner. He can concentrate on deciphering the miserable butchery of the desired destination's name. (The Eiffel Tower, for instance, is the Tour Eiffel, pronounced Tour Eefell, stress more on second syllable than first.) No raised eyebrows, no blank stares. Possibly, in this case, stranger to stranger, the Frenchman will smile encouragingly. And chances are he'll not only tell the foreigner how to get there but also offer to show him the way.

"The Five Magic Words work wonders. I use them all the time," says Julie Winn, a former copy editor, who moved to Paris with her husband, David, director of a bank.

"Exactly," says Rebecca Theobald. Rebecca, on leave from Digital Equipment, "trailed" her spouse, Chuck, transferred to Paris by Federal Express. "We're here with a little six-month-old baby. I'd heard all these tales about the 'rude arrogant cold' French and my experience couldn't be more different. People are always helping me with the stroller to get onto a bus or the subway."

French dietetics entrepreneur Alexandre Chakarian says, "The code is indispensable in France, I use it all day long."

If you add after the Five Magic Words, five more, *"J'ai un problème"* ("I have a problem"), you qualify as a person to be respected and helped to the very limit of the Frenchman's possibilities.

You can use the Words in your struggle with the French administration, and in any store. The storekeeper or salesgirl may spend half an hour trying to match a blouse to a skirt, find the exact kind of light bulb for your chandelier or screwdriver for your reading glasses.

Alex Russell, a Scot, former global marketing director for Groupe Bull, said that uttering the Ten Words in the Gare du Nord (North Station) changed everything. "I had a reservation – my secretary had made it – but the reservation slip was missing. I went to the conductor, said, *'Excusez-moi de vous déranger, monsieur, mais j'ai un problème'*, and he responded instantly, found out what was the matter, and came back with my reservation."

Ruth Blakeslee, a Renault spouse, went to the grocer for some dill. She didn't speak any French, and hadn't even looked up the word for dill in the dictionary. The Ten Magic Words, along with her body language, were so irresistible that the grocer turned the store upside down for her and eventually came up with canned dill, fresh dill and dried dill.

The Words even work sometimes in big department stores, but don't count on it. Department stores seem to have a special effect on French employees. Their concept of "customer service" is often described as customer disservice. Some seem to exult as they hasten to tell you they don't have whatever it is that you want. Your pulse will race less and your adrenalin stay calmer if, when there, you reflect on how nice it is that there is something we do so much better, so easily.

Code 4: Add "Monsieur" or "Madame" to "Hello"

Keep in mind that you must always say hello and goodbye to all of the strangers, including cashiers, that you have an exchange with in stores. In small shops you declare a firm general hello and goodbye on entering and leaving. The form is rigid: *Bonjour, monsieur* (or *madame*) and *au revoir, monsieur* (or *madame*). The *au revoir* can be varied with *bonne journée* (good day) or *bonsoir* (good evening). Never drop the madame or monsieur. "Madame" is fine for any girl over 16, it means "my lady", not necessarily a married lady.

Whatever you do, DON'T ever say *messieursdames*.

"I could see a noticeable change in people's attitude at the office and elsewhere when I started adding monsieur and madame," said Jack Brock, CEO Europe of Wind River Systems. "They should put it in your passport."

If you're on first name terms with someone, then replace the monsieur or madame with the first name. Always. As in, " *Bonjour, Solange*," or "*Au revoir, Didier*."

Code 5: Shake Hands !

An English bank director in France on a stricter time budget than most told me, in some desperation, that he clocked 20 minutes of handshaking per day for most of his personnel.

Handshaking in French offices is to a "hello" as ice cream to apple pie. It's Latin, a way of touching and being close, yet formal. It makes all the difference and is missed if not there. You shake hello and you shake goodbye. *Bonjour, Monsieur* (shake) and *Au revoir, Monique* (shake). A firm, short shake. No pumping, no finger crunching. The person of higher rank extends his hand first.

A Du Pont de Nemours human resources manager (I'll call her Colette) told me, "Jack R. never shakes hands when he comes into my office. And he always wants something outlandish. I feel insulted, and much less like helping him."

I told Jack about this. "So that's what's wrong!" he said. "I thought it was because I was being too persistent – you know what I mean, Colette is one cute piece of work – or that she didn't like my Texas boots!"

You shake hello the first time you see someone each day, whether it's in his office, at a meeting or in the hall. You shake goodbye on your way home. If it's a business visitor to your office, you shake when he arrives and when he leaves.

James Q., a computer whiz straight out of Silicon Valley, slumped into a chair for the second meeting of a seminar. James hadn't had much experience with handshaking in California and was thoroughly fed up.

"Last week you told us we had to shake hands with hello!" he growled. "So I shook hands with my boss the next day right away when I saw him, and then the next time about an hour later. He looked at me oddly, so the third time I really took his hand and gave it a good yank twice, up and down. And then you know what he said? 'But we already saw each other today, James.' What's that supposed to mean?"

It's not enough to know that the first hello of the day gets a shake, and only the first. You have to keep track. If you forgot that you shook in the morning, and extend your hand in the afternoon, you'll invariably trigger, "But we already saw each other today."

For the French guys and dolls at the office who've known each other for ages, double-cheek kissing often replaces the handshakes. As a foreigner, you would do well to skip that, as well as the *tu* form for "you" (see Chapter 16 for more on *tu-vous*).

Outside the office, whether a shake goes with the *bonjour, monsieur* or *bonjour, Monique* is more subtle, or *nuancé*, as the French would say. With the barman at a café, no, unless you've been a regular customer for years. Otherwise, people you know socially, yes, always, on the street or anywhere else; people with academic degrees that you're dealing with for one reason or another, such as your lawyer or tax consultant, yes. Service and tradespeople, maids, concierges and repair men, no.

Code 6: Watch Out at the Door!

In France, a door in front of you, approached in tandem or group, is not to be swept through first just because you got to it first. It's a test of your savoir-faire. Like the formula you use for signing a letter, which depends on who you are and what rank and sex, and to whom the letter is addressed, and their rank and sex (there are 38 choices), you must consider who else is approaching the door with you and their rank compared to yours, and their sex.

It's called the *bataille de la porte* (the battle of the doorway) and also takes place at the elevator. If you're the junior one, insist firmly that the others pass through first, or you'll be forever a hick from the boondocks. And if you're the senior one, tune the degree of your polite resistance to going first to the degree of your superiority of rank.

The battle is just as *sérieux* at business and social dinners, ladies' luncheons (Chapter 14) and even in the bosom of the French family. Older daughters enter before younger ones, married daughters with children enter before married daughters without children etc.

Similarly, at a business or social lunch or dinner, wait to be seated by the host. He will have figured out the nuances of rank. If you're the host, get your secretary to figure it out.

This is all part of the intricate, dense web of relationships written down for eternity in that particular French straitjacket called protocol. The Italians and Spanish courts had their protocol, but Louis XIV elevated it, and above all, seating arrangements *(placement)*, to an affair of State in 17th century Versailles, to keep the courtiers busy and in their places.

At Versailles everyone's precedence at the door and elsewhere, all day long and all evening, was as clear as a number in a waiting line for airplane tickets. It was calculated with astrological complexity according to proximity to the King. No one was allowed to sit down in his presence except the Queen, the Dauphin and the Dauphine (the Crown Prince and the Crown Princess), who were allowed an armchair, and the royal duchesses married to the King's grandsons, who were allowed stools. Royal princesses had to stand up in his presence and were not allowed to go to the door to receive anyone. But Cardinals must be received at the door. What happened when a Cardinal came to see a royal princess? The princess had to pretend to be ill, so that she could stay in bed, and receive him there.

As noted in more detail in Chapter 8, the Sun King still reigns. His rays illuminate French assumptions, values and habits. His protocol affects most aspects of French daily and office life. You can't escape it, so you might as well lean into it, figure it out and enjoy it. It's part of that great creation, quintessentially French, called style.

Chapter 2

French Space
Public, Private and Office

They crowded me so in the post office and at the bank dispensers – looking over my shoulder! – that I was completely fed up. When I turned around and said "Don't do that!" they said, "Don't do what?"

Louise Walker
English Computer Engineer, Honda

The quote above sounds as if it's about bad manners, or downright nastiness.

But, again, it's about different codes, this time spatial ones. Edward T. Hall, the American anthropologist, made the momentous discovery that the use of space is culturally determined. He coined a word for it: *proxemics*.

Rick D. is a brilliant systems engineer from Philadelphia, transferred to Paris with a big computer multinational. The first day of a seminar, in a few seconds, unconsciously, he puts his finger on some of the metaphysics of France which make it baffling and infuriating for northern foreigners.

"Why are people always trying to bump me off the sidewalk? Why do they crowd me so in lines? Why do they swim in circles?"

American cities are often laid out in grids. Paris is a city of connecting circles, surrounded by a circular boulevard. There's no way you can go straight from one side of it to the other. The Louvre, palace of the French kings for centuries, used to have a round wall around it. The center of Paris also used to have a round wall around it, like most old cities, for protection. The French like circles. Thinking and talking in circles comes naturally here. It's a kind of French-preferred protection from showing one's hand too soon, from taking risks and making mistakes. And circles are more aesthetic than grids.

Why *not* swim in circles?

"Because it's disorderly!" bleats Rick.

Maybe it's another kind of order?

Rick moves on to his other woes. "Why do they push and shove and talk in my face? They stand so close when they talk to you – if they talk to you – that you can smell their breath! Bad breath!"

I invite him to sit down, pour him some wine, offer him some cheese and ask him, "How close is too close?"

"How close is too close!" Rick cries. "Everyone knows that!"

Do they?

For Britons and Americans and Germans, about a yard of space feels right if you're talking together socially, or at the office. For Latins, half that. For Arabs, a few inches: an Arab *wants* to be able to smell your breath, to perceive if he can trust you or not.

Rick goes on. "And they sit so close to me on the Métro that their knees are always knocking mine! The cars in the next lane of traffic practically shave your paint off! But the worst is the post office. They practically suffocate you while you're standing in line!"

The sidewalk, the Métro, cocktail parties, cars, the post office... From Canada, Australia, England, Germany, the U.S. – even from New York City – foreigners in Paris have a short fuse just waiting to be lit about what they perceive as French disregard for their rightful elbowroom.

"It seems just so *rude*," said Louise Walker, the English computer engineer quoted at the beginning of the chapter, "and infuriating, until you realize that it's part of their culture – they aren't doing it on purpose."

Sophisticated world traveler Judson Gooding, author, journalist, a former editor of *Fortune*, who has been living half the year in Paris for seven years, has a French wife and loves France. But on the subject of French space he sees red.

"I hate to be touched in public," he says. "It's outrageous the way they crowd you at the post office here. There is absolutely no excuse for it. There is always an enormous amount of room and relatively few people occupying it."

Amy Wyeth, Wellesley class of '90, has a strategy for the post office: "You have to be alert and take care not to leave a gap between you and the person in front of you. If not, someone will nip into it. So the people in back are always crowding you to guard their space. I hate that! But I fox them. Whenever I go, I take a backpack."

Julie Winn's solution: "I now *say* something at the post office, like 'C'est à moi, madame.' It works!"

English speakers and other northerners are sensitive about space in all the queues in Paris. David Buckingham, a New York advertising man, standing in a line at the movies, felt constrained to ask his companion in a loud voice, "Is the man behind me trying to *know me carnally?*"

I used to have talks about this with the English-American poet, W.H.Auden, when he lived in Austria. Later he wrote a poem which sums up Anglo-Saxon space:

> *Thirty inches from my nose*
> *The frontier of my person goes.*
> *All the untilled air between*
> *Is private pagus or demesne.*
> *Stranger, unless with bedroom eyes*
> *I beckon you to fraternize*
> *Beware of rudely crossing it.*
> *I have no gun, but I can spit.*

Body Bubbles

Edward T. Hall, the American anthropologist, quotes these lines in his ground-breaking work, *The Hidden Dimension*. Describing proxemics and the interaction of man and space as being culturally programmed and "out of awareness", he puts his finger on Louise Walker's problem: the body bubble that Americans, English people and many northern Europeans, unlike most of the rest of the world, carry around with them.

The bubble may not be 30 inches, like Auden's, but surely a good three or four inches. Like Auden, we feel antagonized by any unauthorized person who violates it. We're angry at being jostled, bumped, squeezed and grazed.

Americans, especially, take up a lot of space. We swing our arms and often our shoulders when we walk. We sprawl over furniture. An African student, asked to imitate a young American, slid down in his chair until his back was almost flat, his legs spread wide apart. The sitting posture of Dagwood's son, in the *Blondie* strip below, is typical.

BLONDIE by Dean Young and Stan Drake

Reprinted with special permission of King Features Syndicate
© 1993 King Features Syndicate

Grown-up Americans take up more space, too, even sitting for photographers, than Europeans.

U.S.'s former President Clinton

France's former Prime Minister Balladur

Car Bubbles

The Germanic "Get Out, No Trespassing" body bubble is even bigger than the American. It includes their car. Woe be to him who assumes that the fender owned by a German, an Austrian or a German-Swiss may be a momentary resting place for a package. As for a bumper being a shield for receiving bumps – watch out!

One evening in Vienna, late for the theatre, I squeezed my little Austin Mini into a space barely large enough, and touched – very lightly! – the bumper of the car behind. Four Viennese men jumped out from the shadows, shaking their fists at me. I couldn't understand their angry German, and trembled in the darkness. The owner of the bumper arrived on the run, also shouting and shaking his fist. He inspected it. No dent. Not even a little scratch. He glared at me, shouted some more angry words, and they all left.

So you never hear Americans complaining about elbow room in Germanic, Anglo-Saxon and Scandinavian countries.

The problem for them and the other northern foreigners in France is that the French, along with the other Southern Europeans, Slavs, Latin Americans, Asians and Africans, don't have a body bubble. Far from it. The French lack of a car bubble is a tourist attraction. Blond Northerners gather to gape at a Frenchman maneuvering his Citroën into a space only half large enough for it, by pushing the adjacent cars a foot or two backwards or forward. Judson Gooding calls it Contact Parking.

Sometimes when I can't sleep at night, I imagine German drivers at the Etoile in Paris, the traffic circle around the Arc de Triomphe, where cars from 12 major avenues converge and roar around to their various exits mostly without traffic lights or stop signs, in amusement park obliviousness to the other cars speeding lethally at them from all sides. At any given moment about 100 French drivers dive ecstatically into this maelstrom and its definitive test of reflexes, brakes and macho feistiness, to see who can bluff the longest and come the closest without colliding. The French call it *Liberté*. The Germans call it Insanity.

Some Americans never drive in France because of their dread of the Etoile. Others make it a point to live far, far away from it. The moment that I finally dared it was the moment when I really fell in love with France.

I was stuck with the Etoile my first years in Paris. We lived close to it, with the children's school on the other side. Still intimidated by Austrian ire, I avoided it as long as possible. I didn't feel like a collision, an angry crowd shaking their fists at me, all traffic coming to a halt, furious policemen hustling me into a billy wagon, jail, etc. But taking the long way around was tiresome. And...

"Chicken!" said my six-year-old one morning, as I detoured it.

The next day, secretly, without him, I set out. I plunged into it. Terror! Which way to look? Back, front, left, right, they were aiming straight at me! I wasn't half way around the Arc when I bumped into the car ahead of me. Not hard, but enough to stop it. The driver, a dapper, unsmiling Frenchman, got out. I also got out, head humble, heart sinking, waiting for the angry mob.

But no one else took any notice. They kept on boiling past.

The driver inspected the rear of his car in silence and discovered only a slight scratch. He turned to me solemnly and said,

"Madame, in your place, I would take the Métro."

Desk Bubbles

Most Americans don't have a car bubble (Californians tend to, for instance) but at the office they have a desk bubble.

Emily Borel, a devastating redhead who had her own direct marketing firm in New York, married a Frenchman nine years ago and was soon discovered by a major direct marketing firm in Paris. She is now one of their top consultants, but at first she didn't have an office of her own.

"I was in a sort of hall with about 10 other people," she says, "doing a research project with a bunch of magazines and reference books on my desk. The other people in the office came over to my desk and leaned all over me, picked up the magazines and leafed through them without so much as a 'Do you mind?' I had the feeling they didn't know I was there!"

In some way weird to us, they probably didn't.

I had the same feeling when I was photocopying at the only place in Paris with a decent machine available on Sunday, Le Drugstore at Saint Germain des Prés. The machine is on the mezzanine, which you reach directly by a staircase from the street, and is squeezed into a small space between the telephones and the Drugstore offices. To reach the offices you have to circle around the person photocopying.

I was engrossed in my photocopying when I was suddenly knocked to the side by a Frenchman as he passed behind me to one of the offices... without saying a word.

Even for me, after 23 years in France, this was too much. In my nastiest voice before he closed the door behind him, I said sarcastically, *"Excusez-MOI, monsieur!"*

Nothing. The door closed. Presently it opened again and his head came out.

"Madame," he said, in French, "did I bump into you?"

"Bump into me!" I squawked. "You practically threw me to the floor!"

"Oh dear me!" he said. "I didn't notice!"

Then he went down the steps to the street, and reappeared with a bunch of lilies-of-the-valley.

"Please accept these flowers," he said, "with my humble apologies. I really didn't notice."

Sound bubbles

What the French do notice is raised voices. They have a distinct sound bubble, unlike Americans. They're touchy both about being overheard and about disturbing others.

For Americans, air waves belong to the strongest voice. Let it carry where it may. Americans invented the telephone because their voices couldn't be heard coast to coast, only in the next state. You can hear the details of American conversations from the other side of the Grand Canyon, let alone the other side of a restaurant, a post office, or a park. The volume of Americans talking together increases geometrically with each additional person. Four Americans talking together equals one F-16 flying low.

They don't mean to be insulting to all the strangers within earshot who feel abused. Quite the contrary.

"It's not polite to whisper in public," says Charlotte Davis, a Texas broker.

And the French?

"We're taught to modulate our voices in public," says Marie de La Martinière, a prominent Parisian who founded SOS Paris, a conservancy association. "It's *mal élevé* to be overheard."

French conversations between adults in public spaces are as private as the insides of those elegant walled houses foreigners hardly ever get to see. Even adolescents talking a few feet away aren't audible in the little rue de Babylone park near where I live. It's quite close to a school, and groups of five to 10 teenagers are camped every 15 feet or so when the spring sun, a rare sight here, is out. You wouldn't know they're there. I never heard them except once, when one of the young girls in a large circle of companions tickled the feet of one of the boys. He shrieked.

Guarding one's sound bubble is one of the few things the British have agreed with the French about since they burned Joan of Arc. The Germans, Dutch, Belgians and Scandinavians have sound bubbles as impressive as their body bubbles.

But most Southern Europeans are as unconcerned about noise as about stranger-grazing. This goes for the Arabs, most Middle Easterners, black Africans, Latin Americans and Orientals, except the Japanese, who suffer on their stiflingly over-crowded subways as much as any American.

French Light

Let there be light, lots of light, says the English-speaker. The American and the Australian put huge windows in their houses and offices. They equip them with lots of lamps and 100-Watt bulbs, which they switch on at the first hint of dusk.

The French are quite happy in darkness.

One evening at an anglophone dinner, I sat next to a "frog"-loathing Englishman who clearly had not had a success in France. In the middle of someone's sentence, he burst out contemptuously, "The French are so stingy that they don't put their headlights on until it's pitch dark!"

Which is quite true, but not in the sense he meant. French children don't grow up with their mothers telling them they mustn't read without a "proper light" or they'll "hurt their eyes."

On the contrary, they're drenched in stories of the high cost of electricity, and told, "DON'T TURN ON THE LIGHT UNTIL YOU CAN'T SEE THE WRITING ON THE PAGE!" Their parents encourage them to read by bulbs about as strong as two candles, and dress them down the moment a light flickers in an unoccupied room. Electric light is a luxury like champagne and foie gras, not to be taken for granted and to be used sparingly, for the sake of the family budget.

Julie Winn, mother of four, tells of a newly-hired French au pair girl she was showing around the apartment. The girl was plainly anguished at the American habit of having lights blazing in several rooms at the same time.

"When I leave a room," she asked plaintively, "do I have to leave the light on?"

I remember years ago visiting a distant French cousin who lived in an elaborate and beautifully maintained fortified château near Strasbourg, and the twilight dimming to dusk and almost darkness before one lamp with one 40-watt bulb was reluctantly switched on. When the butler anounced dinner, my cousin carried the lamp into the dining room where, again, it was the single source of light.

My mother sent her a second lamp for Christmas, but she never used it.

Non-resort hotels in the French provinces usually provide one, not two, bedside lamps for a double room, with one 20-Watt bulb inside. I take along one of my own.

French and American light habits being light years apart, this is what happens at the office:

"I come to a meeting with a couple of people already there," said Gary Graves, of Cabot, an American chemicals multinational, "and they're sitting in darkness. Well, it's darkness to me, anyway. About as much light as in a child's bedroom with a nightlight. So I turn on a light. And what happens? The next guy who comes in turns it off. And no one says anything."

French Office Space

Frank Lloyd Wright's space revolution, opening up rooms, tearing down walls, letting space go and flow, didn't make it in Europe. Rooms have doors and doors are closed, in houses and in offices. It has to do with privacy, secrecy, security and heat, depending on which country and what the temperature is.

Some closed doors are more closed than others.

A closed door in a German office is closed, locked and barricaded.

The same goes for most northern European countries, including England, and above all, for America, where the doors are usually open unless something extremely delicate is going on

The Mystery of the Closed Door

But in France, in most companies, the doors are always shut. All you see on your way to visit someone in his office in Paris is a corridor with rows of doorknobs.

"It looks like a hotel," says David Santiago, a computer engineer from India with Air Liquide. "All those halls with closed doors."

As French companies tend to be extremely hierarchical, with strict procedures about who reports to whom and no skipping over the various links in the chain of command, all these closed doors are pretty sure to panic a foreign northern manager just off the plane from Tulsa or Newcastle. Even managers who have been here for over a year don't usually pick up on what the closed door is all about.

However, the closed door in Paris, or Milan or Brussels, doesn't have the implications or significance of an American or English or Swedish closed door.

It might as well not be closed at all.

French subordinates aren't fazed. They know the code. They simply open it and enter, after a perfunctory knock, which is a signal rather than a question.

"So that's why !" said the newly arrived director of an American bank in Paris, in one of my seminars. "I was in my office with the door closed last week, firing one of my employees, when one of my assistants simply walked in – after hardly knocking at all, and not waiting for an answer. I was very put out indeed."

Robert Pingeon, now Directeur Général of Cigna Insurance Company of Europe, had the same reaction in a different seminar. Later he reported that he called a meeting of his French employees and staff, when still director of Chubb, and translated the meaning of an American closed door.

"It worked like magic," he said. "No more door crashers."

Foreign directors not briefed on doorcodes may blow their stacks. But non-doorcode-briefed foreign subordinates' invited to the office of their boss, may have a hard time keeping the lid on, like this young Brown-Stanford Business School star now with one of the big banks in Paris:

"I go out to get a drink of water and run into my boss in the hall. He says to come with him to his office, and closes the door. He chats about nothing in particular, small talk, and I'm asking myself what I did wrong, was it that report I handed in yesterday I thought was great – or shouldn't I have spoken up in the meeting this morning... I tell you, the room's getting hotter, my shirt is wet with sweat and still he doesn't come to the point and I'm ready to yell, 'Well, come on, out with it, what's wrong???' when he gets up and says, 'Nice talking to you, let's have lunch some time.'"

The Door Taboo

Room doors in private houses in Europe are closed and meant to stay closed. What's behind them is no trespassing for strangers. A great way never to be invited again is to wander around alone from room to room in a European friend's house.

The hottest spot in a private house in Europe for US-European quarrels is the door to a room with a toilet in it, be it bathroom or *le petit coin* (the little corner), euphemistic French used familiarly for a room containing ONLY a toilet. (The preferred French, correct in all circumstances and levels of society, for this plumbing fixture, and the area where it is located, is *les toilettes*.) Americans and Britons leave this door open when the area is unoccupied. To do so was shouted at them so often when they were growing up that it's automatic, as programmed as not blowing their nose with their napkin. They're usually helpless to do otherwise, no matter how often and how urgently their European hosts have begged them to leave it closed.

Europeans are just as helpless at overlooking it. An open W.C. door is taboo.

Chapter 3

French Time

"Why is everyone always late?"
"Why does everything take so long?"

I can't get my French subordinates to understand that time is an important element in the functioning of a company. There is a great negligence about time in France. Meetings, if the CEO is late, will not start on time. No time is allotted to various subjects and all the subjects are discussed at once.

Günther Lorenz
Managing director of BMW France

You know the joke about the Mexican and the Arab. The Mexican says to the Arab, "I hear you have a word for tomorrow that's similar to our word *mañana.*"

"Yes," replies the Arab. *"Bukara.* But it doesn't have the same sense of urgency."

Latin Americans, Arabs, Asians, Africans and southern Europeans – in other words, most human beings – live rhythmically, around a *mañana* which is perhaps more, perhaps less urgent – maybe next week, maybe next year.

Not northern Europeans! Not Americans!

If Americans, Swedes and Germans are choleric about their elbowroom in France, they're positively apoplectic about the country's time system. Or, as they would say, non-system.

John D. is a financial strategist at a big French multinational which bought the American company he used to work for. He's having a lot of trouble communicating in France. Partly, he admits, because of working for and with foreigners. French foreigners.

"I'm eight minutes late for a meeting – very upset and stressed about it – and racing down the hall at a gallop," he says, "and I run into this French colleague who's part of the same group. He's going in the opposite direction! I say, 'Hey, Jean-Louis, aren't you coming to the meeting?' And he goes, *'Bien sûr*, of course, what time is it called for?' Just like that! Doesn't know what time the meeting's called for! An important meeting! So I tell him he'd better move his ass, it was called for 10 minutes ago!

"So you know what he says then? He goes, 'Okay, I'll be right there, I just have to pick up some lunch.' Lunch, for crying out loud, and he's already 10 minutes late and going in the wrong direction!"

Northern foreigners are stupefied at what they perceive as the casual French attitude, not to say disrespect, of scheduled meetings, agendas, and deadlines, and at how the time is actually spent in meetings.

Kirk Coyne, from Texas, controller at Lafarge Fondu International: "A lot of time is spent studying all the consequences of a decision, which is excellent for the long term. Time has a different meaning here. It certainly isn't money."

Unreported Meeting Changes

"They continually change their meetings – half the time without letting people know!" said Greg McNevin, an agro-chemical engineer with Sandoz. "Drives me crazy! One time, two weeks after I'd spent hours trying to organize a big meeting, getting the date and the time of day that would suit everyone, and then signing up the conference room – that was the worst – this guy comes up to me and asks me to change the date! I said, 'No, it's against my policy. I'll tell you what happened, but I won't change it. He was surprised!"

"For a long time it infuriated me that they would cancel meetings or hold them somewhere else without letting me know," said Chuck Theobald, a systems engineer with Federal Express, "until I realized nobody meant it badly, they just sort of forgot who else was supposed to come. So after a while, you get used to it and don't mind so much."

But sometimes it does seem to be meant badly. In any case, it *feels* like it: "Downright insulting!" says Tim S., a young trainee at Alcatel. "I'm meeting this French colleague for lunch – he finally arrives, half an hour late and doesn't even say he's sorry! He is wrong to waste my time like that!"

Madlyn M. was an executive in New York real estate financing until she was transformed overnight into a trailing spouse. She's cooking up career possibilities of her own in Paris, and was astonished at the non-synched timing of two executives for a job interview at the BNP, a French bank.

"One of them received me on the dot of the appointed meeting,"she said, "and the other kept both of us waiting for 40 minutes. He didn't say he was sorry – and didn't give an excuse. And the one who was on time didn't seem at all bothered. It was as if this was perfectly normal."

Needless interruptions in meetings can be intolerable for foreigners.

"I was in an important meeting with our president," says Emily Borel, "plus about four other people, including a woman vice president. About 15 minutes into the meeting, this vice president's secretary comes into the room – without knocking, of course – and says there's a call for her. It's her maid! And she takes the call! So all of us, including the president, sit there and wait while she talks – for a good 10 minutes – to her maid – about her dog! And no one thinks this is odd except me!"

Insult Time

German managers and executives also tear their hair out over this. "The French don't realize that being 10 minutes late is an insult to a German," said Heinz-Peter Haenlein, vice president of the international division of Clarins, the cosmetics multinational, "or that a deadline is serious. Keeping a delivery date is a matter of honor for us."

"Honor" is a key to the French too, but in what they do and how they do it, not when they do it.

Edward T. Hall made a communications leap of Einsteinian proportions when he perceived, from his studies of various cultures, that time is not an absolute: that time, like space, is culturally variable and programmed.

While Americans, Britons, Germans and Swedes grow up assuming that their perception of "on time" and "lateness" is as universally valid and incontestable as the movement of the planets, the fact is that only the northern, industrialized, business-oriented, Protestant trading countries have similar definitions: Holland, Germany, Switzerland, Canada, the Scandinavians – particularly Sweden – and to a slightly lesser extent, England. "Late" for a business appointment means, for citizens of one of these countries, not on the dot of the scheduled time, and may affect the outcome of the meeting. There are only slight variations in the toll for each accumulated minute of lateness. Five minutes late, the American mumbles his excuse, the German states it precisely, while the Swede is already skating close to insult time. Ten minutes late, the German kept waiting is insulted while an American has a margin of 20 minutes before insult time threatens.

For these nations, time is sequential and rigorously scheduled along an endless ribbon of appointments and obligations. People live in a sort of temporal straitjacket, bullied by a schedule they can change only at the cost of their credibility, and by their religion of punctuality that equates lateness with original sin or lunacy.

Monochronics and Polychronics

Hall calls these cultures "monochronic". He found that countries having the same sense of "when" also share various other perceptions and behavior codes. They have similar mechanisms – management principles, procedures, habits of work, projections, agendas, attitudes towards the task to be accomplished. Their projects have priority over all manner of creatures, including human beings – all of whom, they assume, live under the same time tyranny.

Alice's White Rabbit: extremely monochronic

But for the overwhelming majority of humanity, being alive doesn't necessarily mean being "on time". They have a more indulgent or elastic view of "lateness", if indeed they have a word for it at all. Hall calls these cultures "polychronic": Asians, Africans, Middle Easterners, Mediterraneans, Latin Americans.

The world of the polychronics is abuzz with people. People come first. Projects get completed because of their vast network of people. Time is more like a point than a ribbon, more circular, sort of like a balloon that swells and shrinks according to who's around. The more people around all the time, the better; the more things happening at once, the better. Appointments are for giving a general idea: they're easily postponed or canceled, and not necessarily exclusive. Others may be booked into the same slot, which is probably open-ended, or they may simply occupy it jointly without warning. Polychronics can listen to three conversations at the same time and also take someone's pulse, sign a document or fill out an airplane ticket.

Where are the French in all this?

Figuring out French time is like trying to catch a trout with your bare hands. French men and women are on time if invited for luncheons – two minutes late and they cover themselves with excuses if not with "I'm sorry", but 30 minutes late for dinner and you might not hear anything, though there might be some murmuring about the traffic. French trains and airplanes leave on the very dot of their scheduled departure. Dentists and surgeons are on time, but not gynecologists or GPs, necessarily. Movies usually, but television, well, that depends. Sometimes it's early. Soon after Edith Cresson became the first woman to be appointed French Prime Minister, her interview with TV news star Anne Sinclair drifted 15 minutes into the 8:00 news. All the programs that followed that evening were at least 15 minutes late.

But that's nothing compared to the television upheavals after the death of a beloved personality. When Yves Montand died, all the evening programs were simply canceled. For the next two days, there was little to watch but old Yves Montand films.

In other words, the French are richly polychronic, but are punctual whenever necessary or suitable. Most have an inner alarm about when to be on time – and then they are. They also know when it doesn't matter much, and when it doesn't matter at all. It's part of their *liberté*, like smoking and letting their dogs mess up the sidewalk. In business, it also makes a difference if they are *demandeur* (soliciting someone for something) or *demandé* (being solicited).

The French: Quarkochronics

I call the French "quarkochronics" for the way they defy prediction and loop in and out of both systems. You can tell a quarkochronic who's on time or three minutes late from a monochronic because he's never stressed about it. He's late, too bad, but "the planet will go on rotating." That doesn't mean you can relax and get away with being late to appointments with a quarkochronic, particularly if he's aware of your monochronic punctuality obsession. He will know that you're insulting him. He won't tell you so, because quarkochronics are indirect, but he'll find a way to let you know.

Du Cirque Chez Chantal

A frantic monochronic myself, for 12 years in France I thought that in this quarkochronic country I could safely be a few minutes late, like 10, for my appointments with Chantal, my hairdresser on the rue du Bac. There was never any comment or indication to the contrary. Then one day, my usual 10 minutes late, I was parking my bike in front of her salon when I remembered that I was out of hair conditioner, something Chantal generously lets her clients bring with them, a cheering little economy.

So I waved to Chantal through the window and pointed to the pharmacy across the street, indicating that I'd pick something up and be back in a minute. But at the pharmacy there were several people with endless prescriptions ahead of me. So it wasn't one but 10 minutes later when I crossed the street back to Chantal's door and tried to open it.

The door wouldn't open. Then I saw through the window that the shop was in darkness. My first reaction was to check that it wasn't lunchtime, or Monday morning, when things might be closed. Then I remembered that I'd waved to Chantal before I went to the pharmacy! Was I going crazy, or what?

My face must have taken on a wild look, because at that moment, the lights of the shop blazed on, the door opened, and Chantal and her three hairdressers plus four clients burst out onto the sidewalk, laughing their heads off. They'd all been hiding behind a partition in the dark.

"You should've seen your face!" they roared at me. And then, "That will teach you not to be late every week!"

They still laugh about this. "You should have seen your face!"

Jet Lag

Often, just when it would seem to matter a lot how late you are, it doesn't even seem to be noticed. Stressed to be on the dot for an interview with one of the top nabobs of SNECMA, the huge French jet engine producer, I didn't realize that my car would be inspected as I entered the grounds. After 10 minutes of this, I found that the receptionist in the entrance hall wasn't at her desk to indicate where to go. Another five minutes. So I was 15 minutes late when I entered the director's office. I was shaking with shame, but he was totally unconcerned.

"But Madame," he said as I tried to cover myself with apologies, "everyone is late in Paris! The trafffic..."

Americans who have dealt with quarkochronics in France for a while tend to become a little quarkochronic themselves.

"In general, everyone's late," said Lafarge Coppée's Larry Waisanen. "So now, I'm late too. I used to be half way down the street to meet someone when now, I'm thinking of putting my coat on. No one minds if anyone is late. That's the nice part – no stress about it.

"I figure it's like with space and bumping into you. They really don't notice. For instance, I have to meet quite often with our accounts auditor. He's a high level manager with a big French company, and for months he was always very late, maybe half an hour, maybe even 45 minutes. He never said anything about being sorry, until one day – when he was 50 minutes late. Then I said, 'Well, it doesn't matter, you're always late.' He was really surprised! Now he's always on time!"

Dick Pasley, chief liaison officer between General Electric and SNECMA: "When I came here we needed a projection on how long it took them to build various parts of our CFM-56 engines. No one could tell us. We had to watch the workers for months, and make our projection from that."

Pasley has a recipe for Americans worked up about deadlines and time-wasting in France: "You have to realize that nothing is simple here, everything takes longer, and when you need something from bureaucrats, the one paper you didn't bring is the one they demand."

Monochronic American managers trying to get French subordinates to finish a project on time might as well expect some sleepless nights until they figure out quarkochronics.

Greg McNevin (Sandoz): "We were preparing the data on a new product for registration with the French government. Our whole program for launching the new product – the marketing, distribution, etc. – depended on getting the registration at a certain time, which meant submitting the data by a certain date. Otherwise we'd have to put it off for six months. The manager in charge of it was new – and I'd told her boss that he'd have to keep checking that she was on top of it. He didn't. I found out almost at the last minute. That's how I discovered that the system here is to keep checking everybody, all the time."

Nicolas Bussière, the young French boss of Desgrandchamps, agrees and explains it like this: "French people live their present intensely, without thinking ahead too much. My job is really reminding people constantly, 'Did you call that person? Did you put in that order?' And so on. Our system here is very hierarchical, not made for people taking responsibility. They don't want to, either – or they wouldn't accept the system as it is."

Not Just One Thing at a Time

"French managers may or may not be on time, but they can give their full attention to about eight people at once," said an American financial analyst at the Caisse des Dépôts bank. "You'll be in your boss's office talking over a project with him and he'll also be talking on the phone, signing something for his secretary, answering the question of a colleague who just came in, and then of another one..."

Louisiana State's surgeon Lou Martin says it's the same in French hospitals. "French doctors are very competent, and it is really something for us to see how they function – they'll be examining a patient, looking at an x-ray, answering the phone, dictating to the nurse – all at the same time."

And French CEO's? It Depends

Being on time for Philippe Quennouëlle, CEO for 40 years of Diot, SA, an insurance international, is a matter of politeness and effectiveness in running a company, which sounds monochronic enough until he says a little more, and then he's definitely quarkochronic.

"We have not had to be so rigid about things, we could afford to be more relaxed inside our Hexagon, not to be constantly worried about profits and reporting to our stockholders. Being audited four times a year, as in the U.S., has been unknown here. So we could be more indulgent with people who weren't up to the mark. Firing people seemed terrible to us – our companies felt more like families. With the world changing, France must also change. We have been spoiled.

"Now, to conquer new markets, we must learn new ways of doing things. Your American time system is one of them – but Asian time is also important and quite, quite different from French time or American Time. In Asia, time has no importance at all. Weeks and months can go by for the sort of decision one would expect in a matter of days. When we decided to open up branches in China, we sent a team to Saudi Arabia, where we already had business, simply to learn to let time go by... patiently."

But many CEO's of private French companies are on strict U.S.-German time. Didier Pineau-Valencienne, one of the five or six top executive stars in France, is a passionate monochronic. The Président Directeur Général of Schneider, the giant holding company which bought Square D recently, he was voted the CEO of the year in 1992 by other CEO's.

"In my company," he told me in an interview, "meetings always begin on the dot, decisions are made, and the meetings do not last all morning. As for deadlines: *deadlines are met.*"

What worries some American companies even more than deadlines not being met is that, after a while, their American employees will find out that Quarkochronics is fun, particularly when France grinds to a complete halt for all the holidays – in August, in November, in February and in May.

"Once you get used to it," said an American systems engineer in a computer international, "it's pretty nice, all that time off. And not being stressed about being late. It all gets done, somehow, and done well. Maybe, you know, their lives are more – well, meaningful than ours."

Part II

The French Way in Public

Chapter 4

Street Strangers and Neighborhood Tradespeople

The Good News and the Bad News

> ... the small shop can survive by doing those things that it can do better than large shops, producing and selling goods where personal attention, service and quality are appreciated, and by establishing a relationship of confidence with the customer that goes beyond traditional profiteering.
>
> Theodore Zeldin
> *The French*

There isn't a governessy bone in the French body. If you want to walk on forbidden grass or cross an intersection against a red light, switch traffic lanes unannounced, turn right from the lefthand lane, or drive down a one-way street the wrong way, feel free. No honks, shouts or fist-shaking, as in Vienna, Zurich or Frankfurt. *Liberté* means freedom from other citizens' notions of civic correctness. It's your adult right to decide whether the law is reasonable or your situation exceptional. (But don't push your luck. A nearby policeman might be feeling liverish.)

At the same time, impatient and preoccupied as they rush about their city, Parisians are nevertheless the most considerate and helpful people in the world – to other strangers who are in sync. (No smiley facial expressions.) If they spot something amiss that could give you trouble, like an open car trunk or a carton of eggs about to fall off the back of your bicycle, they'll find a way to let you know.

Strangers on the Street: The Good News

People run after you with something you've dropped. Try dropping something, if you don't believe me.

I left a glove on the Métro one day and was hurrying along the platform when I heard a man calling loudly *"Madame!"* from the train. I turned and saw a big worker standing by the still-open doors.

"Votre gant!" he called. "Your glove!" and threw it to me.

Also, they stick together to bail each other out in any unforeseen emergency. They're all part of a brave and compassionate Us against the pitiless Them of Police, Bad Weather, Government, Accidents, Carelessness, Bad Luck. It makes you feel snug and safe in a strange city.

Bus drivers wait for you. They even make a special, unscheduled stop for you. If someone finds something lost on the street, they prop it up on the nearest window ledge for the distressed owner to find when he retraces his steps looking for it. Yesterday on window ledges I saw a baby's little boot, a guide to Paris and some ski goggles.

Lost Something Vital?

If something vital has gone astray, or needs emergency help, they'll figure out a way to get help to you.

One Saturday I cycled off in a great hurry with a check for a long overdue telephone bill, to catch the last mail at a central post office. At the mail slot, I couldn't find the envelope. Not in my bag. Not in any of my pockets. Later, at home, I searched for it in vain. So it had dropped out of my pocket while biking, onto the street. Or something. Great. That I had my address on the back was no great consolation.

The next day, it was in my post box. The concierge said she'd found it stuck with Scotch tape to the outside door. A thoughtful Parisian, finding it on the street, noting the importance of the destination and cautious about whether the letter was really intended to be mailed, took the trouble to relieve my worries.

One evening, after driving Ande, my husband, to the station and seeing him off on the train, I couldn't find the car keys in my handbag. They weren't in the ignition. I circled the car, then got down on my knees and looked frantically under it. At this point, a woman got out of a car parked nearby and handed the keys to me, saying she'd picked them up from the street and was waiting for someone to be clearly concerned about them.

This wasn't the first time I'd dropped my car keys in the street. The time before, the kind stranger had given them to the café nearest to the car – to save me the trouble of going to the police. No one in the café suggested that I was careless, or possibly a dangerous lunatic. Parisians are endlessly understanding. Someone said quietly that it was helpful to have a second set of keys. I took the advice.

But a year later, I actually managed to lock our car in the garage with the key inside it, along with a briefcase full of slides and overheads I needed for a conference that afternoon. The second key was eight hours away in our house in the country. As I reflected on this disaster, a neighbor, a young Frenchman always in a terrible rush, roared home in his car. On hearing my plight, he groaned, "That's my nightmare!" and whipped out a wallet. "Look! I always have another key here, a key in the house, a key in Eva's purse and a fourth in the garage! But just in case, I always keep a Slim Jim handy too!" And with his Slim Jim we managed to unlock the car.

But my American au pair girl, when I told her, said, "HOW could you POSSIBLY lock your car with the keys inside!!!"

Nelly Dupré, a Philadelphian married to a Frenchman, tells of sitting in the Métro with some letters she wanted to address when she realized she didn't have anything to write with. She asked the leather-jacketed young man opposite her (*"Excusez-moi de vous déranger, monsieur, mais j'ai un problème"*) if he had a pen. He fumbled in all his pockets and finally withdrew one just as the train began slowing down for the next station. He got up – without asking for his pen back. When it was clear that it was indeed his station, Nelly pressed it on him, but still had three envelopes to go.

"Out of the corner of my eye I saw the woman across the aisle rummaging around in her handbag," she said. "I couldn't believe she was looking for a pen for me. But she was!"

Another time, after much shopping at the local supermarket, including about eight bottles of drinking water, I was trying to secure the carton of groceries on the back of my bike with the one elastic bungee cord I had with me. The carton seemed a bit wobbly, but I thought it would hold for the short way home. A middle-aged Frenchman, who had observed the operation, approached me worriedly.

"I am afraid that won't hold, Madame. You need some string," he said respectfully, shaking his head.

I said I didn't have any string and that I thought it was all right. He kept shaking his head. I assured him I would be careful, but after a few more head shakes, he dashed off down the street, making signs for me to wait. He came back a while later with some string. He insisted on weaving it intricately in place himself.

Hooked with Bungees

There's no doubt that bicycling is a fast way to reach the French heart, at least if, like me, you're both forgetful and in a hurry. My most moving bicycle story was the day I forgot to refasten my bungee cord after I detached it to unload the groceries. It was already dark when I set out again an hour or so later. I was speeding blithely along the rue de Varenne, almost as far as the rue du Bac, when the bike stopped suddenly and threw me to the street, just between my local butcher and baker. The bungee cord was wrapped entirely around the axle, the hooks caught in the spokes.

Instantly the owner of the paper shop across the street rushed over with some scissors, asking if I was all right. The *boulangère* appeared with a lantern so that we could see better. When the scissors didn't make any headway in cutting the cord, the butcher came out to inspect the situation. It was clearly desperate. He dispatched one of his assistants out to us with a really sharp butcher's knife and orders to do the job himself. It took him 20 minutes. But he succeeded, to general rejoicing. They sent me on my way feeling warm with encouragement, and not a word about not being so negligent.

Stalled in the Rain

One of my most astonishing encounters with a French good Samaritan happened soon after we moved to Paris. I was driving the children to school in the rush hour in the pouring rain, when the car, a Renault 4L, stalled on a one-way street jammed with businessmen trying to get to work. About 20 were stuck behind me. They honked. The car wouldn't start. They honked louder. Rattled, I leaned frantically on the starter. The honking became deafening.

Just then the driver of the car just behind me, an elegant Frenchman, presented himself politely at my window and asked me if I'd like him to try starting it. I slid gratefully over to the passenger seat. The other drivers apparently took heart at this move; the honking stopped.

But he also had no luck starting it.

He helped me push it to a space on the side of the street and then said, "Madame, I'm afraid you'll have to take the children to school in a taxi. Meanwhile, I'll send someone to look at your car. I'm from Renault."

When I came back later, two workmen in blue overalls were in my car. They said that unfortunately they couldn't fix it there. They'd have to take it to "the shop". Shop? What shop? Where?

"Chez Renault, madame," they said. "On the Avenue de la Grande Armée. We'll have it ready for you at six o'clock."

When I went to get it, I was told there was no bill.

They wouldn't tell me the name of my benefactor.

"Monsieur le directeur prefers to remain anonymous," they said. My French wasn't good enough to figure out what to do and how to thank him. (Answer: Stick around with a long mournful face, refuse to leave until they relent and give you his name.)

It was a long time ago, but I still see him approaching in the rain that day on the rue Duret, rain dripping off his hat, and knocking at my window. Should he read this, and remember the helpless American with the three little children in the back seat, I hope he will tell me who he is.

The Neighborhood Commerçants: *The Less Good News*

Interacting with French strangers in stores, shops, post offices and banks is different. The counter separates them from you: you become Them.

These Parisians tend to be hypersensitive and supercombustible. They've been compared to a hand grenade with the pin ready to come out at any moment. Which means they can be merciless to oafs whose intentions may be the best, but who don't get the codes right.

You have to woo them delicately, patiently, skillfully from Them to Us. As the French would say, for circumstances as far from the boudoir as an Anglo-Saxon could imagine, "You have to seduce them"

Some French multinationals don't give their new foreign employees anything to do for the first weeks – or months. They simply turn them loose in Paris. The foreigners think it's to learn French, which is also a big part of *être* (being), but mainly, it's to talk, and talk, and figure out how things are done. It's the hidden part, the part you're not told, can't guess at and must know, which is always more important in France. Like the root of a tree, it's hidden, but just as big as the visible part, and the determining factor in the strength of the trunk. In French *être*, the root is knowing how to deal with other people.

In other words, like most countries in the world except the Anglo-Saxon and Germanic ones, France is an affiliation culture. It's belonging, being known, which counts.

Monochronics are accustomed to having things spelled out. At home, they are. In France, they aren't. Here are three true newcomer tales (real names changed in the first two) of monochronics who got French *être* wrong. Each tale by itself wasn't exactly a disaster, but when you have 10 a week, it can pretty well curdle things for you.

Three Tales of Newcomer Bungles

Bret at the Bakery

"I was in a *boulangerie*, buying a loaf of bread," said Bret Moran, a banker from Boston. "It was the first time I'd ventured into a bakery on my own, with my dusty French. I was very polite and said *'Bonjour, madame'* the way you told us last week, and ordered *'un pain de seigle, s'il vous plaît.'* She wrapped it in a tiny square of tissue paper, which she twisted together at the ends, and thrust it at me. I asked for a bag. *'Un sac, s'il vous plaît.'*

"She refused. And snapped at me in a waterfall of French nastiness! The bitch! To refuse me a bag!

"I was so hopping mad when I got out to the sidewalk, with this bare loaf in this ridiculous piece of tissue paper, that of course I forgot to watch out. Someone knocked into me. The bread fell down and rolled into the street, losing the tissue paper on the way, and ended up – guess where – in a dog mess."

Furious, Bret went back to the *boulangerie* and ordered another loaf of bread. He refused to pay for it, claiming that it was the *boulangère's* "fault" that the first one was ruined, and again insisted on a bag: "Un SAC! J'ai besoin d'un SAC!"

His anger triggered a French fit that made the first "waterfall" seem like a love song. He not only did not get the bag, but the *boulangère* screamed at him that she'd get the police if he didn't pay. And added that he should never come back to the store again.

La boulangère

At home, he discovered that the loaf was three days old and hard as a rock.

"At this point, I hated not only the *boulangère* but all of France and everyone in it," he went on. "But not as much as my wife did. She'd had to hang around all day waiting for the plumber to fix the washing machine – who never showed. She'd had to cart all the wash for a family of six to the laundromat – where she got in a row with the laundress and had to wait for five loads before she could have it washed. When I got home, she went for me – a tantrum such as I'd never seen. She was ready to dump me and the kids for good and clear out of France right then and there. We were up half the night roaring at each other."

After a moment he added, "The next day at the office I thought my head would split open. Luckily nothing much was going on."

Bret may sound unusually bad-tempered. He's not. Lots of managers with frayed nerves at the end of a day of frustrations explode like this.

Bret's Blunders

- He didn't make himself known to the *boulangère* before doing business with her.
- He didn't grasp the inappropriateness of his request (for the bag) and then devise a strategy for obtaining something he was not entitled to.
- He blamed the *boulangère* for something. This is always fatal. See Chapter 6.

Warren at the Bank

"I went to the bank to get a certified check," said Warren Wood, a Canadian engineer, "and they wouldn't give it to me. The teller said I'd have to come back in three days. I told him I needed it right away. I had to pay the dealer for a new car that day or he'd sell the car to someone else. I didn't tell the bank what I needed it for. It was none of their business – their business was to give me my money. The teller repeated that it was impossible.

"I asked to see the boss. He said the same thing. I asked to see the branch director. By this time I'd just about had it. I mean – the money was there! In my account! 60,000 francs!

"The director was rude! He said it was impossible, that the teller was right, and repeated that it took three days to issue a certified check. Three days! I blew up, pounded on the table and said, 'All right, I'll take it in cash.' You know what happened then? He said, 'Very well.' He piled it up

– himself – in 10 heaps of 6,000 francs each and put them in a big plastic sack – the kind they put garbage in – and told me he was closing the account! Can you believe it? Said I could take my business elsewhere!

"So now I have to find another bank and go through all that horseshit again – I mean, they want to have your pay slips back to Adam and Eve and a truckload of other documents, I wouldn't be surprised if they asked for my great-grandmother's birth certificate next time!"

Warren's Blunders

- He didn't build up a relationship with the director or with the clerk, before he needed something special.
- He made false assumptions: that French banking is the same as in the U.S., and that certified checks are automatically issued to customers with sufficient funds.
- He didn't take the clerk into his confidence about the reason why he needed the money immediately.

Polly at the Supermarket

Polly Maguire, a lovely, quiet-voiced young art historian from Vermont with fluent classroom French, hadn't been in Paris long when, one evening, she went to the small local supermarket, where she'd been shopping for a month, to get some yogurt. Just yogurt.

Standing in a long line to pay for it, she realized she didn't have any small change, only a 100-franc bill. When she reached the cashier, not the one she normally patronized, she explained her problem.

"The cashier said she didn't have any change," Polly said, "but I could see in her drawer that she had plenty of it. She told me to go and stand in the line of the next cashier, who had change.

"I said I'd already stood in line long enough and pointed to the change in her drawer. She still refused to give it to me – and started yelling at me."

Polly asked to see the director.

The director listened to her impassively and then suggested, not politely, that Polly buy something else, or bring smaller change.

Boiling, beaten, Polly dumped the yogurt on the cashier's counter and retreated. She had to walk four blocks to the next store.

Polly's Blunders

- She didn't stand in the line of the cashier she knew.
- She made a false assumption: that, as in most places in New York, change of a big bill for a very small purchase is a routine matter.

- She didn't give the cashier any personal reason for the favor (something she was not automatically entitled to).
- She went over the cashier's head.

Getting It Right With People You Deal With Often

Business is personal in France. It's a tango. You need to know the steps, how to do them and which not to do.

French people like to deal with people they know. As we've seen, they're not wild about strangers. Strangers in a pickle, who are in sync, as in the beginning of this chapter, are different. Otherwise, for all French people, not only storekeepers, "Us" is only family, close friends, classmates, and old, faithful customers.

Working in France has to do with *honneur*. *Honneur* is one of the most beloved words in the language, up there with *logique, séduire, gloire, dignité* and *ambiguïté*, distant relatives of the English words honor, logic, seduce, glory, dignity and ambiguity, but much more treasured for constant reference.

French people are concerned about personal honor, the honor of France, and the honor of their family and friends, and of their long-term customers. School children are taught all these different, separate, vital kinds of honor in the *Chanson de Roland*, an epic poem about Roland, one of Charlemagne's heroic soldiers. It was written down in the 12th century about a battle in the 9th century. Yes. We're talking about a 1,000-year tradition of *honneur*.

You aren't part of that club. There's no rule of honor, implicit or explicit, that says they have to sell or do any kind of business with you, an unknown foreigner, much less accommodate your outlandish requests. The process of selling their wares, or their employer's wares, in shops and stores isn't the point. In fact, small shopkeepers often seem to stand glowering in their doorways, DEFYING anyone to come in and try to buy something.

As for charming new customers, who wants new customers?

On the other hand, if they want to unload some stale bread or rotten apples, why not on you?

Parisians often spend their life in the same quarter. Bakers and butchers have known their clients, maybe even generations of them, forever – all of them automatically Us. When French people move (itself quite unusual), they're careful to make an investigation on arrival as to who are the most *correct* shopkeepers in the new neighborhood. (*Correct* is also a distant cousin of the English adjective, but much fuller. In French it means a lofty combination of trustworthiness, integrity, reliability, good manners and professionalism.) Then they introduce themselves and have a good chat about the particularities of their family, a diabetic husband, a baby with allergies, an anorexic daughter – themes they can refer to later in their subsequent visits.

This is a game you can play too – and you'd better. Don't groan. Yes, it takes time. It takes energy. Look at it as an investment; it pays off.

Ask your concierge's advice about which *commerçants* to patronize. Introduce yourself right away. Take your concierge with you, if you really don't know more French than the Ten Magic Words.

Make it clear that you've heard wonderful things about that bakery (pharmacy, bank, grocer, supermarket) and that you're going to be around for years and years. Help them to remember you – not that they'll have any trouble, you'll be "the American" or "the Swede" to the whole neighborhood, even if they never give you a blink of recognition. Tell the greengrocer, for instance, that you simply love corn on the cob or rhubarb. He'll call to you when the first delivery of the season arrives.

When it was still hard to find, I confided to my greengrocer that I adored broccoli. From then on, he waved to me excitedly every time he had it. We ate an awful lot of broccoli that winter, but it was worth it. The pears and eggplants were always just right.

After 16 years, I found out that the nearest baker, whom I'd taken for the world's champion grouch, and thus had usually avoided, had a dazzling smile. I saw her light up for my daughter's French mother-in-law one day when we happened to be buying baguettes at the same time. When the *boulangère* discovered that we shared the same grandchild, I began getting hints of these smiles myself – and fresher bread. No one's fault but my own that this didn't come sooner. I had never taken time to chat with her.

Once known, be a regular customer. If there's a dog lying across the store entrance, don't grunt while you stumble over it. Coo to it. It's the owner's. Ask about it when it's not there. You'll be served first. Parisians love dogs more than anyone. (See below for how they took care of mine.) Always head for the same cashier at the supermarket. Never mind if her line is sometimes longer than others. Also, she needs special attention. It's said that the highest suicide rate in France is of supermarket cashiers. Even French people don't chat them up. Give them the same *Bonjour, madame* that you give the butcher, the baker, the salesgirls, post office agents and all the other French people you deal with.

More Good News

If you really go that extra mile and become pals with a French supermarket cashier, she may save your life one day. Two have saved mine. That is, they literally rescued Chico, my little dog, from kidnapping or worse, which was more or less the same thing. In other words, if they hadn't, I might not have been allowed home.

Chico

Chico was a chunky, wide-waisted little poodle clipped to look like a teddy bear. He was adorable. French people were wild about him. He was famous in all the stores, even the ones where he had to stay outside. He was not only the delight of the whole family; he was like a sixth child. The trouble was that I had a hard enough time counting the other five, and had a way of forgetting Chico outside the small supermarkets where I went marketing, leaving him tethered on the sidewalk. I would go in one door and out another, and we wouldn't see each other. Usually I remembered him when I was halfway down the street, but twice I forgot him entirely.

The first cashier to save Chico was Françoise, the cashier at the Hamon store on the rue de Seine. I always chatted with Françoise. Chico, my five children and her Sicilian husband she couldn't have children with gave us endless themes for conversations, the kind you'd go in a rage about if you were in line behind me. That day she noticed that two vagabonds were playing with Chico. She remembered that I had long since left. She marched out to the sidewalk, grabbed Chico from the vagabonds, got permission from the director to put Chico in his office while she looked up my name on the check I'd just given her, found it in the phone book and telephoned me.

The second cashier who saved my life, by saving Chico's, wasn't as chatty as Françoise, but I'd made a constant effort with her over the years, in the Félix Potin store on the rue de l'Université, near where we lived then. That day I'd paid with cash. I didn't miss Chico until midnight, when I came home from a dinner party and wondered why he didn't jump all over me to welcome me back home. When he was sick, he used to crawl to the back of one of the children's closets. However, he wasn't in that closet, or any of the other closets. I had a bad night.

At the crack of dawn I ran to the store, to be there when it opened, quaking with fear. The cashier let me in.

"He's here," she said, scowling at me with a look of "Shameless, irresponsible delinquent! Unworthy of owning a dog!" that I'll never forget. Then she added, "We fed him, and gave him a bowl of water and a blanket to sleep on."

Chapter 5

Misery in the Big Stores
Your Weapons and How to Handle Them

How would the French respond to a no-questions-asked return policy? A phone that's answered politely in five rings or less?... The French will buy superior service when given the choice. The trick is to deliver service in a country culturally resistant to providing it.

Jeffrey R. Tarr
Wall Street Journal

On a particularly cold day, I stopped in at one of the small Félix Potin supermarkets where I'd been going sporadically for 15 years or so (not the one that rescued Chico). Selecting a soup, I suddenly felt very chilly. As I'm susceptible to pneumonia, I opened my overcoat to button up my jacket inside, then buttoned up the coat again and finished my rounds.

I wheeled the shopping cart to a cashier who had worked at the store as long as I could remember. Usually she was pleasant enough, but that day when I greeted her, she scowled at me and ordered me to open my coat.

Open my coat? I thought I must have misheard and asked her what she'd said. She repeated the same thing, adding that she had seen me open my coat in one of the aisles. Stupefied – unaccustomed to being suspected of being a shoplifter – I pointed out in some heat that I had been shopping there for at least 14 years.

"Je sais bien," she said. "I know – that's why I was surprised."

Customer Insults

Clearly, one can't be too wary. Insults can rain down seemingly out of the blue on a code-trespassing customer. Lots of newcomer spouses, devastated, hole up in the apartment for weeks after. I haven't been back to that Félix Potin store since. There is glory in not surrendering, and taking your business elsewhere, but there's a limit to the number of times you can conveniently change stores in Paris.

The problem is that while the French language is richly brocaded with concepts, customer service is not one of them. Work places are about giving employment, not service. Thus in the big anonymous department stores and supermarkets, the plight of the customer is desperate. Stay away from them unless your French is good and you're lusting for a challenge.

Selling is not one of the respected professions in France, a country where respect is more important than money. Store management generally has not seen fit either to counter the reluctance of their personnel to do their job with a little upbeat motivation training, or to sweeten it with commissions, merit-based promotions or employee profit-sharing. As far as French salespeople are concerned, customers are strangers, and you know what that means. Danger. In this case, the danger of intrusion. Customers are a nuisance.

I was told so, in so many words, at a store of the Ed's grocery chain.

A young clerk in a white smock was standing on a stepladder, blocking the customer's turnstile entrance. He was trying to hang a poster advertising yogurt on a chain from the ceiling. He had trouble with it. A second clerk joined him, on another step ladder. I was in a hurry, but, a battered customer aware of my lack of rights, I waited in silence. Other docile, silent Parisians behind me in the line were conceivably also in a hurry. I waited about seven exasperating minutes before I couldn't bear it any longer.

Finally I said to the first clerk very quietly, very politely, "Do you think you could come down – just for a moment – and let us through?"

"No," he said, rather rudely. "Can't you see I'm busy?"

"But – I'm in a hurry!" I said, astonished.

"You'll have to wait!"

"But the customer!" I blurted out. "Doesn't the customer mean anything here?"

And then he said – he actually said, "The customer comes last here!"

The Store Director Will Always Back his Employees

A supermarket or department store director and his employees are in the same loyalty club. Relationships are for keeps in France. So the director always stands by his employee, whom he knows and needs, against you, the customer, who is irrelevant. Besides, firing people is difficult and expensive.

You, the customer, can shriek in fury all you want, the director will not hurry you off to a quiet corner and coddle you and commiserate with you. He will tell you his employee is right and you can stuff it.

The Customer Is Automatically Wrong, the Store Never Is

At Ed's, as in lots of supermarkets in Paris, you have to put a 10-franc piece into the shopping cart to use it. One day, the 10-franc piece stuck. I signaled this to a cashier. She shrugged. I asked for another 10-franc piece. She refused.

The attraction of Ed's is the discount. But as with all the big stores, the disadvantage is the employee turnover; you can never get cozy with any of the personnel. I'd been going to that store also for many years, once or twice a week, spending thousands of francs a month.

Curious about the store policy, I asked to see the director. This young man of about 35 with a three-day beard, no tie and a rumpled shirt, informed me that no 10-franc piece had ever gotten stuck before. He implied heavily that it had also not gotten stuck that day. I insisted. He shrugged. He didn't believe me? In other words, he thought I was lying?

He said he didn't say that. I raised my voice and suggested that a customer of 14 years could be given a 10-franc piece even if she were lying, to please her – and keep her quiet.

Now he started shouting, repeating that no one had ever lost a 10-franc piece in that store, and so on.

I gave up.

Customer Contempt or –?

This double whammy was maybe less about customer contempt than about the political incorrectness in France of suggesting that anything or anyone in a store – or anywhere else, for that matter – might have some kind of shortcoming.

One Christmas, I wanted to send something special to Marina Eloy, the human resources director of J. P. Morgan Europe, who had been my first corporate client. She had been transferred to London. What could please a French person more than foie gras? Where to order it sent from but Fauchon, arguably the world's most sublime grocer, which has been thrilling customers nutritionally around the world since 1887?

I did so, and heard nothing from her after Christmas. At the end of January, I asked her the awkward question. Had she received the foie gras? No. I called up the store. They said that if I had ordered the foie gras and paid for it, it had arrived. Period. Next question.

73

Two more phone calls, with the sales slip in my hand, were no more fruitful. Partly out of curiosity to see how long it would take them and in what way they would finally decide to deal with my – and their – embarrassment, I stuck with it. Three more phone calls yielded nothing. I had to visit the store twice, going over the whole thing both times in detail, to get a reaction.

Finally a letter – dated April 16 – arrived. Its entire content was a declaration that the "package" I had ordered sent to England had been returned by English customs; I would find a check enclosed for the amount paid. Which, in the French *formule de politesse*, they hoped I would "well receive with the expression of their great consideration." End of letter.

Did this old, supremely elegant, sophisticated and world-experienced store feel remorse at not having been better informed about British customs? Did they regret causing a vexing incident to a customer? Did they wish to compensate me in some way for the embarrassment and the loss of time insisting on their getting to the bottom of it?

Decidedly not. So much for the shock of a service-oriented foreigner expecting a phrase of astonishment at a possibly new British customs regulation, a soothing phrase like "we are terribly sorry" and, which would be fairly automatic in the U.S. in such a store, a free gift of foie gras to keep me on their client list.

Strategy for Prevailing

The French passion for individual *liberté* mentioned earlier means that every citizen has the right to decide lots of things on his own. Sometimes his discretion and analysis of the situation is openly invited. Have you ever noticed that on some streets, signs tell you that parking is *toléré* (tolerated)? He exercises this right most visibly with his smoking and his jaywalking. As for his driving... well, we'll get to that in the Coda.

And so it is that employees dealing with the public have an enormous amount of room for maneuvering within the parameters of what they're employed or forbidden to do.

In other words, they usually have the power to do what you want, if they want to.

It's up to you to make them want to. To seduce them away from Them to Us.

Everything is negotiable.

Well, anyway, most things.

At the workplace it's different, but when dealing with people you've never seen before and are not likely to see again – salespeople, hotel, theater, post office and railroad agents – the first thing to do is to throw yourself on their mercy, making it clear that you recognize their power and your own helplessness.

Tell them how desperate you are for the thing you need (the bag, the hotel room) or which is missing (a sheet at the laundry) or which you want to exchange (a theater ticket). French people love the theater, so be theatrical. Give them a treat. Make it funny. Remember the joke my hairdresser dreamed up for me, so that she and her customers and assistants could laugh their heads off. Pile on the charm. Persevere. Show confidence and unwavering conviction. Show you mean it.

What *"Non"* Really Means

"Non" hardly ever means "no." More usually: "Persuade me."

"Ça n'existe pas" ("that doesn't exist") means, "It's down in the storeroom."

"Impossible" (the same word in English) means "I'm tired" or "I'm busy" or "The way you put your request doesn't intrigue me enough to bother with it."

It can also mean, "I don't like your looks or the way you behave, so I won't do anything to please you, quite the opposite."

If you ask a hotel clerk for a room, he might say, for instance, *"Normalement* (normally) we're fully booked." Or, *"En principe* (in principle) we're full up." A down-to-earth Anglo-American might understand this to mean, as it would in English, that indeed, the hotel is full up. He assumes the hotel is either booked up, or it isn't. What it means is, however, "We're pretty full, but I'm saving a few rooms for people who really need them, or who appeal to me."

This is not an invitation to take out your wallet. No! It's your cue to paint your anguish in tiniest detail. Be personal. Pour it all out. They want to be coaxed. And they want to be interested; if possible, amused. Then you've moved over to Us, and will always get a room there, thereafter.

It's a strategy that works all over southern and central Europe. My seminar alumni tell me it even works in northern Europe, England and the U.S.! Anyway, sometimes. I call it Persistent Personal Operating, or PPO.

Colin Corder's PPO in Action

English author Colin Corder, an old hand at Paris, rang up a hotel in the Latin Quarter where he had stayed a couple of times before. Told they were *complet* (full), he asked for names of other hotels. He called three of them and got the same answer.

"The only thing I could think of was to call back the first hotel and try to seduce the lady concierge with the gravity of my plight," he said. "So I rang back and said, 'Madame, I have a big problem. The hotels you suggested to me a few minutes ago are also full. I rang your hotel first because I have had such pleasant times there. A group of us comes over regularly for the France-England rugby match and we always stay with you. We always find it very comfortable. I only need a room for two days...'

"There was a moment of silence. Then she said, '*Attendez, monsieur.*' ('Wait, sir.') I waited, my hopes rising. Then she said, 'When are you arriving?'

"And she gave me a wonderful room, not under the eaves as I'd feared, but in the best part of the hotel."

For an uptight, law-abiding, patient line-waiter and turn-taker, PPO can be a little shocking to watch in action. It shocked me as a bride in Salzburg, when Ande was looking for an Austrian loden jacket, called a *janker*. The salesgirl said that the only one there in his size was reserved for someone else. Ande cajoled her, flirted with her, told her jokes, made her laugh and walked out with the jacket.

"Someone else's jacket!" I said, horrified.

"Nonsense," he said. "If she hadn't given it to me, it would have been to the next customer."

PPO is why deliveries are late and why the Germans go crazy over the Austrians, the French and other southern Europeans. It's also a lot of fun when you get onto it, and extremely satisfying when it works. With PPO and the Ten Magic Words, Bret Moran (Chapter 4) could have easily gotten a bag for his bread. *Boulangères* do have bags available on request, but only for very old customers, or those who grovel for them. Faced with her waterfall of French, he should have made an instant reversal of strategy – pleaded that he was on a bicycle, and launched into the drama he would face balancing his loaf of bread on his handlebars. Warren should have appraised his request more accurately, gone with it straight to the bank director, started out with the Ten Words and poured on the PPO. Polly should have headed for the cashier she knew and greeted her with the Ten Magic Words, and then presented her 100-franc note for the yogurt, along with groans about her sprained ankle that prevented her from changing the note somewhere farther from where she lived.

Bargain! Anyway, Try

Prices are not carved in stone, either. Whether you're buying a car, a couch or television set, you can probably negotiate the price down. Again, it all depends on whether the sales person feels like being accommodating, which, again is up to you. He or she probably has the discretionary power, except in one of the huge discount stores where the profit margins are much narrower. It's certainly worth a try. Even during *soldes* (sales).

You go about it like this. First you check the price of the lawnmower, or whatever you need, in various stores. Then, if you're a man, you look at the price tag and say to the salesman, "Well, this price is not realistic – it's for tourists and people who don't know any better. What price are you offering me?" If he refuses, you walk out, or threaten to. If he names a price, you offer a much lower one. This goes on. You creep up very gradually, until you agree.

If you're a woman and you feel this is a bit rough for you, then you look at the price in misery and say that much as you love the chair, or dress, your budget just doesn't allow for such an outlay. Then you pick up the routine above. Remembering to apply all the steps of PPO.

The main thing is to be a regular customer. It pays off, literally.

Julie Winn: "A lot of time they give me five or ten percent off even *without* my asking! They know me! It happened twice in the last two days!"

PPO: Three Tales of Customer Triumph

At Heathrow Airport, London

At the airport in London I found myself in a typical foreigner's mess due to incomplete information. I was on the special kind of cut-rate London-Paris return ticket for 600 francs that you could only get in Paris 24 hours before departure. I didn't know that I was supposed to make the reservation for the return trip in the city of London, not at the airport. So the check-in agent refused to let me on the 4:00 plane.

"But I have to be in Paris!" I wailed.

"You can buy a new ticket, Madam. "

Right. One way – for 1,000 francs. I saw that charm and theater would be of no avail in this Rules Before People culture, so I asked to see the director for Air France. In due course the director showed up – a woman. My heart sank. But at least she was French.

I stated my case. She inspected my ticket.

She was politely brisk. "I'm sorry, Madame, but on this ticket you will have to go back to London to make your reservation for the flight back to Paris."

I carefully did not air my opinion that this was a ridiculous regulation. I said, which was the truth, "But I didn't know that."

"Everyone says that."

"You mean you don't believe me?"

"That has nothing to do with it. In any case, hundreds of people say that every week."

I could see I was losing her. I was tired, but I revved myself up for devastating PPO. "But you see, if I'd known, I'd have done it! I wouldn't have taken any chances on not being in Paris tonight! I have to be there to give a seminar. All these corporate managers will be waiting!" I pleaded.

"I'm sorry, Madame, we can't make an exception. We'd have to do it for everyone."

Then I had what proved to be an inspiration. "But you see – I really am an exception!"

For some reason this got to her. She gave me a long cool look and told me to take a seat and wait a while. Twenty minutes later she came back and said I could leave on the 5:00 plane.

At the Apple Store

At about 5:30 on a rainy afternoon in 1986, after doing a lot of tiresome errands, I forgot all my own good advice. It was when I was launching my cross-culture business. I hadn't bought any equipment, because I wasn't yet sure that it would *be* a business. To get the word around about the wonderful seminars I was offering, I'd borrowed a Macintosh from a young American student friend, who, however, hadn't lugged his printer over the Atlantic. In those days there were no Mac boutiques where you could rent one. So my flyer was only theoretical, as long as it was stuck inside the disk.

My only hope was to throw myself on the mercy of an Apple store.

But by the time I got there that rainy day, I was so exhausted that I forgot to beg. I simply went up to a man behind the counter and spoke to him as I would have in the U.S. Directly.

After "*Bonjour, monsieur,*" I said, in French. "Could you do me a favor, please? I need a printout of something on my disk and I don't have a printer here."

He looked at me with total incredulity. You'd have thought I was asking for a piece of a Martian crater.

"*Comment?*" he said finally. "What?"

I repeated my request.

"Je ne comprends pas," he said, irritably. "I don't understand."

I went through it a third time, adding again that I didn't have a machine available here.

This time, at least, he understood – and was even more incredulous.

"Impossible!" he said, looking stupefied at the craziness of what even a foreigner might come up with.

Finally it dawned on me that I was doing this all wrong. I backtracked, I changed my voice, facial expression and body language from a person asking for a cup of coffee in a café to as close an imitation as I could perform of one of those Salvation Army bellringers.

"Oh dear," I said, "I'm really sorry to bother you with this – I know how busy you are (there was no one else in the shop) and I realize that you don't rent out your beautiful new Macintoshes, but there isn't any place in all of Paris that does – not in all of France, maybe nowhere in Europe – and I'm really desperate --"

I had his attention now, his expression slightly less horrified. So I really poured it on.

"You see, I'm trying to start a new business, giving seminars about France – and how different and wonderful the French are – so that foreigners will get on here better – but I can't give the seminars if no one comes – and no one will come if they don't know about them – so you see, the promotional flyer describing them on this disk is absolutely crucial for my whole future – I don't know where else to turn --"

He studied me for a moment, now frowning reflectively. He was thin and pale, with just a few sparse hairs combed over his bald spot, almost a caricature of the pinched-face Frenchman. From the deference of another salesman who came up to him with a question, I understood that, luckily for me, he was the manager of the store.

After a while he said solemnly, "Wait here a few minutes. I'll see what I can do."

It was then about 5:45. A few minutes became almost half an hour. At 6:10 he took my disk and summoned the flyer to a big screen.

He looked at it. "But this is very ugly!" he exploded.

I said I was sorry that it wasn't terribly elegant, but I was a beginner with Macintoshes and really, it didn't have to be perfect, I only needed just one printout to make copies from...

He wouldn't hear of it. "Sit down and translate for me. You can't send out a mess like this."

For the next hour and a half, until a quarter to 8:00, he worked on that text, shifting it around, changing the fonts and type styles and sizes until it looked absolutely gorgeous. The other salesmen had long since gone home. The store closed at 7:00.

He wouldn't let me pay anything. "Good luck," he said. "Come back whenever you need another."

(Note: I asked Chantal, my hairdresser, how to show my ecstatic gratefulness. She said to send a bottle of Armagnac with his name on it. I did. He was pleased. And I did go back, many times.)

On an Air France 747

This is my sweetest PPO triumph, a misery that ended lyrically.

On a New York to Paris flight I found myself placed next to a baby of three months. Its bassinet was hung from the adjacent seat in such a way that it was over my own knees. Five minutes out of Kennedy and the baby began to scream. The mother gave it its bottle. It spat up all over my lap. Then it began screaming again.

I went to the steward and asked for another seat. He was a DOM-TOM (a French citizen from one of the overseas dominions or territories, in this case Martinique) and very nervous. He refused. The plane was full. No extra seats. Sit down and (it sounded like) shut up.

My options were minimal. I decided that standing up was preferable to sitting down next to a screaming, vomiting baby. I took a book and stood near the galley, reading. This was next to where the steward had his station. He erupted.

"You can't stand there!" he hissed. "Go back to your seat!"

I explained quietly that this was out of the question. I would have my dinner there, and if a seat didn't turn up, well, then I would just stand up all the way to Paris.

His face flushed angrily, but he couldn't think of how to deal with me. I was pleased with my decision, though I hate standing up. I was curious to see what would happen next.

A little while later I saw a trim officer descending the spiral stairway from the cockpit. He came up to me, saluted smartly and introduced himself as the copilot. He said he understood there was a problem?

I explained. He said he'd have a look around, surely he could find me a seat. But after making the tour of the plane in vain, he expressed his regrets.

Then he said, "Unfortunately this happens from time to time... and alas, there is very little we can do. But..." He looked at me and hesitated. "But ... after your dinner, would you care to join us in the cockpit?"

"In the cockpit?" I was dazzled.

"Good. Then I'll come down for you later."

In due course, after the steward gave me my dinner at the galley with a face of thunder, the copilot came to get me.

For the first time in my life I climbed the spiral stairway and stepped into the glass dome of the sky-gods, the heavens and all their stars spread out before me in the vast black night. I'd flown with friends in small planes, but never at night. At night in the cockpit of a 747, try it.

The pilot turned around to greet me with great courtesy and said he hoped I'd be comfortable in the seat behind him, next to the navigator. He was a handsome man in his forties, with a strong back, clear, sharp, kind eyes and a silent John Wayne feeling of competence and cool-headedness, someone who could handle any emergency. If someone told you, "Draw your dream pilot of a 747," this is the man you'd draw.

I sat down in the leather seat behind him and sank into the celestial black silence, marveling, singularly joyous.

I don't know how long I was there. There is no time in the silence of the heavens in an open space ship – maybe a lifetime. Long enough to be swept into another dimension. So that when you come back you brim over. Softly. Tenderly grateful to these star warriors. Ready to assume anything, even a screaming baby.

How do you thank a sky-god for his magic? I tried to. I told him his kindness had healed me. I could go back now.

He said, "Would you like to come back for the landing?"

Would I!

When I climbed back up, the spell of the night had passed with the daylight. It was a different kind of spell to approach what seemed like the whole Continent at our feet, and to watch the teamwork of the crew in bringing that colossal ship down. The landing was so soft it felt like coming down on a cloud. I said so to the captain.

People are People in France

The happy bottom line of all this is that, even being a foreigner at sea in a new culture where you probably haven't yet mastered the language, you're never, or almost never, up against a stone wall of rules and no's in your daily life, once you're in sync with the codes. As you can see, I've found the French to be astoundingly aware and understanding of the anxieties and complications of the lives of their fellow humans. Human beings come first. With PPO, train conductors have let me travel on a discount ticket, although I left my discount card at home. Theater ticket agents have exchanged tickets issued for the wrong night, which I should have noticed at the time, even though on the ticket it said clearly that they couldn't be exchanged or refunded. A news photo agency took pity on me and not only reduced the fee for photos to one-fourth, but also included a photo free of charge. This does not happen in the monochronic countries.

It might even happen with civil servants, as you'll see in the next chapters. But as you'll also see, don't count on it.

Chapter 6

Blame Paranoia
Truth and Consequences

On n'a pas droit à l'erreur en France.
(One does not have the right to make a mistake in France.)

Odile Challe
Professor of Organizational Behavior
University of Paris-Dauphine

It isn't just store personnel who have trouble being graceful about admitting defects or mistakes. Blame in France is a hot potato no one wants to catch, even if justified. Some people might say, particularly if justified. Foreigners all agree about this: the French are paranoid about accepting it. For anything, from a forgotten appointment to a political scandal.

It isn't that the French are "arrogant," as some foreigners have suggested. The fact is that mistakes are culturally unacceptable in France. As Professor Odile Challe says above, French people do not have the right to make them.

"Refusing to admit mistakes goes through all levels of French society," said a young French banker with an American mother. "And at work, it drives me nuts."

"In the U.S., admitting error is not only seen as honest, but important," said Dixon Thayer, vice president of Scott (Paper) Europe. "In an American company, you're not perceived as learning much if you don't make mistakes. Therefore you won't move up, at least not in this company. It's like skiing — you're not going to learn how if you don't take a lot of falls. But in affiliation cultures like France, there is the matter of face involved. If a senior manager makes a mistake, he and everyone below him loses face. If he, or a lower-level manager, admits a mistake it is perceived as weakness."

As Anglo-Saxons consider admitting mistakes good form, fair play and good sportmanship, even taking blame for minor mistakes of other people, this makes for bizarre differences with the French in daily life. In business, it can be expensive, as well as infuriating.

In the English-speaking world, when two people are involved in some kind of minor incident, such as one person knocking over the other's glass of water, inaccurate bidding in a bridge game or getting lost because of inaccurate directions, a ballet takes place with a series of "I'm sorry, it's my fault", answered by, "No, it's my fault, I'm sorry."

The choreography is automatic: everyone knows whose fault it is, but the pretense is played out.

But in France, when the Canadian, American or Briton says politely, "I'm sorry," knowing it's not his fault, expecting the Anglo-Saxon response, "No, no, it's my fault, I'm sorry," he hears instead,*"Ce n'est pas grave."* ("That's all right, it doesn't matter.")

After five years in Paris, Walter Schwartz, of the *Manchester Guardian*, wrote that in France, "not only does no one ever say they're sorry, there isn't even a word for it."

The French response to someone else's clumsiness, for instance, or their own, is also a ballet. The pretense is simply danced in the opposite manner. Some of the examples found to be "off the wall" by Americans:

At Angelina, the fashionable tearoom on the rue de Rivoli, a Frenchwoman rose from the table with a swirl of her cape, which threw over the sugar bowl to the floor. Sugar cubes scattered far and wide. "What a stupid place to put a sugar bowl," she said huffily.

Emily Borel watched a similar incident at a restaurant. The woman at the next table was choosing from a selection of hors d'oeuvres on a wooden tray perched precariously near the edge of the table.

"I was just waiting for the whole thing to go smash on the floor," said Emily. "And what do you know, she turned around to look at something and her elbow knocked over the wooden tray. All the little dishes – there they went, smash onto the floor, all over it. Terrible mess. Her comment to the waiter was, 'Why did you put the tray there?'"

A French dinner guest spilled some red wine on my beige sofa. "What a strange color for a sofa!" was her comment.

An American spilled some red wine on my rug and immediately whipped out his checkbook. "I'm dreadfully sorry," he said. "Will $100 cover the cleaning?"

Similarly, when there's a political fiasco, Americans sometimes seem to be actually chasing opportunities to embrace blame, as in this strip of *Doonesbury*.

Doonesbury

by Garry Trudeau

Blame and Responsibility in the wake of Waco
Copyright © 1993 by Universal Press Syndicate
reprinted by permission of Editors Press Service, Inc.

But if you have grown up being excoriated for all your mistakes, and if, in addition, mistakes might bring the wrath of the gods in some unimaginably dreadful way upon you and your family; or if at the very least, admitting a mistake is considered a weakness in your culture, then it's understandable that you're at pains to reject it in whatever way possible — deny it, color it slightly differently, or minimize it.

A scandal broke which was laid at the door of Georgina Dufoix, the former Minister of Health. As President of the French Red Cross, she had given permission for the second most notorious Palestinian terrorist, George Habash, to be flown to Paris for medical treatment in February, 1992. An outraged uproar ensued. Habash, known as the "Terrorist Führer," had been allegedly responsible for the bombing of a department store in central Paris in 1986, killing 25 and maiming 128 French shoppers and pedestrians.

Madame Dufoix, confronted with the scandal, conceded an *"erreur"* in not having advised the President or the Prime Minister about her charitable act, while maintaining that her action had been "correct" for humanitarian reasons.

An *erreur* is bad enough. But it's a picnic compared to a *faute*. Madame Dufoix, famous for her comment that she was "responsible but not guilty" (*"responsable mais pas coupable"*) concerning a previous scandal, knows her nuances and ambiguities. In French, an *erreur* is a mistake you're not supposed to make, but that you do innocently, if clumsily. A *faute* is an error you make knowingly. It can be anything from a blunder to a misdemeanor, or worse. After Napoleon had the young Duc d'Enghien assassinated, Talleyrand said, *"C'est pire qu'un crime, c'est une faute."* ("It's worse than a crime, it's *une faute*."). You can see from this that admitting a *faute* is a no-no. It turned out that a Castro interview of one of French television's star anchormen, which had seemed to be a one-on-one interview with the Cuban dictator, was actually a montage of the anchorman asking questions – and Castro answering some other unseen person's questions at some other time and place. Said the anchorman: *"J'ai fait une erreur, mais pas une faute."* ("I made an error but not *une faute*.")

Newspaper investigations about who or what is at the bottom of various *fautes* often evaporate into thin air. Whose *faute* was it that 1,800 passengers were stranded all night long at Orly airport outside Paris on what came to be known as Black Friday, May 17, 1991? The airport computer failure was repaired by 10:00 p.m., but the planes weren't authorized to take off until the next morning.

There was food for very few, beds for fewer and no one got where they wanted to go. The passengers stormed and blamed the domestic French airline Air Inter. The CEO of Air Inter, Jean-Cyril Spinetta, blamed the Civil Aviation Authority (DGAC), stating that the fact that Air Inter was giving all stranded passengers free round-trip tickets did not mean that Air Inter considered itself *"coupable."* This was a "commercial gesture." The DGAC also refused to catch this hot potato, declaring in effect that it wasn't the DGAC's *faute* that there was an agreement with an association of residents near the airport that forbids planes from taking off after 11:30 p.m.

As the daily *Le Figaro* put it, "There is no question of DGAC ordering a general investigation in order to know where to place the *faute*."

Truth Is Not Necessarily Beauty

With all this, it is easy to see that George Washington never would have made it to President of France if that story about the cherry tree ever got out. Let's tackle the inevitable corollary of the Not-Me ballet. Truth, or what Anglo-Americans mean by Truth, is relative in France.

Here is the key:

"Truth is less important than not being *en faute*," said Edouard D., an industrialist. "So some people might go so far as to lie from time to time."

This does not make a "liar" out of you. There is no accurate translation for this English battle cry bristling with the three dreads, shame, guilt and dishonor. A *menteur* is someone who plays with the truth. It does not reflect on his morality or his *honneur*. Calling someone a *menteur* will not start a barroom brawl. Don't bother to check in the dictionary, they don't deal with conceptual differences.

Franco-American marriages can crumble over this.

"I remember the first – and last – time I called Harry a liar," said Françoise R. "He was very very angry. While in France, this doesn't mean anything."

An American lawyer married to a French wife: "French people have to be careful, perhaps fantasize, certainly avoid admitting anything that might ever be held against them in an unknown, frightening future, where everything may be different."

Given this general scheme of things, facts may become an abstraction. Facts can be pretty boring, and if there's no compelling reason to stick to them, and perhaps a compelling one not to, the natural thing for imaginative people is to play around with them – dress them up or ignore them, as you please. If you make up your life, it's much more fun. Savoir-vivre means enjoying the present. I give you theater, you give me theater. Besides, what's a fact anyway?

Anglo-Saxons, rigorously fact-oriented, are usually perplexed with how to deal with this. After a while, some of them find that spotting the lies can become a sort of fun game. Here is one who triumphed:

Mark Adamczyk, a financial strategist at Groupe Bull, rented a beautifully equipped apartment in a lovely old building in the Marais section of Paris. He didn't need the garage that went with it, so he rented it to a Frenchman in the building, and gave him the key.

"A few days later he came to see me," said Mark, "and told me I had given him the wrong key. At first I thought I was hearing things. He repeated it. I told him that indeed I had given him the right key. He argued, and showed me a key I'd never seen before. Was this guy nuts, or what? Then I remembered what you'd told us about lying here. So I looked him straight in the eye and said, forcefully, 'I GAVE YOU THE KEY – AND YOU LOST IT! So you – not me – will have to have another one made!'

"You know what? He admitted it – just like that – as if it was nothing. No embarrassment. Just trying. Okay, I won, so he had a new key made."

"In France You Can Tell Small Lies"

How to deal with this at the office?

General Electric, the quintessential all-American gung-ho company, was in for some surprises when it took over a state-owned medical equipment company, Cie. Générale de Radiologie (CGR) a few years ago. Its projected $25 million profit for 1989 turned out to be a $25 million loss. One of the reasons was that French managers, as the *Wall Street Journal* reported (July 27,1990), "simply exaggerated their forecasts about cost cutting, production and sales as well as other key data."

The *Journal* quoted the explanation for this of a well-known French communications consultant in Paris, Bernard Krief: "In the U.S., lying is a serious offense. In France, you can tell small lies."

While Americans tell lies all the time too – the latest survey reported in the *International Herald Tribune* claimed that the average American tells 19 lies a week – they can't hide from that cherry tree. George is looking at them. To be called a "liar" in England or America is a devastating assault which one can't allow. People who are "liars" have lost everyone's respect. In the U.S., lying subordinates are fired. In France they're Through the Looking Glass.

"After a while you learn to spot the lies," said Kevin R., a production coordinator in a French company. "I was pretty burned up when I found out that my assistant had changed the notes of a meeting – and then lied to me about it. The main problem is keeping your respect of the people who are found out. You have to get rid of that American self-righteousness about everything that is different, and realize that all of us are more or less products of cultural programming."

See Chapter 16 for more about handling this at work.

Meanwhile, keep in mind a frequently quoted French proverb: *"Toutes les vérités ne sont pas bonnes à dire."* ("All truths are not appropriate to say.") Old civilizations have an old wisdom all their own. After he retired from politics, Montaigne (1533-1592), one of France's most eminent writers, spent much of his life in a tower of his chateau in the Dordogne, pondering the great questions of existence. Man, he concluded, was powerless to find truth and justice. Both were relative, and depended on your culture. Man was destined to search for truth, but only a greater power could possess it. *"Quelle vérité que ces montagnes bornent,"* he asks in his *Essays*, *"qui est mensonge qui se tient au delà?"* ("What truth is that which these mountains bound, and is a lie in the world beyond them?") One hundred years later, Pascal (1623-1662), the great mathematician and inventor, was struck by the same thing. *"Plaisante justice qu'une rivière borne!"* he cries in his *Pensées. "Vérité au deça des Pyrénées, erreur au delà."* ("It is a fine kind of justice that has a river for its boundary! Truth on this side of the Pyrenees, error on the other side.")

Not Me! à l'Autrichienne

Don't make the mistake of thinking the French have a monopoly on blame denial. Austrians may have similar reactions. I was driving along a country road with an Austrian friend when something caught her eye at one of the roadside antique shops. She drove into the courtyard, where there were several large terra cotta vases, the kind you see on walls of Italian gardens, and went into the shop. She looked around, came out and got back into the car. She had to go into reverse to drive out. She backed into the largest of the terra cotta vases. The owner came running out, shouting and wringing his hands.

"My vase! It's broken! You must pay!" he said

"Don't be ridiculous. It was already broken," she said, and drove off.

I had my first glimpse of the dangers of blame admission in Austria.

It was on one of those after-college tours of Europe with four Wellesley classmates, among them Hannah Green, now a well-known novelist. We were driving down a steep mountain towards Innsbruck, in a hurry to get to Italy, when Hannah saw some caves by the side of the road.

"Oh please stop!" she said. "I must see what's inside the caves!"

We reminded her that we were already hours off schedule. None of the rest of us wanted to stop.

"I'll be very fast!" she pleaded. "I won't be a minute!"

She flew out of the car to one of the caves, and true to her word, ran back across the road just a few minutes later. She was in such a hurry to mollify us that she didn't look up or down the mountain before crossing, and collided with an old woman on a bicycle coming down. Hannah was unhurt and got right up, but the old woman lay on the road unconscious. Almost immediately, the road, which had seemed to be running through empty countryside, was swarming with police and bystanders.

A policeman came up to Hannah and asked her what happened.

Hannah, conscience-stricken, upset about the old woman, then uttered the fateful words.

"Oh, it was all my fault!" she said. "I wasn't looking where I was going!"

"*Wirklich*? Really?" he said, looking surprised. And then, although in many countries the person on wheels in collision with a pedestrian is thought to be legally at fault, he told her she would have to stay under police supervision in Innsbruck until the woman recovered – or didn't. In that case, she would find herself in court.

The rest of us were aghast. We thought it must be a joke. We told him, in our imperfect German, that this was impossible. Hannah couldn't stay there. We were expected that night in Bologna.

However, the policemen, by this time about 10 strong, made it clear that Hannah was not going anywhere. We drew straws to see who would stay with her. Hannah and the "winner" had a week of forced sightseeing under guard, before the old woman's condition improved and they could join us in Italy.

Chapter 7

You and the Bureaucracy
The Système D

I've been driving since I was 16. That's 17 years. And I come to France and have to go to driving school! For six weeks! And then pass a driving test with the police! And because I make a mistake on judging the number of meters between me and the next car, I fail it!

Yolanda G.
Groupe Bull

Now for the big A – tackling that citadel of power known as *l'Administration*. There is no way around the French bureaucracy in some form or other, if you stay for any length of time. You need good nerves, determination, patience and a great sense of identity. You need time, lots of time; all, but all of the techniques in the preceding chapters – reread them before your first visit – and an appetite for adventure, mystery and suspense.

The Big A is Them with a capital T. The good news is that Them are people too, and that France is about personal relationships.

Figuring it out with the other French people you deal with in one way or another is a great warm-up for the Big A. With your Persistent Personal Operating (PPO) and your awareness of never accusing a French person of a *faute* – particularly a bureaucrat ! – you're almost ready to sail through your encounters with civil servants at the Big A.

But not quite.

First you must master that tool which is indispensable in handling things at the Big A, the *Système D*.

"D" comes from *débrouiller*, meaning to untangle, to sort out.

Se débrouiller is to extricate yourself from difficulties. This can take many forms, from convincing a civil servant in the Administration to abridge certain procedures involved in issuing you a document to driving down a one-way street the wrong way to escape a traffic jam. It is *not* doing something illegal. People who think it is inevitably end up in deep trouble. However, it can be convincing a policeman, as a French lawyer explained it to me, "that you have an exceptional reason why the application of the law can be suspended in this particular case." In other words, you can defend yourelf.

For instance, Yves B. was doing 130 kilometers an hour on a back road (90 km/hr speed limit) when his Porsche was stopped. In the bucket seat, his American wife was visibly pregnant, about a month more to go. Yves was now in danger of being parted from 900 francs.

"*Mais, monsieur l'agent,*" said Yves, "look at my wife's condition. It wouldn't be good for her to go more slowly on these bumpy roads!"

The gendarme cracked up. Yves drove on, soberer, at 90 km/hr, not minus his 900 francs.

Or take Becky C., an English student, at Avignon. She failed to come to a complete stop at three signs in the outskirts of Montélimar at 1:00 in the morning. Two gendarmes pulled her over.

"You have committed three traffic offenses," they told her. "Each one is 450 francs. You must pay on the spot."

She pleaded, "I'm working here to pay for my university; 1,350 francs is two weeks' wages."

No response.

She tried another tack. "Why didn't you stop me after the first time – that way, it would only have been 450 francs?"

The gendarmes saw her point, and settled for 450 francs.

France is a very old, legalistic country where laws are taken very seriously. Inside the great big box called the Law, there is a stupefying maze of exceedingly complicated and time-consuming procedures for applying the laws that the French refer to as a behemoth. Whatever document you need means a series of visits to whatever state institution involved, interminable waits and inconclusive interviews with perhaps brusque, perhaps ponderous bureaucrats, who often seem to be searching for insurmountable obstacles to solving your problem. The *Système D* is finding a person in a position willing and able to cut through the procedures for you... to take you straight through the behemoth, fast forward. "Without the *Système D*, life in France would be intolerable," a French banker told me.

First, a word about the French civil servants who are responsible for the behemoth's frunctioning.

Privy to the centralized state's millennium of laws, decrees, regulations and counter-regulations, empowered by the state to have them respected, civil servants – referred to by the French as *ils* – have their finger in every imaginable pie concerning their compatriots, except the boudoir.

Ils are known as *fonctionnaires*. They make up one-fourth of the French work force and they're unfireable. Their employment is for life. The French word for this state of permanent unaccountability for magistrates is *inamovible*, which means not only that their employment is for life, but also, that particular job. The rest of the *fonctionnaires* can be shuffled around between ministries and state industries – but never fired. As no civil servant, from the clerk to the *grand commis de l'Etat* (high civil servant) can be fired, and as all of them have special rights (*droits acquis*), you can see why French mothers battle for their son to become a civil servant, the higher the better, comfortable and secure in his rank, with a specific power that he can guard jealously.

Think about it. It translates to mean they have the invincible power to bulldoze through a pet project by strategically ignoring directives, or to stop one by infinitely refined delaying tactics.

It means they have the decisive clout of inevitable, exasperating eternity.

In *Le Mal Français*, former Minister Alain Peyrefitte describes how hard it can be even for their supposed masters, the politicans of the government, to get their policies implemented. Politicians are voted out. Governments change. But the *fonctionnaires* are there for the duration of the Republic.

Fonctionnaires are well trained and competent. They've passed tough, demanding exams. They're probably the world's most brilliant, dedicated, scrupulous and conscientious corps of civil servants at all levels. Except for the *grands commis de l'Etat* just one or two steps below the cabinet ministers, they're poorly paid. They make up for this by the exercise, or refusal to exercise, a certain parcel of power in a rigid and scrupulously maintained hierarchy.

L'Administration is about rank as much as power. Everyone has someone over them and someone under them, all with corresponding power levels and privileges, and they mean to keep it like that, all the way up to the top. In other words, it's a resounding echo of feudalism, the back stairs of the French soul: there, unseen, an immutable link with the ancient past.

The French Revolution only changed the labels and the criteria. Today's dukes are the *grands commis de l'Etat*. They're running things now, not because their blood is blue but because their brain is a whiz at civil administration. But the system is similar, except for the concept of duty towards the rank just above, and that instead of the lord for protection, they have their statute of eternal unfireability. The President rules at the pinnacle, where the King used to, alongside God. The French press often blurred the two, referring to the late Mr. Mitterrand as God (*Dieu*).

President Mitterrand as God giving life to France (Marianne) assisted by his Ministers Rocard and Jospin as angels
(Serguei, *Le Monde*)

The *Système D* is first of all knowing how to find the human being at the right rank who is in a position to put your request through, and secondly knowing how to convince him to do it. Otherwise, you might be told that, according to Article L103B 12/2, the answer to your request is on page 1,001 of .... (phone rings, papers rustle) you'll have to come back tomorrow – except that tomorrow, we're closed, next week I'm on vacation...

The Surgeon and the Préfecture de Police

One of the most dreaded of the *Administration's* cells is the Préfecture de Police, or police headquarters. Non-Common Market foreigners have to deal with it for their *carte de séjour* or residence permit, if they want to stay in France more than six months. And if they want to work there. And for lots of other vital documents.

Lou Martin, the handsome surgeon and professor at Louisiana State University Hospital, is about 40, with a caressing voice and a shy, disarming smile. He was much missed by students and patients alike when he came to Paris on a sabbatical, doing thyroid research with INSERM, the French government research institute. He often had occasion to wonder if it had been such a great idea. He spoke no French. He didn't know about the *Système D.*

"I tried to get my *carte de séjour* right after I got to Paris," Lou said, "because I knew how easy it was to do the wrong thing, and was afraid of getting in terrible trouble – for instance, if I had an accident with my car. I arrived when Americans still had to have visas, and I'd seen people without one thrown out of the country at the airport.

"I'd already had an unpleasant experience on the Métro. I'd gotten my *Carte Orange* (a monthly Métro subscription) and was very pleased with myself – I thought I was doing things the French way. But I didn't realize there were then two classes on the Métro. We don't have to deal with trains too much in the U.S., and the only subways I was familiar with don't have a first class.

"Well, so I'm sitting in the first class and this inspector comes up and asks something. My French isn't good enough to know what. I show him my Carte Orange and he looks at it and growls, '70 francs!' I recognize the 'francs', and realize it has something to do with money. I try to talk to him – to plead with him – it seems obvious to me that I'm foreign, and innocent. But he just keeps repeating over and over, '70 francs! 70 francs!' Like whacking me across the face. That's what it felt like."

Surgeons aren't used to being treated like delinquents, and it put Lou in shock for a while.

"It's unsettling. You arrive in a new country and assume that if you do things with good will and good intentions, people will be nice to you, and make allowances for the fact that you're foreign.

"After that I was even more nervous about being *en règle* – having all my papers in order. For the *carte de séjour*, first you have to go to the nationalization center of the *mairie* (city hall) of your arrondissement. There I had to prove I was living somewhere and paying rent. But as the American I was subletting from didn't want anyone to know he was subletting, the bills for gas, phone, etc, all stayed in his name. So although it was clear I was working there -- I had my salary checks – I had no document that I was actually living there."

Then Lou had his first glimmer of a French technique with the bureaucracy:

"The next week I went back to the *mairie* with this American's mother, a little old lady who was French. She screamed at the bureaucrats that I was living there, whether I had a phone bill or not, and they had better take her word for it! And they did!"

"I was launched.

"So then I went to the Préfecture. After hours and hours with what seemed like the whole population of the Third World, including babies finally I got to the head of the line, where, again, I was treated offensively – like a defective member of a primitive tribe. I was given only a piece of paper with an appointment – months from then – to come back with various documents.

"I came back. More hours and hours of waiting, and then a bureaucrat looked at my passport and said, 'But your visa says you're the guest of INSERM. That's a government agency. Therefore, they're the ones who have to handle this.' It's 'their responsibility' was the way he put it."

The merry-go-round was just starting.

"So I sent the application to the central INSERM office. For weeks, nothing happened. Several times I called the woman there who was supposed to handle it. She kept saying Yes, yes, but nothing happened. Then one time I called – and was told she'd resigned! I was getting pretty desperate, but they didn't take it seriously at all."

Lou had a revelation about the different mentality in France during an incident involving his car.

"I began to understand that being *en règle* is a sort of state of mind when something happened on the autoroute. A policeman stopped me. I feared the worst, and quaked with anger and dismay at the prospect of a large fine for what I couldn't imagine, as he asked me something I couldn't understand. Finally I actually understood what he wanted to know – which was why I didn't have a license plate on the front of the car. I explained somehow in my broken French that I was an American, and that in Pennsylvania, where the car was registered, we don't have license plates in front. To my amazement, he accepted that politely and waved me on.

"This made me feel better – it gave me confidence that people really would try to understand, and helped me to make the effort to improve my French. Once you have a successful interaction, no matter how small, it encourages you to keep trying.

"I discovered that there is really is one brand of reliably, unfailingly nasty official in France, and that's the ticket inspector who prowls the buses and Métro looking for offenders. But other officials, and French people in general, do make allowances for your being a foreigner – it's just that their curt manner *seems* offensive to an American at first."

You might have thought that someone at INSERM would have told Lou in the beginning that they would take care of his papers, eventually, and not to worry, meanwhile. But that's not the way it works here. The French figure you know everything, the way they do, and would be insulted if they told you. So they don't go around handing out unsolicited information (see Chapter 16 about what you have to do to get it).

The key to Lou's getting as far as the Préfecture is the little old lady, with her perfect understanding of the way her country works: on human relations. She made it clear that, phone bill or no phone bill, Lou was living in her son's apartment.

Without the *Système D*, Lou Martin had to waste a great deal of time and had a lot of unnecessary anguish. Had she applied it, Yolanda G., who is quoted at the beginning of the chapter complaining about failing the driving test after having had a U.S. license for 16 years, would probably have had little trouble getting her license.

The Professor and the Ministry of Finance

Here is a tale of a foreigner who, speaking fluent French and an old hand at Paris, applied the *Système D* brilliantly :

Bob W., a bilingual Canadian, is a professor of French and literature at the University of Toronto. He had been coming to Paris for years when he stumbled on the *Système D*. Now he applies it with confidence and a big dose of PPO. Here's how he got a document recently – quickly.

Soon after he arrived in Paris on a research sabbatical, he bought a Peugeot 504. As he was staying in France only a year, he wanted a tax exemption for the car. This was a simple matter, providing he hadn't set foot on French soil for 18 months prior to the sale. But he had. So, according to the regulations, he could only have an exemption for the six months prior to exporting the car. Bob, however, skimping on an academic salary, thought the regulation unfair and was determined to have an exemption for the whole amount.

At the Ministry of Finance, a civil servant, Madame Y, told him that he would have to make an application at the Automobile Club. At the Automobile Club he was told to go to such and such a stairway at a different office of the Finance Ministry. There he was sent back to the first office and Madame Y.

"I pleaded," he said. "I told her I was desperate, a penniless professor with a wife and 6 children. She sat and looked at me for a long time. She rustled some papers and made a couple of phone calls. Seeing I was still there, she said, 'We're told never to give out the names of any of the *fonctionnaires*!' And then she did just that! She told me to go and see Monsieur D... I still remember his name today because it's the same as one of the Balzac characters that runs through all the books of the *Comédie Humaine*.

"My luck was that Monsieur D. was interested in that car. 'Ah, the 504? You like it?' he asked me.

"'Yes, it's a marvelous car,' I answered enthusiastically.

"'Oh, isn't it!' he agreed. It seemed that he had one too. Then he asked, 'Do you write French?' I said I did. So he dictated me a letter, stamped it and that was that.

"When I took it to the dealer in Boulogne, he said, 'Oh, I see you know someone.'

"But, you see, I didn't!" said Bob, with a dazzling smile of victory.

The Big A is *People Too*

Jacques Coup de Fréjac, a former high civil servant, describes how you can prepare the way for the *Systeme D* when you need it:

"Establish a personal relationship with the Administration before you ask anything of them, no matter what. If you don't take this precaution, when you arrive with a request, you're in an inferior position – *demandeur* – which he will not fail to demonstrate.

"So whenever you have a tax to pay or a declaration to fill out, stop by and ask the fonctionnaire if you're *en règle* – if you've done the thing properly. If you have – divine surprise – thank him warmly for his advice.

"Then, when you do have something to ask him for, he'll do it, amazingly fast, or direct you to the right person. Whatever you do, show respect for him, and respect for the hierarchy."

Part III

French Context

Chapter 8

History Matters
What Was, Is

On this bridge, how many pilgrims from America, from Henry James downwards, have paused and breathed in the aroma of a long-established culture, and felt themselves to be at the very center of civilization?

Sir Kenneth Clark, "Civilization" (BBC Series)
standing on the Pont des Arts over the Seine

"History? It's irrelevant," said a computer whiz in one of my seminar groups.

Well, maybe in the U.S., where business comes first, history is irrelevant for making or selling computers. In France, the person comes first, then the business. A recent survey of 30 countries compared their answers to the question, "Is it more important who you are or what you have achieved?" The U.S., the U.K. and Australia were at the head of the countries putting achievement first. France was at the head of the countries ignoring it in favor of valuing the whole person.

In clear language, this means that French people like to know who they're dealing with and if they're *sympa*, in sync with that person. They want to know if he has any culture... and culture in France is everything important – history, art, food, love, it's all part of culture. They'll make it a point to find all this out, probably during a business lunch with you.

So... if you want to do business with the French...

Look at it this way. Knowing that the midday meal is a favorite French moment for clinching a deal, you've invited an important prospective client to lunch. French etiquette forbids the mention of business until *entre la poire et le fromage* (between the pear and the cheese), that is, until after the meat course (*le plat principal*). That permits a lot of time for culture talk. At some point he might observe, "As a Cartesian, I can't take that seriously..." If you suppose he's claiming membership in some kind of religious or ethnic group and don't know the significance in the French mind of Descartes, the 17th-century French mathematician, scientist and philosopher, you're in trouble. But if you say, "Oh yes, Descartes, wouldn't you say that he's a direct descendant of Peter Abélard in the 12th century?" you're off and running... towards that trust that brings the contract.

Or maybe you're talking politics, and he says that a certain politician has "gone to Canossa." You'll get a lot of credit if, instead of saying "Where's that?" you can come up with a knowledgeable, "Really! What sin did he commit to have to eat humble pie?"

A foreigner who asks why so many Métro stops are named for German cities is not going to make a great impression. (They're named for Napoleon's great victories.)

Then again, your French lunch partner might speak with special bitterness about the English, the usual comment being that "they're hypocrites." He would tell you that the English have nothing good to say about the French, and then shake his head in disbelief that Lord Clark, an Englishman, could have uttered the quotation at the beginning of this chapter. You might be confused at these comments, knowing that the English and French were allies during two world wars, but not if you were up to speed on the 12th century, and knew what a narrow escape France had from becoming part of England – and England from being totally French. You'd be aware that the French and the English have been quarreling off and on ever since, most notably at Fashoda in the Sudan in 1898, when Kitchener, with more soldiers, bulldozed the French explorer-general Marchand into giving up the whole Nile basin, and at Mers-el-Kebir in 1940 where the British sank a major part of the French fleet, drowning over 1,000 sailors; not to mention French opposition to England's joining the Common Market. Despite having been invaded by the Germans three times in the 70 years between 1870 and 1940, the French get along with the Germans and do not get along with the English. "With the English, it's a family feud," they explain.

Thus each nation has subtle ways of insulting the other. Leaving a party abruptly in French is *filer à l'anglaise*, while in English it's taking French leave. A condom in French is often referred to as a *capote anglaise* (English hood, literally), while in England, it's a "French letter." Speaking of which, here's a Franco-English historical anecdote to slip into that business luncheon: in 1749 Louis XV, who had an aversion to his mistresses' bearing children, ordered 300 condoms from England. Because of a papal ban, he wrote, he couldn't get any of these "preventive machines used by prudent young gentlemen" in France.

All this is to say that history envelops everything in France, including business. French people live and breathe it. It's all around them and always has been, for 2,000 years. They consider themselves the heirs of the Greeks in abstract thought – mathematics and philosophy – and in art and scientific investigation. From the Romans they inherited engineering, hierarchy, imperial pomp and glory, male hegemony and their beloved language. They have no precursor for two treasures they themselves gave the world in the 12th century – Gothic architecture and romantic love as a lifelong commitment.

If there is one Frenchman who caught all of this, poured it into the French soul and made it French, it's that larger-than-life great king who, from the remote 17th century, throws his light or his shadow, depending on how you look at it, on almost every aspect of modern French life – Louis XIV, Louis the Great, Louis the Sun King.

Your lunch companion is perhaps another American or Englishman, who grumbles that his French CEO decides everything, but everything, down to the *cantine* menus and the newspaper subscriptions, so that larger decisions take forever? Of course. Louis XIV signed every chit at Versailles and tirelessly supervised all the activities of his ministers, architects and artists, making all the decisions about everything.

How come bureaucrats have so much power and prestige? The Romans gave it to them. Louis took this over from them and Napoleon kept it up.

Business is a little looked down on? Louis's courtiers were not permitted to be "in trade." Aristocrats had one business: military distinction.

Engineers are idolized? Engineers, designing his fortifications and machines of war, gave Louis the possibility of military triumphs and, in time of peace, the architectural glories of a great capital... Louis's signal to the world that Paris was the new Athens, the new Rome of might and of art.

You're frustrated at the rules of hierarchy in the company you work for? Whether it is a French company or the French branch of an American company, you most likely have been caught short for skipping levels of hierarchy or applying horizontally in your company for the information you need. The organization of French companies is quite military, to give it clarity, elegance and importance.

French people are dragging around two millennia of triumphs, upheavals, discoveries, tensions and struggles. How do they always spring back from the brink? Where does all the talent come from? Other countries look like still ponds in contrast to this violent whirlpool. It's the complexity and density of the happenings, and of the personalities of the movers and the shakers of the two millennia which are startling and significant for modern France and its ingenuity, paradoxes and contradictions.

Here I would like to shade in some early layers of the French subconscious, reinforcing that favorite saying of theirs, *Plus ça change, plus c'est la même chose.* As the 12th century was a turning point, and relatively little known to Americans, I've lingered on that period perhaps more than its share, particularly on two figures whose influence did much to shape the French mind, the inimitable Abélard and that glorious queen, Eleanor of Aquitaine. Alas, it's impossible to include all the prodigious kings and characters down the centuries who have had a bearing on the richness and complexity of the present. What I'm hoping is that you'll pick up a history of France and absorb the rest on your own.

The way they talk about it, you'd think it happened yesterday, not in 52 B.C., that the Romans marched in behind Julius Caesar and conquered Gaul.

This was the moment of glory of the first French hero, Vercingétorix. Never mind that he was a Gaulois, the Hexagon being then inhabited by Gaulois, 400 tribes of squabbling individualists with 72 languages. Nor that there was not yet the slightest hint of the France that was to be, except that the divisions among French people, and their love of debate, are often attributed to these ancestors.

Vercingétorix has been immortalized as French because he was a valiant David who succeeded in uniting the quarreling tribes against the Roman Goliath. He's up there with Joan of Arc on the hero citation lists of politicians today. Like many French heroes after many startling successes against overwhelming odds (Joan herself and Napoleon), he lost the decisive battle (at Alésia). He was taken to Rome to be shown off in a cage to the populace. He was later beheaded. His latter-day reincarnation, Asterix, a cartoon figure, who is constantly running rings round the great and powerful is nationally popular.

Engineers and Power

Meanwhile Roman engineers began planning the straight, tree-lined roads which are still, many of them, the pride of the French countryside. As are the magnificent three-tiered arcaded aqueduct in the Gard; the arch of triumph in Orange, the temple in Nîmes, the arena in Arles. Later generations built the Roman baths under what is now the Cluny Museum, in Paris.

In the 17th century, Louis XIV had only to look around him to see that engineers, the spearhead of an army, were a nation's passport to greatness.

Greatness was what Louis had in mind. Anyone doubting this has only to observe his portrait as a young man on a fine charger, dressed as a Roman general.

If the 16th century had been Spain's, the 17th was to be his. Louis put his army engineers to work streamlining the war machine that was to forge a greater France. To secure it, Marshal Vauban threw up border fortifications which are still studied for their ingenuity. For the greatness of Versailles, at once Louis's center of power, his court and his residence, his engineers built an aqueduct and rerouted waterways, so that his new palace could be reflected in cascading fountains and splendid wide canals.

The message of Versailles was to dazzle: France was at the head of all other nations in greatness – military, economic, artistic, literary, scientific. It was to be copied by monarchs all over Europe.

For the splendor of his capital city, Louis had his engineers build the wide boulevard sweeping down to the royal palace of the Louvre, the Champs Elysées, one of the most beautiful streets in the world.

Louis had ambitions for Paris to be the center of art as well as power. Not to be outdone by the great domes of the Cathedral in Florence or of St. Peter's in Rome, he commissioned Paris's crowning glory, the golden Dome of the Invalides.

Napoleon, whose tomb is appropriately underneath, was as apt a student of ancient Rome as Louis. He made the Roman style his very own, in furniture and in dress. He did Louis one better. In 1798 he reinvented the school of engineering, the Ecole Polytechnique, which had been founded in 1794, and made it a military institution at the service of the state. The school, known as X, is still considered by many, and certainly by itself, as the best in the world, and the most prestigious.

The French word *ingénieur* is a very distant cousin of "engineer." It has multiple undertones of brilliance, integrity, class and general marvelousness. It guarantees supreme competence in many areas, particularly conceptual rather than practical, and above all, in higher mathematics.

The word descends from the medieval French word *engin,* which meant war machine, and which today is the generic term for all material used at war. Back we go to the Roman formula: Great nations have great armies have great engineers.

In modern France, with such a past, guess who's running things? *Ingénieurs.* Not the government, at the moment (though ex-President Giscard d'Estaing is one) but much of business and industry.

More, *lots more,* about *ingénieurs* in general, and X in particular, when I come to education. Not knowing the connotations emanating from these words in France is like coming to America or England without a feel for the aura of Harvard or Oxford. Only much, much more so.

Gods, Bureaucrats and Laws

After Caesar, the soldiers and the engineers, came the rest of Roman civilization: the gods with their temples and the bureaucrats with their laws and regulations.

The gods gave up to Christianity eventually, but the bureaucrats have never flourished more than right now.

Roman bureaucrats had ranks and privileges as fiercely defended as army grades in a highly centralized hierarchy, leading straight up to the Emperor. Louis XIV adapted this system for France. He expanded the ranks of royal officials and centralized them into a rigid pyramid culminating in himself, God's deputy on earth. With the help of the brilliant Colbert (an *ingénieur*, what else?) and an enterprising secret police force, he knew all the details of what took place in his realm, partly because he made it a point, as already noted, to personally approve every expense at Versailles.

Napoleon, who often posed for his portraits as a Roman Emperor with a crown of laurel leaves, romanized France with even greater zeal than Louis. He tightened the ranks of centralized hierarchy. As the Roman governor in Gaul had been a prefect (*préfet*), a high civil servant either in the army or the administration, with pretty much divine rights and answerable only to the Emperor, so Napoleon installed prefect-gods in all the departments, answerable only to Paris. The prefect system is still maintained, though with less power in the last few years.

Women, Lunatics and Criminals

With his passion for order, Napoleon rewrote the Roman civil code of law for France, in which every possible situation was supposedly foreseen. Its 2,281 articles, though updated since, are still a model of clarity. In them he managed to outdo Rome in his subjugation of women. French women, who since the late 16th century had been little more than chattels (the word comes from capital, or property), were now legally classified with children, lunatics and convicted criminals. No vote until 1944, not even for the three female ministers in the cabinet of Léon Blum in 1936. No bank account without their husband's permission until 1966. The first woman member of the Académie Française was elected in 1974 and there are still just two, out of 40. Only one Métro station is named for a woman and only two women have been deemed worthy of the state's greatest accolade, burial in the Panthéon - Marie Curie and Sophie Berthelot, and she only because her husband, Marcellin, is buried there, and because they died at the same time.

Power to the Dukes, Briefly

In the 5th century, the Romans in Gaul were battered and finally defeated by waves of wild tribes from the East. Gradually one of them, the Franks, took over, settled in and presided over the period of privation, desolation, terrorized rural life and disintegration of cities known as the Dark Ages.

Not only centralized government but much of western civilization itself, almost sank without a trace. Had the Franks not beaten back the Moslem invasion as far north as Poitiers in the 8th century, not only would France never have become the France we know, but it would have been part of the Moorish empire.

The cultural breakthroughs vigorously undertaken by the Frankish Emperor Charlemagne in the 9th century, with the help of an Anglo-Saxon monk, began to blossom, albeit modestly, in the 11th century, when the fearsome Vikings, who had been devastating France since the 8th century, began quieting down as Norman farmers.

The regions had had to fend for themselves. By the 10th century they had worked out the system of reciprocal obligations known as feudalism, which flowered in the 12th century. The chiefs at the top, the dukes, protected everyone inside their fortified castles in times of siege. Until the 15th century, the Dukes of Normandy, Brittany, Burgundy and Aquitaine, and the equally powerful Counts of Toulouse, Anjou and Provence were mightier, and ruled over much greater areas, than the Kings of France.

Hierarchy was back – but not centralization, not yet.

For a few hundred years, women were people too. Thanks to Frankish law, they could study and practice medicine and law. They could manage their dowry after marriage and retrieve it if their marriage didn't work out. It was not to last long. Eleanor of Aquitaine's taking just about all of France southwest of the Loire with her, after divorcing the King of France in 1152 and marrying the King of England, was a state disaster. That one woman – and what a woman! more about her later – could thus revise geography and cause hundreds of years of ferocious battles over these borders, and that they were partly restored to France through the charisma and military leadership of another woman (Joan of Arc), was too much for the male Establishment of the time to bear. In 1431, Joan of Arc, for trying to undo what Eleanor had started, and expel the English from France, was burned as a witch. Not a single Frenchman lifted a finger. The message to women should have been clear. It was from then on that women's rights were inexorably curtailed, so that Napoleon in the 19th century had no trouble legally embalming them as sub-people.

Regions have long memories. Louis XIV's 17th-century strategy for royal preeminence, bringing back centralization and transferring the ducal hierarchy to his appointed officials (sometimes called the twin curse of the Romans on the French), was continued by Napoleon and has suited the purposes of monarchical presidents of the Fifth Republic. But the regions are stirring. They have been demanding more automony, and under the Socialists achieved some. In 1982, much of the *préfet's* power was reduced. Alain Peyrefitte, distinguished former Minister, Académicien and author, argued in his book, *Le Mal Français* (1972) that French industry wouldn't be able to score globally until regional questions stopped being decided by faraway Paris bureaucrats.

Brussels is even farther away. Small wonder that during the debates of the Treaty of Maastricht in 1993, "Franco-French" quarrels erupted over the wisdom of allowing bureaucrats in Brussels to ram unpleasant regulations down French throats.

The Papal Empire

With the collapse of the Romans in the 5th century, the Church stepped into the vacuum with its "soldiers of God" in the monasteries to keep civilization alive. No one else could read or write. This world was such a mess in the Dark Ages that most people were only too ready to invest in the next one. Faith in that was all people had.

The Popes wielded their great spiritual weapons — interdict and excommunication – all this time, and up to the 16th century, with great effect. A kingdom under interdict was a kingdom forbidden church bells. No Christian sacrament – no Christian baptism or burial! – meant no access to heaven's grace for anyone in it. Kings and emperors thought twice before defying the papal wrath. Few laymen cared to risk eternal damnation through excommunication.

Gregory VII topped it all with the papal bull of 1075, announcing that the Vatican had divine origin: the Pope could commit no error, and was empowered to depose kings and emperors. The Pope had armies to back up his bulls. When Henry IV, the Germanic Holy Roman Emperor, tried to appoint his own Bishop of Milan in 1077, he was excommunicated and almost lost his throne. To get back in the Pope's good graces, he had to give proof of his penitence: to spend the night in the snow, and then to walk three kilometers on his knees, in the snow, to the castle of the Pope at Canossa, in northern Italy.

Nine hundred years later, the imperial shame still vibrates in the French language. Thus it is that modern politicians, obliged to eat humble pie, are described as "going to Canossa."

By the 10th century, things began to improve. The invasions were over. The barbarians settled down. The land was cleared for crops, and various inventions made agricultural life easier: the chimney, the flour mill, a plow that turned more easily at the end of a row. The Moslems were under control, so trade was picking up around the Mediterranean. Cities began to live again.

When the world failed to come to an end in the year 1000, people began to think it might be around for a while. They started to build.

Thus was the stage set for the tumultuous, gloriously exciting 12th century.

The Royal Crusaders

It was the Crusades that launched it. The Pope had the clout and the wherewithal. To save their souls, the people were willing to do anything for God's deputy on earth.

So when Pope Urban II told his flocks at Clermont in 1095, "Free the Holy Land from the Infidel !, " the first group, all French, set off joyously for the dangerous months-long journey to Jerusalem. Everyone was massacred. All seven of the crusades, from the 11th to the 13th centuries, were mostly French, and mostly led by French kings. They were multicultural, to be sure; but the language – the lingua franca – was French.

The dividends for France were enormous.

First of all, the revival of learning. Only a miserable few dog-eared manuscripts, mostly scriptures, had made it from antiquity through the Dark Ages, closely guarded by the monasteries. The crusading knights straggled half-starved into Constantinople to find a flourishing, magnificent city. No Dark Ages had hit the Byzantine, or Eastern Roman, Empire. It was steeped in splendid, lavish elegance – and books! Bursting with all the books from ancient Greece on. Books on geometry, mathematics, astronomy. Poems and plays, Aristotle and Plato.

Savvy Suger Creates Glorious Gothic

The knights shipped the books back from Constantinople to Paris and caused a sensation more earthshaking than astronauts landing on the moon. In fact, the mathematics that got them there descended directly from the Euclidean geometry rediscovered in the 12th century.

Geometry! It was to change the face of Paris forever, and the way Parisians thought. They loved it. *Ingénieurs* were back.

One of them was the Abbot Suger, a monk who was one of France's ablest diplomats, administrators and royal counselors, and incidentally a passionate and discriminating art collector. Louis VII left him in charge of the store when he went off on the Second Crusade in 1147. Pondering Euclidean coordinates and spatial relationships, he hit on the arches, weights and balances for a totally new way of building, ogival architecture. He immediately began blueprints for the Church of Saint Denis. Gothic was born, and barely 50 years later, Gothic's great gift to humanity, Chartres Cathedral, intellectually, emotionally and spiritually transcendent, one of the most beautiful covered areas in the world.

Chartres was also a hotbed of mathematicians. Scholars are still deciphering the secrets of their sacred esoteric numerical combinations in the Cathedral.

Inimitable Abélard

The word got around that things were moving in Paris, and scholars began flocking there from all over Europe to read the books, or at least learn from the French teachers who had studied them. By the 13th century, the University of Paris was the acknowledged center of learning, attracting the greatest minds of Europe, and dominating the whole Christian world with its spiritual and moral force.

In the 12th and 13th centuries, academic degrees were given in the studies of theology, law and medicine, and the five liberal arts of grammar, rhetoric, dialectics, arithmetic and now geometry. The material studied was controlled by the all-seeing, all-powerful eye of the Church, which taught that faith was a matter of intuition and believing. Reason had nothing to do with it.

Enter Plato and Aristotle. They blew the mind of Peter Abélard, the star dialectician and crowd spellbinder of his day. After reading Aristotle, Abélard (1079-1142) was determined to investigate things rationally. Including his faith. "I must understand in order that I may believe. By doubting, we come to questioning, and by questioning we perceive the Truth," he said. These were heretical words in the 12th century and they got him in deep trouble with the Church. He challenged the venerable mystic Abbot of Clairvaux, Saint Bernard, quarreled with Rome, was excommunicated, then vindicated, and continued to persevere in his critical and rational approach to Christianity. He was persecuted again and again all his life for it.

Abélard was a pivotal historical chararacter, a towering figure in a momentous period of outstanding people, who cast his shadow into the 20th century, if not farther. His theory of conceptualism and his theological-philosophical system, called scholasticism, gave France some of its dominant thought patterns, to be taken up by Saint Thomas Aquinas 100 years later, and in the 17th century, by Descartes. This genius blasted through dark, subterranean ecclesiastical labyrinths into a reasoning daylight everyone could understand. "I think, therefore I am," said Descartes. His principles of investigating nature and reaching conclusions through examination of demonstrable facts and logical arguments have carried the day in France until now.

Frenchmen today describe themselves with some pride as Cartesians.

Individualism

Peter Abélard not only presaged the dominance of rhetoric, theory and rationalism in French mental processes. He was the first individualist. The son of a nobleman in Brittany, and expected to become a knight, he was determined to spend his life using his brain rather than his sword. He rebelled against paternal authority, and, like a provincial American drawn by New York, set off to seek his intellectual fortune in Paris. At 22 he was out-debating his dialectical teachers, and turned to the study of theology, the path that led to his confrontation with the great of his age. As we've seen, he eventually took on the whole Church of Rome.

First Western Romance

Abélard was also the hero of the first Western romance, and owes his name recognition mostly to that.

For another contribution of 12th-century France to the West was the concept of romantic love. The historian Joseph Campbell signals it as the beginning of a "distinctive Western consciousness, the romantic idea of the choice of the individual as an ideal to be lived for, which became a social system in the West."

Until then, there was what Campbell calls the "zeal of the organs" for each other – sexual desire. Marriage was a matter of property, and was arranged by third parties, so the zeal of the organs had a way of taking its course outside of the marital bed. Cupid sent his arrows at random, towards any targets that might be around. The targets succumbed, and that was that. There was no nonsense about sighing and moaning, much less dying, for the object of the zeal.

Then the troubadours, Tristram and Isolde, and Héloise and Abélard changed everything.

In the ancient legends of Tristram, first written down and popularized in the 12th century, Tristram, sent to escort Isolde as a bride for his King, is given a magic potion by mistake, and falls like a ton of bricks for Isolde. He is in excruciating, marvelous agony. He doesn't care if he is caught and executed for this, or, more astonishing, if his soul will be tortured in hell for eternity. Don't forget, people of the 12th century *really* believed in hell fires. But Tristram was ready to burn. His love for this one woman, Isolde, was greater than life or death. This person-to-person relationship, exulting in the soul's counterpart, was totally new.

Héloise and Abélard were real flesh-and-blood people, French intellectuals who fell passionately in love, were imprudent, married and were parted, not by fate, like Tristram and Isolde, but by Abélard's self-appointed mission of bringing Truth to the Church. In his memoirs, Abélard describes giving up Héloise and their child, thereby bringing on the wrath of her uncle, who sent some thugs to castrate him, or, as he put it "to separate me from that part of my body which had caused distress." The couple continued to write letters of love until they both died many years later, separately. They are buried together at the Père Lachaise cemetery in Paris.

The letters were published in 1874 in editions still available. Héloise sounds like a remarkably modern heroine, beautiful, brilliant, full of spunk and ready to sacrifice her life with the man she loved for the sake of his professional integrity, peace of mind and eventual glory. Marie Einstein, considered to be as brilliant a mathematician as Albert, did the same thing 1,000 years later.

Abélard, persisting in his mission, lived up to Héloise's hopes and justified her sacrifice. The historian Pierre Gaxotte calls him the "dominator, the dictator of thought in the 12th century. He enlarged the field of reflection in every sense. Great stimulator of ideas, incomparable professor, he initiated an academic movement the like of which had never been seen before. In Paris, he had audiences of up to 5,000 people. Among them, one became a pope, 19 became cardinals and more than 50 became bishops. Although he never ceased to recognize the traditional authority of the Church, he was denounced by Saint Bernard as guilty of new ideas which were heretical. He was condemned to silence and ended the most tormented of lives in a priory."

The Muse and La Divine Eleanor

Most historians agree that it was the southern troubadours, the nobility of the courts of Aquitaine, Toulouse and Provence, who launched the new phenomenon of organizing one's life around "what the eyes have made welcome to the heart," as the troubadour Guiraut de Borneilh sang in one of his romantic love songs.

Pierre Gaxotte calls it "the gratuitous and magnificent gift of France to the Western world."

Where did they find their Muse? Some say in the love poems of the Moors in Spain. Some say that the songs are the coded language of the underground Albigensian heretics. Others claim it was the Roman poetry of antiquity, particularly Ovid's "Art of Love", brought back from Byzantium during the Crusades. Still others credit the Crusades themselves, and the exotic influence of the Saracens.

Whatever inspired this great leap for humanity, the ladies of Provence and Aquitaine knew a good thing when they saw it, and promoted it with all they had. With their lords off in the Holy Land for years at a time, they were left to run their castles alone. These women and their daughters suddenly had a great deal more power and freedom. With gentle love in the air and the younger nobles left behind pining for them at their courts, the ladies could call the shots, and they did. They encouraged personalized lyrics celebrating their charms. They drew up rituals and rules of long, drawn-out, often inconclusive courting that came to be known as courtly love, and were the model for the "love map" or *carte du tendre* that the *Précieuses* in the 17th century – and not a few today – demanded their lovers stick to for any hope of success.

The courtly love code that the 12th-century ladies worked out ruled that the lovers, guilty or not, separate for the sake of honor (Tristram) or duty (Abélard), to be reunited only in death. The Arthurian legends, with the dishonorable twist of Lancelot living shamefully alongside his great love and mistress, Guinevere, the wife of his best friend and liege lord, were written down around the same time as Tristram by Gregory of Monmouth, in his *History of British Kings,* and translated from the Latin into French on the order of... Eleanor of Aquitaine.

If anyone's enchanted hand is behind this personalizing of love, and the glamorizing and promotion of gentle, courtly behavior and chivalry, it is that staggering comet of 12th-century exploding energy, Eleanor.

Eleanor of Aquitaine (1122-1204) grew up in the sumptuous southern court of Aquitaine. Her grandfather, Duke Guillaume IX (1064-1127) was

113

the first troubadour. Known as the "Prince of Troubadours," he was the author of seven celebrated songs and one of the first Crusaders. Her father, Duke Guillaume X (1075-1137), a far more cultivated lord and far greater landowner than the King of France, was a man of immense charm and talent. A troubadour himself, he was also, like his father, a Crusader and a famous womanizer. When he wasn't chasing mistresses – many of whom, once discarded, joined the convent of the barefoot ascetic monk, Robert d'Arbrissel, in penitence – he was composing lyrics and songs. His court was a sunny, joyous place, elegant, cultivated and polished, lively and exhilarating, with musicians, artists and poets. Women were treated with courtesy and encouraged to demand exquisite manners.

Eleanor was married off to Louis VII of France at age 15 with a dowry of Aquitaine and Poitou, all of what is today southwest France. Her dowry didn't do her much good in Paris, where she froze in the dismal stone walls of the pre-Louvre royal palace. The manners of the North were still crude, and the sweet life of music, poetry and troubadours non-existent. The "universals" of Abélard and the other teachers didn't interest her. She was an exuberant, beautiful girl married to a retiring, studious, pious young man who had been brought up for the Church. His older brother, who had been groomed to be king, had been killed at 16 in an accident.

Louis VII had no stomach for the battles Eleanor was constantly goading him into against various lords who had designs on her territories.

When his soldiers burned down a church, in a village called Vitry-le-Brûlé, that turned out to have about 1,000 refugees in it, Louis was aghast. The Pope was outraged and put the entire kingdom under interdict. Louis had had enough. He decided to go on a Crusade, the Second. Eleanor was delighted. She pined for the hot South, the songs and the court manners of home. She jumped at the chance to go with him to the exotic East.

Splendors of Byzance

In Constantinople, the capital of the Eastern Roman Empire and a great trading center between East and West, she found a civilized international metropolis, with architectural splendors, exotic gardens and fountains and a sumptuous, dazzling court. Eleanor realized what she'd been missing in Paris, and it was probably there, talking in her own Provençal language with her uncle, Raymond, the reigning Prince of Antioch, that she decided she'd had enough of dreary Paris and pious Louis VII.

Louis VII wasn't any happier with the marriage than Eleanor was. He not only couldn't handle her, but, worse, she hadn't produced an heir, only daughters. They stayed in the Middle East for two years, and on their return, after a pilgrimage to Vitry-le-Brûlé to plant some cedars brought back from Lebanon – which are still there – they decided to divorce.

Little did Louis suspect that in just one month Eleanor would marry Henry Plantagenet, who, two years later, would become Henry II of England – and take her Aquitaine-Poitou dowry with her. The Kings of England were still, since the Norman invasion, Dukes of Normandy and Counts of Anjou and Maine. Henry II was in charge of what now became known as the Angevin Empire: most of what is the western half of today's France – territory a great deal larger than that presided over by the French King.

French had been spoken at the English court since the Norman invasion, and Eleanor, now Queen of England as well as Countess of Poitou and Duchess of Aquitaine, and in her prime, threw herself into making the courts of Poitou and London even more civilized, cultivated and lyrical than her father's. Already a living legend, the Seven Muses rolled into one, she worked closely with troubadours and poets, composing with them their tales of romance and fatal love. It was she who commissioned the writing down of the legend of Tristram by Thomas of England, one of her court poets, and Béroul, a Frenchman, thereby launching romantic love in the western world once and for all.

But this was to be only a short lull for Eleanor in her continuing battle, after the death of Henry II, to keep the Angevin Empire out of the hands of the next French King, the son of Louis VII and her own stepson, Philip Augustus. Ultimately, she failed, but not because of lack of will. She traveled ceaselessly from one end of her Angevin realm to another to reassure her barons and distribute alms, fiefs and justice. At 77, she covered more than 1,000 miles in the heat of three summer months. At 80 she even traveled to Spain to choose from among her royal granddaughters the bride of the future Louis VIII, Blanche of Castile, who was to be the mother of Saint Louis, Louis IX. Her labors for her posterity failed for three reasons beyond her control: the sudden death at 42 of her strongest son and ally, Richard the Lion-Hearted, the notorious unreliability of her son John Lackland, and the consummate military and diplomatic skills of her adversary, Philip Augustus.

At the end of her life, she came full circle, in perfect symmetry, from the pleasures of love, song and luxury through the excitements, duties and anguishes of sovereignty to join another and opposed strong 12th-century current, the extreme asceticism of the Abbey of Fontevrault. It had been founded at the beginning of the century by Robert d'Arbrissel, the same barefoot monk who had attracted the discarded mistresses of her father. She died there in 1204, just after the end of the exceptional century which had suited her so well – and which she had done so much to make resound through time.

It would be another 50 years before a French king would be able to reconquer all of Aquitaine.

Philip Augustus and the Great Battle

Philip Augustus won a large part of it back, as well as Normandy, Poitou, Maine, Anjou and Touraine, in his battles against John Lackland, and the Holy Roman Emperor.

His victory against all of them, at the Battle of Bouvines in 1214, was the real beginning of the Kingdom of France and the national dynasty of Capetians. This, any Englishman will tell you, was the last great French victory over the English, and is therefore greatly cherished in the French memory – not an easy date to slide into a business lunch, but one to keep in mind for foreigners seeking to astound French friends or business contacts.

Philip Augustus was a great general, a clever, subtle diplomat, and an able administrator, instituting many improved administrative procedures. He set up the Royal Archives and a more coherent tax-collecting system through appointed provincial bailiffs, who rendered their accounts three times a year to the King. He paved malodorous mud paths near his palace and established a police force to keep order. He built ramparts around his city to protect it. He started building the Louvre to house his modern government, and the Sorbonne to people his government with trained administrators, rather than hereditary nobles or superstitious prelates.

This was a king with vision, and he is often credited by historians with being France's most brilliant. Maurice Druon, eminent historian and doyen of the Académie Française, told me in a tone of finality that he was not only the most brilliant and able of French kings, but also the real founder of the French State.

But like Eleanor of Aquitaine before him, and like the country he is credited with founding right down to the present day, he accomplished this feat of moving towards a rational humanist future while grasping ever more tenaciously at a spiritual past.

It was during Philip's watch that the Inquisition seized hold of France. With the King's consent, if not enthusiasm, Simon de Montfort, on an appeal from the Pope, took an army south in 1208 and massacred the heretic Cathars, or Albigensians. With them was also massacred the artistic civilization of the South, along with its nobility, for the troubadours had supported the Albigensians in their opposition to Church corruption. Thus Philip Augustus, the stepson of Eleanor, wiped out much of the heritage of civilizing arts and manners that she had given to France, squaring accounts with the Queen who had at the same time taken so much away from it.

The Albigensians were the first French Protestants, ancestors of the Huguenots. This was the opening bloody chapter in what were to be hundreds of years of merciless religious wars. A particularly horrible carnage, known as the St. Bartholemew's Day Masssacre, took place on the order of Catherine de Medici, Queen Regent of France, in 1572, when 3,000 unsuspecting Huguenot wedding guests were slaughtered during the marriage of her daughter to their chief, the future Henry IV, at the Tuileries palace.

In the 17th century, the German states were reduced to chaos during the Thirty Years War, partly due to the religious zeal of French armies commanded by Richelieu politics. The end of the century saw the massacre of all the Huguenots in France not able to escape the country.

Yet the 17th century was also the *Grand Siècle* (the Great Century) of the Sun King, with scientific breakthroughs and unsurpassed works of art and literature. It was the century of giants, Pascal and Descartes, Racine and Corneille, Molière and Poussin, and it rang with honor, beauty and religious faith – and also with treachery, debauchery and bigotry. It opened the way for the Encyclopédistes and the Age of Enlightenment in the 18th century, for the idyllic paintings of Watteau and the exquisite ornamental taste of Madame de Pompadour and Marie Antoinette. It also brought on that goriest of revolts, the French Revolution, and yet bequeathed to the West that most sublime of humanist doctrines of faith, the Rights of Man.

The complexities and paradoxes of French life were in full play.

Conservatism vs Change

At the end of the 12th century, the patterns and tensions of creation, the clashes of mindsets, the talents, ambitions and ambiguities of modern France were all in place, ready to evolve: intellectualism and mysticism, science and religion, centralization and regionalism, individualism and authoritarianism, monarchy and "clanarchy," or the anarchy of striking guilds, now unions; plus the French passions for poetry and language, love, elocution, debating, style, fashion, military superiority, glory and grandeur.

Change has never been easy in a country with as much of a past and with as much of a need to hold onto its past as France. The Frenchman's willingness to launch his country into the future goes hand in hand with the desire to make that future compatible with the past. To do anything else would be not only to abandon a great asset, but would also be to say that Frenchmen in the past had been guilty of errors, and to admit that the efforts of present day Frenchmen were subject to error. (See Chapter Six, on blame, for why such a course is unlikely.) Thus this is the country that builds a modernistic pyramid as an entrance to its greatest Renaissance palace. Where there was once a 19th-century produce market with a soaring glass roof, Les Halles, now there is a modernistic underground shopping mall topped with a park. Its trellised walks preserve the form of the old market. The French don't like to forget.

The time the French forgot to hold onto their past was during the Revolution that started in 1789. The changes went much farther than cutting off the heads of the King and Queen, and letting the heir die in prison. Many other people lost their heads too. Some died for being of the wrong social class, but others died for thinking the wrong way, or just keeping on with some old ways of thinking.

The Revolutionaries changed the calendar. Year I was 1792. They changed the names of the months. Formal forms of address were eliminated, all with a Cartesian thoroughness and logic, and all with a hostility toward the past.

The result was a series of revolutions and counter-revolutions throughout the 19th century.

Napoleon reestablished a government more authoritarian and centralized than anything Louis XIV had had. He effectively ended the first Revolution by focusing its energies on French nationalism and directing it outward, towards overthrowing the old monarchies surrounding France. Finally those monarchies ganged up on France and put Louis XVI's brother, Louis XVIII, on the throne in 1814. Do we even have to note, *Plus ça change...?*

When that brother of Louis XVI died, he was replaced by another brother, Charles X, who made a conscious, if foolish, effort to set the clock back before the Revolution. Of course that ended in another revolution, known as the Revolution of 1830, and he was replaced by a cousin, Louis Philippe. He was an improvement on Charles, but by 1848 a revolution took care of him too, and for the second time France had a republic.

This Second Republic was no better able to satisfy the people's idea of what France and French life should be than the First Republic or any of the kings.

In 1852 France had another emperor, this one named Louis Napoleon, a nephew of Bonaparte. It took defeat by a German army to oust Louis Napoleon in 1870. He was replaced by the Third Republic. This one lasted until another defeat by German armies ended it in 1940.

The point of all this is not to try to make anyone's head spin, but to show the disruption caused to a country like France by such a radical break with the past as the Revolution of 1789. To govern this country for long, a politician has to have a vision of France's past as well as her present and her future. Louis Napoleon's name connected him to the great French past of his uncle; and his support of industry and the rebuilding of Paris prepared France for the future. The Third Republic achieved stability because by then, there was a republican history in France and its tradition was very well taught to the French through symbols and in school.

No French leader has understood France's past and recalled it better, and at the same time stirred his country to stride forcefully and positively into the future, than General Charles de Gaulle. A student of history as well as a career army officer who had fought in World War I, de Gaulle echoed Louis XIV in several ways. He was a military strategist, he had vision, he had a total and disinterested dedication to his role as servant of his country, and he had personal grandeur. Not just because of his height was he known as *le grand Charles*.

Charles de Gaulle

During and after the Second World War, de Gaulle gave his country back its soul and, probably, its very existence. Still reviled by some, he is revered by many as the savior of his country – not once, but three times. He saved its soul on that fateful day on June 18, 1940, when he addressed his countrymen from London as the Germans took over Paris, and called for their resistance to the invaders, a movement which he led, first from London, then from Algiers in 1943, and finally in Paris in 1944.

This Resistance made all the difference to France's credibility after the War and to its ultimate recovery. He left the government in 1946 in protest against the multi-party "revolving door" governments. Recalled to pick up the pieces of his country in 1958, he saved it again by giving it a new constitution with a presidential form of government. He gave his countrymen back their pride, and the sense of glory so vital to them, through a policy of military independence with a nuclear deterrent, and a stepped-up campaign of transforming France from an agricultural to an industrial, high-tech nation. At the same time he saw that, contrary to the passions of his countrymen, he must end the disastrous civil war in Algeria. It became clear that Algeria, considered as an integral part of French territory, would have to be given independence. The decision, resulting in a revolt of the generals and several assassination attempts, limited his own democratic hold on power. When his policy was rejected by a referendum in 1969, de Gaulle left his office the very next day. His probity was legendary. Over 20 years after his death in 1970 his influence remains strong, and this is not limited to the political party he created, the Rassemblement Pour la République, or RPR. He is part of the past, but continually present. If you fly into Paris, you will most likely land at Charles de Gaulle airport, and if you ride the Métro or the RER, you can't avoid the Charles de Gaulle station, suitably located just under the Arc de Triomphe... which is the appropriate centerpiece of the traffic circle also named for him.

Living in Paris you can see this reverence for the past all around you, and the clever ways the past is mixed into the present and the future. Signs like the park trellises at Les Halles and the pyramid in the bosom of the Louvre are everywhere.

Look closely at the birds on the Arc de Triomphe, decorating the names of French victories. There are eagles, the symbol of Napoleon's empire. He designed the arch. But there are also roosters that act like eagles – their wings outspread, one foot raised. This is the symbol of the French Republic. By having the two together, one monument can celebrate both Napoleon's victories, like Jena and Austerlitz, aggressive battles of Empire, and Verdun, the great battle for the defense of the Third Republic in World War One. In the process, the monument makes a coherent history out of conflict.

Or look at the Place de la Bastille. Surely the column in the center should celebrate the storming of the Bastille prison on July 14, 1789. But the dates on the column are three days in July 1830! In fact the column celebrates the revolution of 1830 that put Louis Philippe, the most moderate of the monarchs, on the throne, getting rid of his wildly conservative cousin, Charles X. It moves the Place de la Bastille forward from the famous site of the country's bloodiest insurrection to a monument to moderate government.

Marianne

And who is that gilded fellow on the top of the column, and what is a regal lion doing at the base? Where is Marianne, symbol as well as nickname of the Republic? Usually represented by the bust of a woman in a Phrygian cap, she is the central figure in Delacroix's famous painting celebrating that same Revolution of 1830 – a militant, bare-breasted woman. It seems that when the Bastille column was built, Marianne was considered too traumatic and explosive. For that reason, the column is a hodge-podge of symbols, the lion at the base and the golden-winged figure on the top that looks like Mercury, messenger of the gods, in full flight, but is actually meant to be the spirit of Liberty. Liberty? Next to a lion, symbol of power, authority and glory? Well, historians will tell you that they're handy symbols to smooth over memory, when other symbols are felt to be too potent.

Marianne wasn't considered safe until the 1880's. You can find her at the other end of the Boulevard Beaumarchais from the Bastille, appropriately at the Place de la Republique. Aha, but this is a different Marianne. Not the warlike bare-breasted Marianne of Delacroix's barricades or the wild, bellicose Marianne of the Arc de Triomphe. This Marianne is a sober, modest, queenly type, more like Athena, Greek goddess of thought, art, science and industry, quietly presiding over representations of the nobler moments of all the revolutions. We see the reading of the bill of rights, for example, not the guillotine. But even in this gentler form, it took nearly a hundred years, from 1789 to 1883, to allow Marianne in public at all. Now you see her portrait in the lobby of the Hôtel de Ville, with the face of a famous working beauty that changes every few years. First Bardot, then Catherine Deneuve. The current face is of a fashion model turned designer, Inès de la Fressange.

The Marais

The game of past and present is played out in the transportation system of Paris as well. Most of the great boulevards in the central part of Paris are the work of Baron Haussmann, who worked under Louis Napoleon from the 1860's on. The Métro runs under the boulevards. But certain quarters aren't served well by either system. For example, Haussmann wasn't permitted to plow through most of the Third and Fourth arrondissements, the Marais, because there were too many fine old houses of nobles there from the reigns of Henry IV, Louis XIII and Louis XIV. Also, since the time of those kings, the area had become working class, and walking was good enough for workers. This is frustrating when you're in the Marais and want to go somewhere else. On the other hand, you can keep your wine in the cellar and it won't be disturbed by passing trains.

These huge old houses of the Marais are treasure troves of Paris's continuity. Many are restored, but lots are still hidden under layers of industrial and commercial ugliness, furniture and clothing factories, and wholesalers of the last century and this one. For along with all those political revolutions in the nineteen-hundreds, Paris had an industrial revolution as well. American cities were built by industry. In Paris, industrialization just added one more layer on an edifice already standing.

The furnishings of these old houses, the ones that have been lived in continuously, are codes of past-present allegiance. All the kings, from 1550 on; the Directoire, that ran things at the end of the 18th century after the Revolution; Napoleon, the restoration kings, Louis Philippe, and Louis Napoleon had furniture styles named after them. By setting a new style, they left their mark on France. The ones your ancestors picked, and the ones you pick today, not only display their and your taste, but also your political affiliation. The furniture statement was clearer than the clothes you wore in Marcel Proust's day, and not that different right now. I know a royalist who refuses to have furniture in the style of the upstart tyrant, Napoleon, in the house. I know a Communist who has only unidentifiable, upholstered department store furniture in his large, comfortable house. Upstairs in his office, though, where you're not likely to see it, is the piece of furniture that he loves – a Louis XV desk.

The codes of these furniture symbols sometimes give out mixed signals, which makes them more difficult to decipher. For instance, Charles X furniture is the most expensive and the most coveted of the 19th century. This might be because Charles didn't last very long and wasn't very popular, so there isn't much of his style around. It might also be because there is a lot of worksmanship in the style, and after him, machines became more important in furniture manufacturing. Perhaps it's expensive because it appeals somehow to current fashion. But it could also be expensive because Charles X was the last of the legitimate kings, and so his is the last of the legitimate styles. The last of something is always valuable.

Presidential Style

Nonsense, the late President Mitterrand would have said. The history of style goes on. Presidents are just as legitimate as kings. Having built his controversial pyramid at the Louvre, he then ordered yet another heatedly debated monument, the Bibliothèque Nationale, or TGB. It will be remarkable and, to many, inappropriate for books – four glass towers to house the books, black glass to protect them from the sun, air conditioning to protect them from the heat; and a kind of sunken hole in the ground between the towers for the researchers and students to work in. Aside from questions of cost and practicality, the President imposed his style on the country of style. A stunning modern engineering feat will house one of the world's great repositories of history, just as another stunning modern engineering feat, the pyramid, was built a few years ago by the same President as an entrance to one of the world's great repositories of art... and just as a stunning engineering feat of the 19th century, the Eiffel Tower, is the symbol of Paris recognized around the globe. The new will accommodate the old at whatever cost.

Plus ça change, plus c'est la même chose.

Chapter 9

The French Family
Rules, Closeness, Wit and the Esprit Critique

> *French childhood is an apprenticeship, during which one learns the rules*
> *and acquires "good habits"; it is a time of discipline, of imitation of models,*
> *of preparation for the role of adult. As one French informant told me, "We*
> *had a lot of homework and little time to play."*
>
> Raymonde Carroll
> *Cultural Misunderstandings*

A French bourgeois family (that is, a family of some substance) is run like a mini-kingdom, with a mini-Louis XIV in charge, even if he does change a few diapers these days.

The King (the father) decides, in concert with his *égerie,* usually his wife. *Egérie* is one of those words you have to know to understand the French. As it doesn't exist in English, the English-French dictionaries give varying, usually misleading, definitions. The French-French dictionaries are clear: an *égérie* is a woman who is the counselor of a man or a political group, or both. The official mistresses of the French kings, who were French, were *égéries* and the queens, who were foreign, were not. Even during the 350 years between 1600 and 1944, when women had lost all their civil rights, they maintained a great deal of power by being *égéries* to the kings, emperors and presidents, and to their husbands.

Louis XIV was a very secretive and reserved French king. French fathers, and French families, are also very secretive and reserved. To understand the dynamics of French families you really have to be born into one.

Everything else is hearsay. If you're a foreigner, you can find out a lot about French families if you make friends with a French person in kindergarten or first grade. If it's too late for that, then there is only one other good way, and that's to marry into one.

Otherwise, like me, you read books and question endlessly people who have done one of the above... been to first grade with them (like my children) or married into them (like my children and many of my friends).

Soon after I moved to France, a Frenchman of the *grande bourgeoisie* – that is, one who comes from an established old family and can move around amongst all the classes, up or down – told me encouragingly (at the cocktail party of a mutual Hungarian friend, with whom he had been in kindergarten), "You'll never be invited to a real French party, like a wedding."

It was startling to me that the mere fact of being foreign, never mind how fascinating you were, could bar you from festivities where you might very well wish to be. NO other Western country functions like this.

And for many years it was true. The good news is that I've been to lots of French weddings in the last few years. Like much else in France, it all depends on you.

There's a third way to find out about French families, which may be the most significant. This is to interview French parents after they've spent some family years in America. When they come out of shock (if they survive), they have a lot to say about how differently (read dangerously) children are brought up over there in the U.S. Then they may tell you what they think is the right (and only) way to bring them up and live in a family.

Parental Hopes and Techniques

French and anglophone differences begin in the womb, with the prospects and plans the parents have in mind for that future child. As for how to go about implementing the prospects, the countries, as might be expected from previous chapters, couldn't be more opposed.

Raymonde Carroll, a French anthropologist married to an American anthropologist and living in America, points out in her wonderful book, *Cultural Misunderstandings*, quoted above, that expectant French parents are presenting France with a future citizen who must learn to conform to French society. Their duty is to require certain behavior and set certain goals so that he will be a credit to France and to them, and be able to survive the system in the pleasantest way for the child — and for them. Their contract is with the state, but the parent-child relationship, and the family fabric in general, is densely interwoven and continues relatively unchanged throughout their lives. They probably talk to each other on the phone every day, and dine together once a week as long as the parents live.

French children are not told they must "stand on their own two feet." There is no implicit agenda about making a pile of money, expectations of happiness or effort-oriented rewards. They're expected to do their part in a network of relationships. Their "identity" comes from that and I've never heard any French person worrying about it. In school, this nation of celebrated individualists is taught early on that it's knowledge which is important... not what they happen to think about it. The moment they write "I feel that..." on a term paper, they get a zero. What they worry about is France "losing its identity" in the new Europe, or in the floods of immigrants.

Expectant American parents are presenting the world with an entirely new, unknown person, and their parental duty is to help that person develop his/her own individual potentialities to the utmost. Their contract is with the child. How the parents train him is no one's business but their own. Once he's grown up, he's no longer part of the family routine. He recognizes no one's claim upon him, nor is it found acceptable, let alone desirable, that he live at home after he's finished his education. He's off to the races and he feels confident of winning. Where there's a will, there's a way, if you work hard enough.

Madame Carroll uses an agricultural metaphor: if future parents are imagined to be growing a plant, French parents know exactly what kind of seed they're putting in the ground, what to expect and how to make it come up to their expectations: how much water, sunlight and fertilizer to give it, when to prune it, when to splice it, transplant it, and so forth, to produce the kind of plant they have in mind.

American parents, on the other hand, have no preconceived ideas about what sort of a seed they're planting and how it will or should turn out. They hope the children will learn by their example. Constraints or harsh discipline might warp the perfect growth of this unique new wonder on the earth, who might — why not? — grow up to be President of the United States. So the parents encourage his self-expression. It's an exciting experiment to grow something entirely new, and they simply have to guess at how much sun and water and fertilizer it needs in order to flower to perfection. Sometimes they wonder, when the child seems to be warping anyway. They can only hope they've got it right, and wait and see.

French parents are doting and loving, but the perspective is different. There is no time to be lost in pounding, hammering, molding the little savage into a civilized, effective, seductive, responsible citizen, who will some day reward their efforts with him by taking care of them in their old age. Hundreds of years of tradition and experience, which will be tirelessly

127

recalled to the parents by neighbors and relatives, are there to guide this serious mission. It demands authority as much as tenderness. It is not for softies who want to be "pals" with their children. The interesting thing is that when these children grow up, they *are* pals with their parents, perhaps more than American children.

Becoming *Bien Elevé*

Thus, French mothers launch potty training at, say, 6 months. If a child isn't fully trained at 18 months, he may be seen to be retarded, or to have a malfunctioning mother. Baby-care centers might not accept him.

By two and a half, French children shake hands with grown-ups and say *"Bonjour, monsieur,"* and *"Bonjour, madame."* One of the first and most important things French children have hammered into them is not to speak to strange children in the park, and above all, not to share their toys with them. (So don't be surprised that, once grown up, they don't speak to you, either, in the supermarket queue.) At three, they're qualified for kindergarten. Their education from now on is serious, demanding, and free. By the age of four, they've acquired the basic social courtesies. They have also learned to sit still for hours at a time.

So, when French parents see American children running wild in a restaurant, they need to be told it's not because they're retarded or autistic. It's because the parents are against those possibly warping constraints. When American parents in France see five- and six-year-olds sitting with their families at restaurants for hours at a time without moving, they need to be told that the children aren't ill, they're simply *bien élevé*, or well brought up.

A four-year-old trying to interrupt her mother talking with a friend is ignored (she is being rude and should realize it), while the American mother will probably ask the child what she wants and spend the next five or 10 minutes (interminable, to the French visitor) trying to figure out and answer the question (encouraging the child to express herself, in the interests of that perfect flowering).

French *education*, in the French sense of the word, which means training in manners, morals, style and general behavior, is a very serious matter, and unrelenting all through childhood. There is constant criticism and pressure to be perfect. Very soon the child learns, *"On n'a pas droit à l'erreur."*

For Americans, it seems excruciating. Where an American mother would hesitate to bruise the child's ego, the Frenchwoman, with all those centuries of unbroken tradition behind her, doesn't hesitate to call attention to stupidity, bad taste, bad manners, boring comments, inappropriate reactions and any lapse in impeccable appearance. Punishment can escalate from verbal reprimands to facial slaps in public, spanking, threats about attacks from monsters, and being locked in a dark closet. Most Americans would consider this a strategy to put the whole nation in the nuthouse by age 20. It's strange how well-balanced they turn out.

French mothers continue to harp on their offspring's shortcomings throughout life. A French countess of about 65 told me that her mother, a grand dame of the old aristocracy nearing 90, was going blind, but nevertheless never failed to dress her down about what she was wearing. "She'll never be so blind she stops telling me I have a spot on my dress or why am I wearing those dreadful shoes," said the countess cheerfully.

Even around the French family dinner table (and the family still gathers there every evening!), a child's question is not necessarily answered. "That's boring," or, "You're just trying to get attention" ("*Ne joue pas l'intéressant*") is often the reply. The child learns from the older siblings that he can only get answers by being witty. It's surprising how fast they learn. And not surprising that they grow up with the same taste and appreciation of wit as their parents.

The Crucial *Rallye*

As nothing must be left to chance in the child's *education*, his social life must be organized so that he is sure to meet the right people. Steps must be taken so that it is in full swing before adolescent revolts start. Parisian mothers of the traditional upper classes have a unique system for this. A few friends with 11-year-old daughters get together to make lists of all the people they know or know of with children the same age, who will form what is known as a *rallye*. At first only 12 or 16 of these are selected to meet with their own children at age 12, to play bridge. At 13 a few more will be invited to join, now for dancing classes. The group will gradually be enlarged each year, so that they get used to each other comfortably. By age 18, the last year, there will be balls of up to 500 in the smartest places in town.

The girls' mothers are called on to give a party each year. The most sought-after girls may belong to several *rallyes*, if their mothers can afford the tab. Very eligible boys will obviously be deluged with invitations for all the *rallyes*.

French mothers with ambitions but few connections are hard-pressed to find a *rallye* for their daughters. And some *rallye* invitations are more fought-over than others.

The young people likely to be left out are foreigners. Foreign mothers who are keen for their daughters to be part of all this have been known to have nervous breakdowns over it. They rarely have close French friends who happen to be *rallye* organizers or know someone who is, so that their daughters are automatically on the list. Nor are foreigners likely, as we've seen, to be considered particularly desirable as friends for their children. One girl I know of was refused admission to a *rallye* with these words, from one of the French mothers in charge: "She's not only foreign, she's the daughter of divorced parents!"

Shrewd foreigners put their daughters in the schools, read French Catholic schools, where they have an opportunity to make friends with the *rallye* girls.

Rules and French Mothers-in-law

As for mothers-in-law, American wives of Frenchmen feel they cross the insult barrier in a way that their own mothers would never dream of doing at any age, and certainly not once they're out on their own.

Donna G., an elegant and sophisticated New York lawyer who has a *good* relationship with her French mother-in-law, put it like this:

"They have about 200 rules that don't exist in America, so the first few years in France, of course you're always breaking at least one of them, and they have to tell you, not only so that you'll shape up yourself, but so that you'll bring up their grandchildren properly, and not disgrace the family.

"For instance, you can't put a foot out of the house or apartment in the morning, even to go get a baguette, without being properly dressed. One spring morning, I tried to go and get a newspaper without stockings on, before my legs were tanned, and got told off about it.

"At my parents-in-law's house, they always end up the meals with a bowl of fruit in the center of the table. I had a lazy way of plucking a grape from the center bowl. Finally my mother-in-law slapped my hand. 'Don't pick, take the whole bunch from the bowl, Donna!' she snapped.

"The stress on appearance is not to be believed. Look at the children in the parks – half the time the little girls are dressed up in white dresses!"

Gladys H., another American wife of a Frenchman: "I like my mother-in-law a lot, but sometimes – really! It took me a long time to find a hairdresser who could cut my hair properly. One time it was really a mess. I was embarrassed enough about it, and so then my mother-in–law goes, 'Goodness Gladys! Your haircut! You look like a poodle!' Then she imitates a little dog. 'Woof woof!' It doesn't make you feel exactly great.'"

Gladys's mother-in-law is a picnic compared to the one Joan H. is stuck with, who was against the marriage from the beginning. One evening at a party, Joan and her husband, Jean-Marie, and his mother were talking with a friend of his mother, when Jean-Marie's mother said to the friend, "Jean-Marie hasn't had a promotion lately, and I'm sure it's because he has an American wife."

Like the government, like big business and industry, French families are pyramids of strict hierarchy.

Even though French fathers are becoming familiar with the inside of a kitchen, they don't seem to do much there, even if their wife works. Their authority is unquestioned. That more mothers are working, and a third of French children are now born out of wedlock, usually in normal two-parent but not yet legally certified homes, doesn't seem to have chipped noticeably away at it.

It is interesting watching my American niece, Nell Platt, bringing up her little children with her French husband, Bernard Rivière.

"Eat your carrots, Mathieu," says Nell, coaxingly.

Mathieu, 5, whines. He doesn't like carrots. "Why should I?" he says, fiddling with them.

"Because they're good for you. They'll make you big and strong."

Mathieu is not impressed. He goes on whining and fiddling.

Bernard steps in. "Eat your carrots, Mathieu," he says quietly but sternly.

"But I don't like them," Mathieu whimpers, about to cry. "Why should I?"

Bernard now measures his words, articulating them not only sternly, but very slowly. "Because - I - tell - you - to," he says.

Mathieu eats his carrots.

French Families in the U.S.

French families are not independent, nuclear units. They're part of a complex interlocking network of relatives of various generations that they keep up with all the time. French families usually live in the same area all their lives, so the network is always there.

If one family is amputated from this close-knit, formal, rules-oriented system and is put down in a culture with a different, non-hierarchical, informal system of operating like the U.S., trouble clouds will gather.

The adventure of the French families who came to suburban Cincinnati as part of a SNECMA-General Electric program, started out reassuringly.

They were astonished and moved at the friendliness of the neighbors. The Welcome Wagon! They couldn't get over it. Everyone was helpful in showing them around and helping them get settled. All the families were invited to dinner by their neighbors.

They began to be uncomfortable when they invited the Americans back.

"They helped themselves to drinks," said Madame D. "They followed me out to the kitchen! I'm sure they only wanted to be helpful, but it was very strange for us, particularly when they wanted to see the whole house. And then, they eat differently, and so early... dinner at 6 p.m.! We just can't eat at that hour.

"But the American children, this we couldn't believe. The friends of our children would come to our house, barely say hello – no shaking hands, of course – and go straight to the refrigerator. Our refrigerator. And help themselves. Our own children aren't allowed to do that."

There's no French lycée in Cincinnati. In order to be able to rejoin their former classmates in the excruciatingly rigorous French school system two or three years later, French teenagers had to do homework for their French school in the evening.

It would have been a killing load, had there also been homework for the American school. There wasn't. The parents were shocked and worried. Were their children going to forget how to study in this country? Were they going to learn anything? This made them even stricter about the French studies.

For the children, it meant they couldn't take part in the fun things the Americans were doing after school, like singing or painting or playing hockey or football, or going to the local swimming hole in the spring. They resented it, particularly as they knew that, once back in France, there would be no singing or painting or swimming after school. Studying. Period.

If parent-teenager tension began building over the French lessons, it got much, much worse, as the children began making friends and feeling integrated. Gradually everything that happened around the teenagers made the parents feel desperate, as if they were in a jungle, and helpless.

Cross-cultural Pitfalls

Monsieur and Madame R., let's call them the Raynauds, prosperous bourgeois and devout Catholics, had two teenage girls with them, one 13, Brigitte, and one 19, Cécile.

Cécile lived at her college in Cincinnati. Brigitte, as long as her English was poor, continued to be the docile girl she'd been in France. But by the second year she was fluent, and began being asked to spend the night with American friends.

She heard her best friend, her own age, then 14, talk back to her father. She heard the friend's older brother announce – not ask, not beg, but announce – that he was taking the car that night. She heard the older sister sassing her mother.

Amazed, Brigitte told her own older sister, Cécile, about this, sure that her new friend's family was just weird. But Cécile assured her that this was how it was in America, and wasn't it great? Imagine! Say what you think! Do what you like!

Cécile, living at college, away from the parental eye, as that was the American system, was a convinced American after one year. When she was at home for vacations, the two of them began acting like Americans. They horrified and scandalized their parents. The mother felt ashamed. The father was shaken. His world simply fell apart when his daughters began talking back to him... and refused to do what he said.

Both girls fell in love with American boys and were deeply involved, particularly Brigitte, who was head over heels with a boy called Harry. Brigitte and Cécile didn't tell their parents how serious they were about their loves. They were loathe to leave the U.S. when the time came to go back to France.

For Monsieur and Madame Raynaud, returning to Paris was a huge relief. For all its freedom from prudishness, Paris is probably the only comforting city in Europe for parents bringing up adolescent girls. Its reputation for licentiousness, which comes from the goings-on in red-light districts like Pigalle, is one of the paradoxes of France, which has the strictest rules and constraints on young people in Europe. Drummed in all through childhood, they're later enforced by the father and mother, by the relatives, the neighbors and the Church. The Catholic schools, where the children of the *bourgeoisie* tend to go, are unisex. Teenagers have to study so hard there's little time for playing around or daydreaming, and parental discipline is respected. French families are able to postpone "meaningful relationships" till much later than other countries. Virginity isn't considered humiliating for 20-year-olds, or even for 25-year-old girls – or boys.

But Brigitte and Cécile had tasted foreign ways. If the family situation of the Raynauds was miserable in America, it barely avoided tragedy when they got back to France. Cécile took up with a divorced Lebanese Moslem twice her age, and married him, bringing an alien element impossible to assimilate into this formerly close-knit family.

Brigitte fared worse. Having lived in America from the age of 13 to almost 16, she felt completely out of things back in formal, rule-oriented France. And she missed Harry terribly. The French school gave her homework that kept her up half the night and even so, she could hardly understand it. Her marks were depressing, and the comments of her teacher were searing, on the order of, "Well, what do you expect, if you spend three years among savages..." and "You seem to have lost all power of reasoning in Disneyland."

She didn't want to go on living like this. Finally she decided she didn't want to go on living at all.

Her mother came home after shopping one day and found a suicide note under the door. Madame Raynaud phoned the firemen and rushed upstairs. She got there just in time.

Chapter 10

School Days
The Survival of the Smartest

Where America extols money, West Germany work and Great Britain blood, France has nailed its flag to the post of cleverness. It is achievement in the educational field which determines inclusion among the decison-makers of French society. The nation is governed by its star pupils, and the higher reaches of management are no exception.

Jean-Louis Barsoux and Peter Lawrence
Management in France

In the country of Voltaire and Balzac, Chateaubriand and Zola, Descartes and Pasteur, brains are the way to measure worth, and education is the way to furnish and train the brain, leading to the power and the pleasures of body and mind that French people find make life worth living.

Education is the consuming concern of all French people. I said all. It unites them. It gets them out in the street, regardless of their politics, their religion, their color, their region. If you ever need a conversational topic with a French person, ask him about the recent reforms. You don't have to know which. There are always reforms in progress, because every new Prime Minister and every new Minister of Education have to show that they realize that education is closest to his electorate's heart.

In 1984, the Socialist government ("the Left"), voted in for the first time since the Second World War, decided to live up to the anti-clerical doctrines espoused since the French Revolution, and incidentally collect some money for its seriously depleted coffers. It proposed to take away the government subsidies from Catholic schools. This meant that these schools, attended by a large minority, would become a great deal more expensive.

The Catholic Church organized one of the public processions (*manifs*) for which the French are famous. About a million people took part – from both the Left and the Right. They were taken out to Versailles in special trains. They walked the 12 kilometers to Paris. The government backed down.

The French were marching for their *liberté* and *égalité* – their freedom to choose the school for their child without undue regard for expense, probably the most critical decision they would ever make for him. Whether worker or CEO, French people demand the right to decide on a secular or religious education.

Whichever they choose, it will be among the best offered anywhere in the world, it will decide his whole future and it will be a compelling commitment for the whole family.

That Brigitte Raynaud tried suicide after years of being in the U.S. and off the track, and not being able to get back on, isn't surprising. What is surprising is that she seems to be an isolated case.

School is the most harrowingly demanding thing a French person may ever have to endure. How he fares there determines, for all but a few rich, enterprising or artistically gifted individuals, how agreeable his life will be. Rank and pay in French industrial, financial and governmental hierarchies is directly related to documented evidence of intellectual superiority. Forget your notion that experience counts.

Like the sacrament of food, the school system, and the national priority of brains it represents, has the support of the entire country.

It would have to. Otherwise the suicide rate would have killed off the population long ago. Even the most irascible of francophobes usually restrains his French-bashing when he hears what poor Pierre and Gaston have to go through.

National Fever

In fact the school system in France is a national fever. It affects everyone.

The whole country trembles and quakes from September to June. Whether you have school-age children or not, French television and newspapers will drench you in the periodic pulse-taking of the children themselves.

First, *La Rentrée*. This means The Return from vacation in September. From vacation to work? No. From vacation to school. From May to August, no French person ever mentions September, but *La Rentrée*. At the end of August already begin the first statistics of how many millions of cars are clogging the autoroutes for *La Rentrée*.

The actual day of the *Rentrée*, the first day of school, is referred to by the media as *"J"*, for *jour* (day) with a capital J. They start counting the days at *"J-10"*, or J minus 10: that is, 10 days to go till the big one. As they roll by, each day brings interviews of school preparations in towns and villages all over the country, and spreads and interviews on various school concerns. What sort of book bag should the parents buy? A sack or a briefcase? 15 possibilities are presented, along with diagrams of the points where each one might strain the back. What kind of haircut is in this year? For boys? Girls? Short? Long? or half way up the back of the head?

Whole sections of newspapers are given over to health care for school children, a major preoccupation, for missing even a week can make a difference in your class rank. The competition is such that you can't expect a schoolmate to show you the material you missed. The role of sleep, exercise, brushing of teeth and proper diet in getting top marks is emphasized, along with the obligatory injections for contagious diseases.

As for what to wear, this subject is so consequential and the possibilities so numerous that J-3 and J-2 (the last two days to the *Rentrée* but one) are usually given up entirely to it. Little girls of six must already make the fatal choices of Look which will affect how they're regarded. Skirts or dresses, Bermudas or trousers, and what cut? Anyone faintly alive this year (1994) can report that the *caleçon*, or tights without the feet, that often looks suspiciously like long underwear, is in for all females under 70.

Don't bother trying to buy any office supplies from August through *La Rentrée*. Everything you might need has been shoved back to the storage rooms to make room for schoolbooks, notebooks, notebook paper, crayons, bookbags, etc. etc., usually displayed back of huge color posters of grinning girls and boys waving as they march joyously back to school.

Now we've reached J-l, the big *Jour* minus one. This is the day of the teachers' *Rentrée*. They meet at the school to hear a speech from the director (the *proviseur*) and find out about their classes. They're the vanguard of the French Ministry of Education. Now that the Soviet Army is no more, this institution employs possibly more people than any other in the world, something over a million. Its budget is 20.1 percent of the national budget.

For the French, it is this army which is of supreme national importance.

The teachers, the elite troops of this army, are interviewed, photographed, followed and invited on television talk shows. Is French secondary education still turning out supremely literate graduates? Can they still recite lines from *Phèdre*? Do they still perceive the resonance of words like honor and glory from *Le Cid*?

A fairly young, attractive teacher, a woman who just wrote a book on the subject, is asked, "What is the hardest thing about the First Day Back?"

"Deciding what to wear," she says. "A *caleçon* or a short skirt lacks authority, and a long skirt seems dowdy. So we mostly wear jeans."

And the second most difficult?

"Séduire les enfants," she says.

Help! Seduction in the *classroom*? I can see you blanching. Do the sexually obsessed French stop at nothing?

Here we go with one of those *faux amis* (words that look the same in both languages but have different meanings) that start wars. *Déception* is another. *Séduire* (and its noun, *séduction*) has splendor in French, with none of the nastiness that Webster attributes to "seduction", of "leading astray, enticing to disloyalty, inciting to wrong." It means a fullness of pleasing, of charming, of appealing because of certain wondrous qualities. It can be applied to vacuum cleaners and lampshades as appropriately as people. In other words, there are no moral implications. Here's an example from *Les Echos*:

Hypermarché à la française séduit l'Europe du Nord

What that teacher meant was that seducing the children – charming them so that they would like her, be intrigued by her, respect her, and listen to what she said – was her greatest difficulty at the beginning of the year.

Finally J Day dawns. Half of the 1:00 p.m. and 8:00 p.m. news broadcasts are devoted to children coming back to school. Now we toil through countless media interviews with them. How much schoolwork did they do over vacation? As much as the school counseled them to do? How do they feel being back? Do they understand and approve of the current reforms?

The camera zooms quickly over three-year-olds in tears and brings us the happy faces of the six- to 18-year olds, grinning like the store posters.

Everyone knows these are the last grins until July.

This goes for the parents too. Playtime with your child is over on J Day of first grade.

On J Day the parents are handed their first assignment: a list of all the things they have to prepare for the child to bring to school the next day.

For a foreigner, the list is about as easy to put together as a treasure hunt in Mongolia.

Emily Borel, whose little boy, Julien, just started school in a village in Normandy, reports from the front lines:

"They have all summer to give you the list, right? But they hand it out as you come to pick up your child the first day. A whole page full of everything from about 20 textbooks of different sizes – and their covers – and pencils with 3 different kinds of eraser to a real pen with real ink, and a piece of felt for the ink blots. So, 40 mothers, most of us with smaller children also in tow, go to the paper store at the same time to get all this stuff, because the children have to have them – must have them – in school the next day.

"So I'm standing in line trying to puzzle out the list, and Anaïs – she's my two-year-old – starts screaming. Then all the other toddlers in the store start screaming. Finally I get to the counter and order the textbooks and their covers. You know what the salesgirl says? I have to make the covers myself! For 20 textbooks! They don't sell them! Is this the Middle Ages or what?

"I go home and try to make the textbook covers with paper and Scotch tape. After two hours I give up. Then I tackle the rest of the list, with my dictionary. I come to *une ardoise*.

"The dictionary says this is a roof tile. A roof tile? Well, maybe they're going to build something. So I go to the barn and get a roof tile. Julien takes it to school the next day, along with the uncovered textbooks and the rest.

"When I go to pick him up, he tells me that the *ardoise* was supposed to be a writing slate and that he was the only one in class not to have his textbooks covered.

"I said, 'Julien, nothing in my life until now has prepared me for this.'"

After J Day, the fever rises as the mission to learn, and get better marks than anyone else, goes into gear. We quiver and shudder until at last All Saints, Christmas, February, Easter give us a respite and we're told how many millions of French families are gasping for the desperately needed air of the mountains, etc. The parents need the vacations as much as the children, having been up every night helping them with their homework.

The *Bac*

Finally we have the paroxysms of June with the *baccalauréat*, known as the *bac* : a series of exams at the end of secondary school that take a whole month. Its outcome determines whether the child will have automatic free entry to university – or not. Photos of children scribbling exams (to prove they're still alive), interviews with them about how they think they did and how they feel, and what they hope to do now.

All the questions are published in the dailies. The first exam is philosophy: one question to write on for the entire morning. "Being or becoming? Which is more important?" In 1993, the question for the literary *Bac* A pupils was, "Is human reason led to suppose more order in the world than is actually the case?" Four hours. The outline (*le plan*) counts 50 percent of the mark.

There's no nonsense about multiple choice for the exams on any of the subjects – although, to the shame and horror of many parents, there were a few in June 1992.

The *baccalauréat* comes in many shapes, which open different doors to the future, the one called "S" opening them all. Whichever section the student chooses, any *bac* diploma certifies a certain level of intellectual achievement qualifying the *bachelier* for university studies.

For the children, the 12 years of French secondary school are like competing every day in an Olympic Event. They're ranked in their class according to their marks from the first grade on. Good health, determination and stamina have to back up the superior brains, if they want to be number one in the class and please Papa, or at least be somewhere near the top and avoid a thrashing. If the whole country weren't out there cheering, clapping and stamping their feet, the system would collapse. Because you can also compare it to a prison sentence:

- Your superiors (the teachers) treat you like dirt. (That teacher interviewed on television, who wanted to *séduire* the children, is a notable exception.)
- There's no demand for creativity. (That comes later.)
- No one cares what you personally think or feel.
- Punishment for any aberration is severe.
- There are no sports but gymnastics.
- There is no escape.
- There's no certainty you'll get a job when you're out.

It's possible that French secondary school teachers will at some future date treat their pupils like suffering creatures who need encouragement. Two things make me think so: the guns that some immigrant ruffians of the suburbs produced to shoot at several of them recently; and the popularity in France of *The Dead Poets' Society*.

The spectacle of pupils in that movie being encouraged to speak up in class, not to memorize but to think, and to climb up on a desk to see the world from a different angle – this blew the minds of both teachers and pupils in France. Bernard Pivot, the country's most popular television personality, devoted a whole program to what school administrators, pupils and teachers thought of it. The pupils expressed being "thrilled and amazed" at this teaching system. The teachers and administrators were so restrained in their condemnation that I had a feeling they might come 'round – some day.

French secondary education is about the transfer of knowledge, not, as in the U.S., about awakening the slumbering mind to the excitement of learning and the possibilities of how and where the child himself can get the information. The word for schooling in France is *formation* – forming the mind, not opening it up – and the pressure from the parents and the teacher to perform is unrelenting. It seems to work better than the American system at turning out independent analytical thinkers, generalists with well-stocked minds.

The teacher is at school the figure of authority that the father represents at home.

Knowing the child – having any sort of relationship with him or awareness of his individual skills and quirks and needs – is not part of the deal. On the contrary.

The strategy of bringing the little savage in line that starts in the family is thus backed up and reinforced by his teachers. The teachers of my own children were angels of compassion according to the tales of most of the American mothers I know who have children in French schools. In general, American mothers go into shock at their children being slapped in the face or shamed in front of the class. Slaps from teachers are fairly infrequent, but shame and ridicule belong to the teacher's daily arsenal as well as to that of the parents. In fact, it is just as well that French parents criticize their little tots mercilessly, to toughen them up for what awaits them at school. They don't seem to end up inevitably on psychiatrists' couches, as an American might be inclined to expect, possibly because they let out their rage out on their roads, statistically among the most dangerous in Europe.

It's the American mothers faced with these situations who need help – in not burning down the school or murdering the teacher. Their children seem to be able to sail through them perfectly smoothly.

But in some cases, professorial ruthlessness in class can be disastrous, particularly if there's a slight handicap. Anne-Marie Chevalier, a Frenchwoman who lived in Washington for several years with her family, has had experience with both and prefers the American way. Her daughter is dyslexic.

"In America they don't murder the child's confidence," she said. "I came back to France when my daughter was eight. The teacher ridiculed her in front of the whole class, saying a four-year-old spelled better than she. Luckily I found another school for her – the Alsatian School in Paris – that had a different policy."

Once the *bac* is over, the misery is only just beginning for the brilliant ones who have big career ambitions and are aiming at a *Grande Ecole,* one of the super-difficult-to-get-into, high-powered academies that exist only in France.

I guess it's hardly necessary to add that there is no such thing as "school spirit" in French secondary schools, as there is no time to do anything but study. Exams are too important to trust with anything as delicate as the honor system. As far as I know, no French student was ever caught singing in school, and certainly not "School days, school days, oh for the good old golden-rule days...."

Chapter 11

The Grandes Ecoles :
The Selection of the Elite

Il n'y a sans doute pas de pays au monde où les diplômes soient mieux respectés, leur validité aussi persistante. En France, le diplôme est une fusée longue portée qui, sauf accident, vous propulse jusqu'à la retraite. (There is surely no other country in the world where academic degrees have more power or longevity...In France, a degree is a long-range missile, which, unless there is a mishap, carries one through to retirement.)

> Alain Peyrefitte, of the Académie Française
> *Le Mal Français*

This was the headline in the business section of a recent *Figaro*:

David (X, inspecteur des Finances) intègre Stern

French-speaking foreigners might suspect that this meant that a Monsieur David was going to take over the Banque Stern, but that's about all they'd glean. For French people, the headline resounds with coded information that Monsieur David is one of the most brilliant men in France; *donc*, as the French say, a man headed for, or already in possession of, great power.

"X" is the code for the most prestigious and difficult engineering school in the world, the Ecole Polytechnique, in Palaiseau, near Paris. Inspecteur des Finances means that in addition, he not only went to the world's most difficult and prestigious civil service school, the Ecole Nationale d'Administration, known as the ENA (pronounced "enah"), but also that he graduated among the first 10 in his class, thus qualifying for the State's most devastating power network, the Inspection des Finances.

Power in France is about X's and *énarques*, graduates of X and the ENA. Diplomas from these two academies, and, to a lesser extent, a few other high-powered engineering schools, are the point of about 16 years of excruciating school misery. Graduating among the first in your class at one of them, let alone both, guarantees positions of leadership until the end of your career. As Alain Peyrefitte comments in the quote above, they're long-range missiles.

Hence when a Frenchman asks, *"Qu'est-ce qu'il a fait?"* ("What has he done?") about another Frenchman he has just met, the question is not about what jobs he has had, but what degrees – and where from.

X comes first. As we saw in Chapter 8, France loves engineers. The country's symbol, recognized far and wide, is not, for instance, Versailles or the Bastille, but a feat of engineering.

The Eiffel Tower is a many-sided beacon. It reminds travel-befuddled foreigners where they are. Ascending its heights gives the intrepid a glorious view of the pride of France, the world's loveliest city.

For the French, it is much, much more. As a work of mathematical precision and building innovation exploiting a new material, it puts the world on notice that whatever the world may choose to think about France as Fluff and Frivolity, France thinks of itself as a nation of brilliantly creative and daring *ingénieurs*... sometimes of a tour de force, and sometimes of something very practical.

Eiffel's tower is both. He put it up as an outrageous challenge to the heavens; but also as a way to get up there in the winds and study what they were doing, thereby founding the science of aerodynamics.

For French fathers, it's as powerful a symbol as Abe Lincoln's log cabin. While the American father says to his son, "You too can grow up to be President of the United States," the French father says, "You too can master the secrets of the universe, and become an *ingénieur*."

Power to the Mathematicians

The difference in qualifications for the two careers says a great deal about the way the two countries look at life: the one, pragmatic, the other theoretical. For a future *ingénieur* shaker and mover, aiming at a powerpacked degree in France means choosing the harrowing math-physics path to the *bac*; single-minded dedication, starting at age 15, to ever higher realms of mathematics in order to qualify for several more years of total grind, open only to the most brilliant, and survived only by the toughest and most determined... in order to qualify for still more exorbitantly demanding exams for entering the gates of heaven to one of the *Grandes Ecoles* of engineering mentioned above.

If he passes them brilliantly, he is set for life. I said *life*.

That French power is about mathematical brains is one of the fallouts of the French revolution. Despite all the singing and banner-waving about *égalité*, the revolutionaries recognized that, while you could give the vote to everyone (everyone being males), some people were still going to be more equal than others. So they aimed at a different basis for inequality than birth. But based on what? Money? Property? Horrors. Physical appearance? Worse. What's left? Intelligence.

But how to measure it? Fairly? By math exams! What a wonderful way to stimulate mathematical research and crown *ingénieurs* with the rewards they merited. The French had been in love with math since the Crusaders brought geometry back from Byzantium. All through the Middle Ages and up to modern times, Paris had been a mecca for learning of all kinds, and as science developed, Paris was its center. There were more scientific institutions in Paris in the 18th and 19th centuries than anywhere else. Lavoisier, the father of modern chemistry, Pasteur, Lesseps and Eiffel were the heirs of the Gothic cathedral architects, of Abélard, Saint Thomas Aquinas, Pascal, and Descartes.

The country has always admired intellectual adventure and treasured innovation and progress, accepting it, reconciling it with the past. The greater the bookworm, the more eggheaded you are, the more likely you are to win friends, influence people and above all, be accepted at a *Grande Ecole* of engineering.

If possible, at X.

The system of *Grandes Ecoles* is unique to France. These high-powered academies are separate from the university system. They're also free, or provide pay for their students, and the privileges don't stop there. They are utterly unlike universities, to which anyone with a *bac* can go. Entrance to *Grandes Ecoles* is on the basis of competitive exams. Universities are underequipped, dilapidated and overcrowded. *Grandes Ecoles* are equipped with the best material, the classes are small and the professors are the best in France and well paid.

Lionel Jospin, Minister of Education (1989) as waiter in front of a "university":
"I don't care if you're the professor. Do you have a reservation? " (Serguei, *Le Monde*)

Future academics and research scientists try for one of the "Normales Sups", short for Ecoles Normales Supérieures. As for the business–bound: despite the lofty reputation of the Ecole des Hautes Etudes de Commerce (HEC), the most prestigious, it boasts few CEO's of the leading French companies. The best and the brightest are not yet applying. Why would they? It hasn't the official sanction of 200 years experience, but only 48. It's not free, but very expensive. Above all, the entrance exam demands little math. If you're a math star in a country which idolizes math stars, why hide your light under the HEC bushel?

The *Prépa*

So let's look at what these math stars have to do.

First of all, from age 15 at the lycée, do your 20 hours of math a week and eight of physics brilliantly for the next three years. In the last year of the lycée, known as *terminale*, the level is already altitudinous – now you're

146

ready for protons, Black Holes and expanding the universe. Pass the *bac*. If possible, do better than average, with a *mention*, or even – oh, joy – a *mention bien*.

Now you solicit acceptance at one of the preparatory cram schools, or *prépas*, to rake your mind over for the entrance exam to a *Grande Ecole* of engineering: two years minimum and probably three years of excruciating grind in higher math, math, math.

But stop and think a minute. Do you really want to become one of those sunken-eyed green-skinned youths you've seen slinking into *prépa* classrooms, looking as if they just escaped from the Gulag? Is it worth it?

Every *bac* season, the newspapers inform prospective *prépa* students what they're letting themselves in for, and suggest they tick off the following qualities in themselves besides brilliance in math:

- a strong constitution
- good health
- good memory
- resistance to temptations not to study all day and most of the night
- desire to excel
- zest for competition
- reserve intellectual capacities
- an organized method of study
- above all, a determination to dominate all tests and trials

If you're still undaunted, you put a file together of all your marks and professors' comments throughout your school years and present yourself at the *prépa* nearest where you live. For the next years you can't afford to waste any time on the Métro. If you have a *mention bien* or high honors on your *bac*, you'll try first at the two *prépas* with the highest rate of acceptance at X, therefore the most popular and the hardest to enter. These are the lycées Louis le Grand and Henry IV: the *prépas* take place physically in lycées. If they accept you, and if you live farther away than a 10 minute walk, you find lodgings nearer. Fast.

The first year is called *Maths Sup* (Mathématiques Supérieurs). If you flunk the exam at the end of the year, you're finished. No repeat. Forget engineering and switch. Either to a university or Sciences Po. More about Sciences Po later.

Otherwise, if you haven't gotten mononucleosis, or dropped dead of cardiac arrest, you drudge on into the second year, known as *Maths Spé*

(Mathématiques Spéciales). At the end of this killing year, you qualify for the entrance exam. X has a special one: nothing but math.

If you're willing to consider another of the great *Grandes Ecoles* of engineering, you can also take a different exam for them, which includes physics. These are: the Ecole des Mines, the Ecole Centrale, the Ecole des Ponts et Chaussées, France Télécom, the Ecole des Arts et Métiers, and a few others. If not, and if you fail the X exam, back you go and repeat *Maths Spé.* Good luck. You're only allowed to repeat once.

If at the end of this repeat year, you're not accepted at any of them, listen to this:

You can now go back to Square One. I mean, where you were just after you passed your *bac.* You have no piece of paper, no document whatever, that shows you were accepted and completed three perfectly hallucinatingly difficult years.

About 10 percent of *bacheliers* go to *prépas.* About half of these are accepted at *Grandes Ecoles.* But of those who do the *prépas* for X and the other leading engineering schools, only two percent are accepted. And one percent for X.

Never mind the others, one of them is you! Bravo! You're an X for life! You'll be in all the newspapers, with the 350 other new X's. Newspapers devote pages and pages every summer to the candidates accepted at all the *Grandes Ecoles.* The lists are not in alphabetical order, but in order of how well the candidates did on the entrance exams.

And now, since part of the aura of X is that Napoleon established it as an elite corps of military *ingénieurs,* you get to wear a glamorous Napoleonic uniform and sword – and you get a monthly paycheck as well!

The Elite Corps des Mines

But there's little time for gloating over your laurels. You have three more years of grind, with one thing to keep in mind: to outdo everyone and finish first – number one is forever thereafter referred to as *major* of his class. Too bad, you missed that, but at least you're among the first 10. Now you've really made it. You are an automatic member of the Corps des Mines. This means you are a member of one of the grand Corps de l'Etat, with the right to high-level, strategic positions in state institutions and industries like the Air Force and Elf Aquitaine. You will be watched and courted by the boards of directors of private industry. You have a fail-safe network of other *ingénieurs* of the Corps des Mines to rescue you should you (heaven forbid) ever make a mistake. Annual dinners are held so that you can mix and meet the older members. You have a right to call all of them by the familiar form of "you", or *tu*, even if it is the President of the Republic. Just imagine what a determining wedge that is, in itself. An annual directory indicates job openings for X's, as well as where other members are working who could be of help to you.

You also have certain privileges for life that can never be taken away from you. What privileges? One of them is secrecy. No one really knows what they are, except the other members.

The first thing you do is rush out and have your visiting cards printed, with *Ingénieur du Corps des Mines* under your name. This will insure the proper consideration from people who wouldn't otherwise know about your elevated status. Also from foreigners. It behooves them to know that they are talking to one of the most brilliant of the brilliant math stars of France.

One of the striking results of this system is not only the quality of brain power out there, but also the hang-ups of the also-rans.

I'd have thought that being one of the two percent to survive not only the *prépa* but also actually to attend and graduate from Mines or Centrale would comfort even the most power-hungry of almost-X's. After all, Eiffel was a Centralien. But some of them go through the rest of their life dragging around a feeling of failure.

Jacques Maisonrouge, who retired a couple of years ago as Number Two at IBM, is one of the few Frenchmen to get to the very top of a gigantic American multinational. He went on to become Minister of Industry and write an autobiography called *Manager International*. In it he mentions several times that he "only" went to Centrale. Not X.

The Rebel

One of the talks during my U.S. speaking tour for the Alliance Française was in Fort Collins, Colorado, where I met a charming Frenchman who turned out to be an *ingénieur* of the Ecole des Ponts et Chaussées.

"You're a Ponts!" I cried, "For goodness sake! What is a Ponts doing here in Fort Collins, Colorado? Why aren't you running your country?"

"Madame," he said, "I didn't get into X. *Donc*, no matter what I achieved the rest of my life, I knew that I would never be appointed to the number one spot at the top of, for instance, Total. I was 21 years old. I decided that a country with this absurd system of deciding a man's whole future on the basis of an exam he takes at the age of 21 was not a country I wanted to live in." An American can hardly fail to see his point.

Back to Square One

The ones who have my unlimited commiseration are the ones who tried and failed totally – the ones who submitted to the entire *prépa* torture and didn't get in to any *Grande Ecole*.

Suppose it's you. Your only choice is go back and start over at the University. Six more years before you can earn a significant degree.

Or if you're still eaten by ambition, you can hope for the ENA and spend the next three years at the Institut d'Etudes de Sciences Politiques (IEP) always referred to as Sciences Po, another prestigious school, which is technically not a *Grande Ecole* because no year or years of *prépa* are required, only an entrance exam. Sciences Po branches into specialties the second year: international relations, economics, etc. The section known as *Service Public* is the Royal Road to the ENA, but you probably won't be accepted in it if you've not already been to one of the *Grandes Ecoles*. Catch 22.

Why not just go into retailing, cinema, computers or "communication?" Help yourself, no diplomas needed.

Or best of all, start your own business. There are actually a few French tycoons who are *autodidactes*, or possessors of no degrees.

The ENA

On the other hand, if you're accepted in the *Service Public* section, don't think this Royal Road is an automatic pass through to the gates of power. There are 300 of you in the class. There will only be 40 admitted to the new class at the ENA. The written exams are brutal tests of knowledge of economics, history, finance, politics, geopolitcs.

The oral exams, quizzing the candidate's general culture, are the most dreaded. The 13 judges make a point of being as intimidating as possible and stare at you mercilessly as you enter the examination room. The exam has already started: you're marked on your poise in entering and on how you greet them. Desperately trembling, your whole career, your whole life staked on the next 30 minutes, the room and the judges in it a blur, you had better notice whether or not there is a woman among the judges. If so, and if you don't say exactly this: *"Bonjour, madame, bonjour, messieurs"*, you get a fat round zero.

The exam questions may be on poetry, finishing a verse by Verlaine or Apollinaire, say, or giving your opinion of the Grande Arche. Or they might ask you a puzzle: you're given three sets of initials and required to spot their common denominator. Answer: they're the initials of wives of former French presidents.

Many of the questions are simply to test your spirit and wits. Here are some past winners:

Q. How deep is the Seine under the Pont Neuf?
A. Under which arch?

Q. What is the difference between us and the Last Supper?
A. I don't know which of you is Judas.

Q. What is temerity?
A. Candidate doesn't answer. He walks out of the room.

Here's one for you:
You are the President of France. You must choose a Prime Minister. The short list is very short – just two men. One of them is brilliant, but, alas, corrupt. The other one has an integrity which is irreproachable. Unfortunately, he's stupid. Which do you pick?

If you blink for a second in answering this one, sorry, pal, no ENA for you. This country is about brains. You can't do anything about stupidity but, *"La corruption, ça se soigne."* ("You can heal corruption.")

The nervous collapse of the ENA candidate after this oral is not to be believed. He goes into shock, sure all is lost, until he hears the results weeks later, even if he (or she – 10 percent of the class is female) is a future *major*, or at the top of his class.

Once accepted, he is officially a salaried civil servant, and has two years more of learning about finance and administration, part of which will be spent working in industry or the government, in France or abroad.

If he graduates among the first 15 in his class, he can choose which of the Grand Corps de l'Etat, with their attendant perks, network and innumerable privileges, he wants to join. The plum for the top two or three is the choice of Monsieur David, of our headline, the Inspection des Finances, which sets up state government and industry budgets and fiscal policy.

Next in line of prestigious Grand Corps are the Conseil d'Etat, the high administrative court of justice; the Cour des Comptes, the State's auditing arm, and the Foreign Office. Unless he chooses to *pantoufler*, and buys his way out, the *énarque* owes the state 10 years of service on graduation. Then he is on his own. After these 10 years, Inspecteurs des Finances are particularly in demand for top posts in the private sector as well as state industry, not only because of their certified brains, but because of their 10 years experience in the Ministry of Finance, and their intimacy with its *grands commis de l'Etat* and intricate procedures.

More are going into the private sector than before, but the attraction of the government is still strong. That's where they tend to be. It's a government of trained pros. The most powerful civil servant in France is the Inspecteur des Finances who runs the Trésor, the beating heart of the Finance Ministry.

Like X's, all *énarques*, whether or not they made a Grand Corps, now belong to a powerful network. They 'll be parachuted into an upper-level job in the government. They have the right to *tutoyer* all other graduates, which can create colorful scenes on television. With the change of majority parties in the Parlement in 1986, Prime Minister Jacques Chirac (RPR, a right of center party) turned over the official P.M. residence, the Hôtel de Matignon, to the new occupant, Michel Rocard, a Socialist. During the traditional changeover ceremony of handshaking and so forth on the front steps, it was startling to hear these two political adversaries address each other as *tu*. They are both *énarques*.

Enarques graduating among the top 20 of their class have luster, and power. But the ENA is simply a school, and it dates only from 1946, which is like about 10 minutes ago for a Frenchman. It isn't in the same class at all with X. The Ecole Polytechnique is 200 years old, it is a military institution with an ancient tradition and an aura of great generals and great battles won, as well as great inventors, great mathematicians and great scientists.

Being an X not only entitles you to classmates' crossed swords at your wedding. You now have a title. On your wedding invitation you have a right to put *Ancien élève de l'Ecole Polytechnique*. No title for *énarques*.

The really motivated, the really tough, the real stars of France are both.

Chapter 12

The Music of Their Tongue
A Passion or a Religion?

The bond of the French-speaking community is the recognition of an intangible sovereign: the French language, which shines, splendid, on a throne of words. It does not dispense justice: it dispenses accuracy.

Maurice Druon
Doyen of the Académie Française, 1987

Language of simplicity, of clarity, of truth, which seems like the perfect vehicle for forming the subtlest thoughts, the highest conceptions, the most generous assertions. Language of liberty... language of pity, language of justice... language of friendship, language of love... it is the genius of our race, it is the glory of our past... it is the invincible hope, it is the solid anchor of the future.

Georges Clemenceau
Statesman, 1896

No effort you make is more important or will count more for your fun and triumph in France than learning French. A few words are better than none. The effort itself will go to the French heart and change the way they perceive you. Understanding them will make the difference between uncertainty and frustration, and not only coping but managing, with confidence and pleasure – whether at work or on vacation.

There are two reasons why learning French is critical for the success and enjoyment of your stay. The first is the personal, intimate and emotional relationship of the French with their language.

The second is the fact is that most French people don't speak English. If they do speak it, chances are they learned it at school, have hardly ever spoken it, and are ashamed of their clumsiness in it. Speaking well has always been the mark of a person of distinction in France. They suppose that the English-speaking world values correct use of language as much as they do. So they don't want to butcher English. They prefer that you butcher French; they will put up gracefully with your mistakes – mistakes which they wouldn't tolerate from an educated Frenchman.

An American banker in Paris says that coming to work early to learn French every morning for a year made him famous in the bank.

"They introduced me in a tone of wonder as the guy who's at his desk every morning at six a.m. to learn French," he said. "They said it with a kind of awe. For me, nothing has been more important. Learning the language has been like turning on the light in a dark room, where you've been stumbling around and falling over the furniture, and suddenly you know what's going on – and feel great."

Verlaine's Word

Our nearest neighbor in Paris is a charming and frenetic French businessman of about 42, Didier Bernardin. When he isn't vacationing in the Seychelles or Tahiti, which, as with many Frenchmen seems like a great deal of the time, he has always given me the impression of being mostly preoccupied by food, wine, and politics, in that order.

I found out how wrong I was about this when he and his lovely Swedish wife, Eva, invited Ande and me to lunch one Saturday. There were about eight other guests, all French but us. The men were business friends of Didier, self-made entrepreneurs, not an intellectual or a *Grande Ecole* graduate among them. The talk got livelier and livelier as the courses multiplied. The subjects hopped from domestic to international to regional politics, then to armaments and the ozone hole.

Around 5 p.m. (weekend lunches in France may last until 6 p.m.), it got to wine. Didier told a heartrending story about being invited out to dinner and noting, during the fish course, a bottle of vintage Pétrus on the mantelpiece. Pétrus is one of those Bordeaux vineyards that only squeezes out four or five bottles a year, so that it costs about $100 a drop. Didier told us how his palate began mobilizing for this sensational treat, which would surely be served next, during the meat course. No. Well, then for the cheese. No! It was not served at all! Not during the whole evening!

The French guests were appalled. The table shook with outrage at this *manque de savoir-faire*, this *manque de politesse* (lack of politeness) - how *mal élevé* (ill-mannered) could you be?

For some reason this reminded Didier of a verse from Verlaine, the 19th-century poet. He began reciting it:

"Je fais souvent ce rêve étrange et... "

He paused and then continued the verse:

"D'une femme inconnue, et que j'aime, et qui m'aime,
Et qui n'est, chaque fois, ni tout à fait la même,
Ni tout à fait une autre, et m'aime et me comprend."

("I often have this dream, strange and...
Of an unknown woman whom I love and who loves me,
And who each time is neither quite the same
Nor quite another, and who loves me and understands.")

"Beautiful, isn'it?" Didier surveyed the table, looking pleased, and then frowned. "But what's the last word of the first line?" he asked sharply. "What kind of a dream? *Etrange et... surprenant...* or *pénétrant*?" ("Strange and... surprising... or moving?")

The table buzzed with opinions and proposals of other possibilities. No one was sure, but all were concerned, and uncomfortable not knowing. Didier got impatient. He took two 500-franc notes out of his wallet and placed them in the center of the table with a startling cry. "There! Find me the word!"

Eva, Ande and I, the three foreigners, stared at each other. One thousand francs for a word in a poem by a 19th century poet?

None of the French guests seemed surprised. The buzz simply amplified. The booty did concentrate the mind. One of them phoned his brother and asked him to look it up in his collected works of Verlaine. But he couldn't find it.

Finally, exasperated, Didier put the bank notes back in his wallet and phoned his mother on the Riviera. She would know. She did. It's *pénétrant*.

French Language as Lover

This anecdote about the excitement stirred up by a word in a verse of poetry is to show that it isn't just French intellectuals who care about their language. It's everyone, from statesmen to businessmen to farmers and fishermen. The bonds of a Frenchman with his language and his literature are one of the mysterious glories of Frenchness.

The French talk about their language as if it were a person, a living marvel who is their mistress, and whose delicious qualities they're continually discovering anew.

Listen to Anatole France:

"La langue française est une femme. Et cette femme est si belle, si fière, si modeste, si hardie, si touchante, si voluptueuse, si chaste, si noble, si familière, si folle, si sage, qu'on l'aime de toute son âme, et qu'on n'est jamais tenté de lui être infidèle."

Very strong stuff, which translates: "The French language is a woman. And this woman is so beautiful, so proud, so modest, so tough, so touching, so voluptuous, so chaste, so noble, so familiar, so crazy and so wise that one loves her with all one's soul, and one is never tempted to be unfaithful to her."

Mastery of this mistress is the definitive distinction for a Frenchman, grocer or clerk, *énarque* or *ingénieur*, mathematician, CEO or cabinet minister though he may be. This is the greatest mission of French education. Children learn that French history equals French culture equals civilization, and that the source of this planetary radiance is the French language.

An Honor to Speak French

They learn it, for instance, from authors like Joseph de Maistre.

In 1870, Joseph de Maistre, a Savoyard, wrote of the "dominating qualities" of the French language even before French literature had produced masterpieces, that "people loved it and recognized it as an honor to speak it. What is called the art of speaking is eminently the talent of the French, and it is by the art of speaking that one rules over men."

He went on to say, "The good writers of this nation express things better than those of all other nations, and make their ideas spread throughout Europe in less time than a writer of another country would need to get his ideas known in his province. It is this talent, this distinctive quality, this extraordinary gift that has made the French the distributors of fame... perhaps nothing is properly understood in Europe until the French have explained it."

All through school the intricacies and subtleties, the richness and profundities of French and the brilliance of French writers are relentlessly, rigorously drummed into the pupil by his teachers and the books of the writers themselves, extolling the virtues of this gift of the gods they are privileged to call their own. And that they had better live up to it.

Later, throughout a Frenchman's life, various venerable institutions like the Académie Française and the Conseil Supérieur de la Langue Française remind him of this. The excruciating annual *dictées* (dictations) of Bernard

Pivot, which, as someone said, are to a spelling bee what chopped liver is to foie gras, give him a chance to see how his own French measures up.

On a speaking tour around America in 1990, I met many French professors teaching at Alliance Française centers in the U.S. They were cut off from their linguistic heartland. They suffered. They pined. You could feel their pulse quickening at the sight of another Frenchman.

Once I said to one of them, "It's amazing to Americans, the passion of the French for their language. I mean, we appreciate English, but we don't exactly think it's such an astonishing marvel..."

"Madame!" he cut me off. "Not just a passion! A religion!"

Pivot's *Apostrophes*

Bernard Pivot, the editor of a weekly literary magazine, *Lire*, became a cultural institution after he started a television program called *Apostrophes* in 1974. It was soon breaking all records of popularity. What was it about? Four or five authors discussing their most recent books.

Parisians stopped giving or going to dinner parties on Friday evenings to stay home and "watch Pivot." They discussed the program all week. Everyone rushed out to buy the books, which turned into immediate bestsellers. It became crucial for book publishers to get their authors on the show. Soon, scientists, celebrities and heads of state with books just out were scrambling for this decisive spotlight.

Pivot knew what he was doing: 44 percent of French adults read 10 or more books a year; 18 percent read 25 or more. Every year there is a stampede to buy the books awarded the three most prestigious prizes for newly published novels, the Prix de l'Académie Française, the Prix Goncourt and the Prix Femina.

In a nation of readers and language lovers, authors are heard when alive and mourned when dead. Six hundred thousand people followed the funeral processions of Victor Hugo in 1885 and of Jean Paul Sartre in 1974. Streets are named after them almost immediately. Statues of poets are all over Paris.

In addition, in this country of readers, where literature often outranks politics in influence, authors are elected to high office – Lamartine, Tocqueville, and Chateaubriand all served as foreign ministers – and high officers of the state are authors. The memoirs of Charles de Gaulle, a career army officer before he became President of the Republic, are models of elegant, lucid French. Each of the five volumes was a bestseller. Together, they sold 3.8 million copies. President Mitterrand has written nine books.

Former President Giscard d'Estaing has written several books on Tocqueville and Maupassant; former Prime Minister Barre is an authority on Baudelaire.

One of Pivot's shows featured Jacques Chirac, mayor of Paris and head of the RPR, the Gaullist political party, as well as a former prime minister. Are you ready for this? Chirac, this consummate politician, said, without a blink and with about four million Frenchmen listening to him, "Poetry is a necessity of daily living." He added, "I never go to bed without reading one of my favorite poets, Apollinaire or Verlaine."

Reading books 12 hours a day for 15 years, and producing a live show with amateurs who sometimes got badly off the rails, finally wore Pivot down. Despite the uproar of protests, he couldn't be dissuaded from depriving the country of its Friday evening literary feast.

He made sure that it went out with a bang. Pivot's last broadcast of *Apostrophes* in June, 1990, was a sensational hymn to the glory of French and its most able practitioners. What he did was to invite over 100 of the country's leading authors to come to the studio with a farewell present: a favorite word, and the reason why he loved that word.

Pivot once described the French language thus: *"Elle est la langue de beauté et de tolérance, et elle est charnelle."* ("The French language is the tongue of beauty and of tolerance, and it is carnal.") I promise you, it was a beautiful and sensual experience watching these authors, some of them ex-ministers of state like Alain Peyrefitte, speaking their word. Slowly. Up the throat, through the mouth, lips forward, the word emerged into the room, and into the rooms of perhaps seven million viewers. *"Nuance,* because it's sonorous and is the finesse of our language." *"Tendresse..* because it's both active and soft..." *"Silence..."* *"Nostalgie..."* *"Plaisir..."*

Pivot's Spelling Bee

"The French language," Pivot wrote in *Lire*, in the words of a lover, "remains in our eyes a precious good, a heritage to defend, a living body of unending astonishment whose vagaries, exceptions to the rules and inexhaustible richness never cease to entertain us."

He was explaining the magical hold of another of his literary innovations, his annual *dictée*, on the imagination of his countrymen. An institution since he started it in 1986, Pivot's *dictée* is known as the Spelling Championship of France. Its popularity is up there with the Tour de France (the bicycle race) and the world soccer championships. It consists of two or three paragraphs of extremely difficult prose riddled with traps. Last year, and please note the gastronomic theme, the text was about the miseries of hunger in a library, noting the impossibility of intellectual nourishment replacing eating and drinking.

Each year the *dictée* mobilizes over 300,000 officially registered candidates around the world, and perhaps seven million more taking it by television. Among them are always celebrities – politicians, government ministers, athletes, movie stars as well as authors. A few years ago, Laurent Fignon, the bicycle-racing star, was among the finalists.

Semifinalists and finalists descend on Paris from all over France and the rest of the francophone world – from New Caledonia, Canada, Louisiana, francophone Africa and the Caribbean. The winner and the full text, the esoteric words and grammatical traps carefully explained, are in all the newspapers the next day.

A spelling bee? 300,000 candidates? Yes! Writing and speaking French perfectly is as crucial as getting the right wine to match the cheese you're serving. Françoise Giroud, author and former cabinet minister, one of the finalists in 1988, made seven mistakes.

"I am ashamed," she said. After another Pivot broadcast, headlines in the next day's *Figaro* scolded the spelling mistake of Jacques Toubon, the Minister of Culture. He forgot an exception to a rule, and fell into the trap of saying that *interpeller* was spelled with just one "l."

But as for anyone, venerable or no, daring to spring these spelling traps, forget it. In January, 1990, a government commission, the Conseil Supérieur de la Langue Française, decided to propose an overhaul of the spelling of many French words, in order to simplify it. When the Académie Française, the high priests of the French language, agreed on the changes, the country went into an uproar. Take away the *g* from *oignon*? The circumflex from *maître* and *huître*?

Never!

The War of the Circumflex Accent

Overnight 24 of France's leading authors launched a national petition against the reform. Two associations, the Free French and the Association for Protecting the French Language, sprang into action and geared themselves for battle in what came to be known as the War of the Circumflex Accent. Five Nobel prizewinners joined ambassadors, actors, doctors and authors in laying siege to the Académie Française. This linguistic war was dropping its bombs at the same time as the Gulf War. The headlines, too, were on the front pages each day, in the same size of type, with long interviews with outraged anti-reform celebrities in various fields insisting on the sensual and aesthetic effect of the spelling exactly as it is. An opera singer was interviewed in *Le Figaro* declaring that the circumflex was an integral part of the musical notes of the French language.

The Académie Française backed down. It turned out that most of the Academicians were against the reform too. Apparently they hadn't been present the day the reform was voted, or they were asleep.

The Forty Immortals

That some of them may have nodded off isn't surprising. These senior citizens, members for life, are celebrated for their longevity, and, indeed, are known as the Forty Immortals. What is surprising is that any of them voted for the reform at all. The last reform was in 1835 and was simply a matter of changing the oi diphthong to ai in accordance with modern pronunciation, in words like *français*.

Historically, the Immortals have looked on themselves as custodians of the language, not reformers. This was the mission conferred on the Académie by Cardinal Richelieu when he founded it in 1634. He wanted a definitive dictionary of the French language, and only the most brilliant and most eminent men in the land – authors, scientists, scholars, generals, anthropologists, statesmen – were deemed worthy of this trust.

Ever since, becoming a member has been, for many, the crowning achievement of a distinguished career: taking part in the magnificent challenge of meeting once a week to define the present usage of French words and of acceptable foreign ones for a new edition. It took 60 years for the first edition to come out. The ninth is on its way, at the rate of about one letter a year, with the first volume, A through Enzyme, appearing in November 1992.

One letter a year? Well, how do you define white? White as snow? Snow is often not white. White as a sheet? Same problem. White as egg white? And what new foreign words do you let in – le drugstore? le cowboy? Yes, in both cases.

The competition to fill the chair of a deceased Immortal is not for the fainthearted. A candidate must campaign energetically, pleading his case to each of the Forty. The results of the voting are published in *Le Monde*. The also-rans are noted with names and votes, an ego-basher to make an Anglo-Saxon reader blush. Even a recent candidate who got no votes at all was carefully mentioned.

Ah, but glory to the happy elect! Besides joining the single most illustrious group in the world, he gets to wear the *habit vert*, a dark green cutaway splashed liberally with gold embroidery, and a golden sword. His reception at the Institut, one of the capital's most beautiful buildings, with the finest of its baroque domes, will rival presidential receptions of visiting royalty in pomp. In fact, the President of the Republic himself may be among the several thousand guests.

But there's a catch. The new Immortal has to prepare a 55-minute maiden speech, a eulogy to the deceased whose chair he will occupy, in pure, elegant, flawless French, with, if possible, a cascade of imperfect subjunctives – and no franglais.

This will also be published in the next day's *Monde*, all 55 minutes of it, as well as in the other serious Paris newspapers. Every single word. If there are any mistakes in grammar, and any phrases not considered worthy of the "genius of the French language", the editors will excoriate him, tear him to pieces and throw him to the tabloids.

"French is the universal language," wrote Antoine Rivarol in 1784, in his *Dictionary of the Universality of the French Language*. "Everything universal is French, and everything French is universal."

Not so far-fetched, if you remember that French was the only internationally accepted language until the Treaty of Versailles in 1918, when English was also accepted for the first time. Educated people all over Europe spoke French together from the 17th century on, and for aristocrats, it was often their only language. Frederick the Great wrote only in French. William of Orange grew up in Holland speaking only French, and took his French-speaking courtiers with him to London when he became King William III of England in 1686.

A Frenchman's words are his baubles. He loves to play with them. Coining a new expression is much, much more satisfying than a hole-in-one for a golfer. Happy the man who came up with *l'esprit d'escalier* (wit of the staircase) for the retort you only thought of after you left the party and were on your way home, or *renvoyer l'ascenseur* (send back the elevator) for repaying a favor.

"One is a little bit in awe of the language," said an engineer, "because there is so much you can do with it."

Make an Effort!

The belief that the French are merciless with foreigners who don't handle French impeccably is as untrue as the one that they're rude, cold and arrogant. You can mangle it to friends and strangers alike and be praised for your effort. If someone insults your French, he's doing it in fun, giving you an opportunity to rib him back; or else you've done something unpardonable that has nothing to do with language, such as neglecting to say, *"Bonjour, monsieur"* before ordering your cheese or chicken, and he's using your linguistic clumsiness to club your uncouthness.

This is not to say that they don't suffer in silence over your grammatical errors. Remember, they were harangued mercilessly at home and at school for the first 18 or so years of their lives about prepositions, subjunctives, unaspirated h's, etc. Burglar alarms go off in their heads when they hear a blunder. Use the subjunctive after *vouloir*! Not after *après que*! *De*, not *à*, comes after *jouer*, if it has to do with playing a musical instrument! Subordinate clauses must be introduced by a definite conjunction! Adjectives have to agree with nouns, words that sound the same are spelled differently and you had better get it right, bozo, or you get a zero at school and a whack at home!

Not foreigners. Foreigners are forgiven everything except not trying at all. But do give it your best. You'll have a lot more fun if you understand what people are saying. And you'll get a lot more smiles.

But there are some translation traps that bring smiles you could do without – or worse. They're called *faux amis*, or false friends.

Déception in French means disappointment. A former American ambassador told me that this practically caused an international incident with the French prime minister of the time, whom he understood to be accusing him of a deception.

Rude means harsh, tough, not rude.

Une demande is not a demand, but a request.

Assister doesn't mean to assist but to attend.

Sympathique: someone likable who gives you good vibes.

To *réaliser* something is to create it, carry it through.

To *contrôler* something is to check it, verify it, not "control" it.

An *entrée* has 13 meanings, mostly to do with different kinds of entrance. In connection with a meal, it's the first course (one enters into the meal with it).

Correct might mean accurate, but often means proper, or upstanding in business affairs.

If someone says something is *clair* (clear), it means that he has heard and understood, not necessarily that he agrees.

Passer un examen does not mean to pass an exam but to take it.

Someone's *éducation* is how he was brought up, what kind of manners he has. The word for the English meaning of "education" is *formation*. There are various ways to translate the English "formation."

That there are fewer words in French than in English means that French words tend to have more multiple, deeper, sometimes more hidden meanings than words in English. Thus understanding the importance of nuances is essential. A straightforward English word like dignity, for instance, becomes much more meaningful and resonant in French. In English it means "the quality or state of being worthy, honored, or esteemed" and a "high rank or office." In French, *dignité* means the respect owed a person or a thing, or oneself; it also means reserved and serious behavior, as well as a position bestowing high rank. *Dignité* is of great importance to French people. After the dramatic rescue by a special anti-terrorist force of six little children, who had been held hostage for 40 hours in a suburban Paris school in May, 1993, the wife of a café owner said, "We have won back our *dignité.*"

As might be expected, the word "nuance" itself gets entirely different treatment in the two languages. Webster gives it three lines. In French dictionaries – same word, same spelling – it gets two-and-a-half inches. French people know their nuances and like to speak in them rather than directly – another reason for their reluctance to speak a foreign language, where their knowledge of nuances would be limited.

Nuances and *faux amis* and badly accented words can bring alarming bewilderment or, worse, guffaws for foreigners.

An American manager, happy to exercise his French, didn't know that being hungry in English translates to "having hunger" in French. He got the phonetic emphasis wrong, as well. Asking his boss if he was hungry, instead of *"Avez-vous faim?,"* he said, *"Etes-vous faim?,"* pronouncing the "m" in *faim* so that it came out *femme...*"Are you woman?"

Joseph Voelker, a professor of English at Franklin and Marshall College in Lancaster, Pa., wrote in the *Washington Post* of several gaffes he made on an early trip to France. He told his hostess about his mother's wonderful jelly and that she never put condoms in it *(les préservatifs).* He asked a neighbor for directions to a famous château and wanted to know if she'd seen it. *"Vous l'avez vu?"* he asked. He mispronounced *vu* (seen) so that his question sounded like *"Vous lavez-vous?"* ("Do you wash?")

Another time, in a grocery-store line, he tried to answer a Frenchman's question, to which the Frenchman replied, *"Oh, monsieur, vous ne parlez pas français."*("You don't speak French.") Voelker writes: "Instead of letting it go, I said, *'Mais, essayez-moi'* ("Try me"), unaware that the phrase is a standard homosexual come on. Only the Frenchman's wife derived any enjoyment from the scene, and her *'Oh, Jean-Pierre, oh-la-la-la-la-la!'* will stay with me until I die."

163

One of the big pitfalls is the word *baiser*. As a noun, it means to kiss. Fine. But in its verb form it means, and the words are firmly printed in my Robert & Collins French-English dictionary: "to screw, lay, fuck."

Another word to skip altogether is *queue*. Its first meaning is "tail" (of an animal, an airplane, etc). The second meaning is a line you stand in, the British "queue." It's a handy word you're tempted to use a lot, usually in rage, at line-jumpers. But don't. It can easily get out of hand. Robert & Collins are definite on this too. Their third meaning is: "penis, cock, prick."

With a simple article, there's no problem. *La queue* is a line, no nonsense there, depending on the context. The trouble starts if you happen to slip a possessive pronoun in front. I did this once at an unfamiliar open-air market. All I wanted was a head of lettuce. People kept shoving in front of me. It was unclear who was ahead of whom, sort of a bunch of people, and the salad vendor was serving them all ahead of me. Finally, in some annoyance, I said loudly and clearly, *"Mais, monsieur, où est votre queue?"* ("Sir, where is your cock?") Roars, but roars, of laughter on all sides. I held my ground bravely. As the laughter subsided, the salad vendor responded in high hilarity, *"Eh bien, madame, voulez-vous que je vous le dise?"* ("Well, Madam, do you really want me to tell you?")

I didn't dare tell Ande, who was buying fruit somewhere else, but at least I made their day.

Chapter 13

Plaisir
Flirting, Food, Language and Love

La faim et l'amour sont les deux axes du monde. L'humanité roule toute entière sur l'amour et la faim. (Hunger and love are the pivots on which the world turns. Mankind is entirely determined by love and hunger.)

Anatole France (1894-1924)
letter to George Sand

La séduction: s'aimer un peu pour plaire beaucoup. (Seduction: to love oneself a little in order to please a great deal.)

Yves Saint-Laurent

Catherine Deneuve, the iceberg icon of French cinema, opened a window on the mystique of the Frenchwoman in *Le Figaro* on January 30, 1992, when she said that wearing the clothes of Yves Saint-Laurent had been 30 years of "infinite sensuality."

"I would like to be naked under his dresses," she said, "in order to feel on all my skin the satiny silk that they're always lined with."

Take that, you casual, hearty, sporty, hurried American women who throw on Woolworth underwear under your Ralph Lauren suit! A Frenchwoman dresses from the inside out. Or, as she would say, she starts dressing with what is most important – with what she puts on first and takes off last, her lingerie. It is chosen for her very own body, which she bathes, creams, plucks, scrutinizes, massages and scents daily without shame. It's hers. She likes it. She wants others to like it too. She takes care of it lovingly, and cares about what she puts next to it.

She cares about all the other layers, too. When she gets up in the morning, the outer visible envelope that she puts on last, whether she is going to work or just around the corner to pick up a baguette, is not a track suit.

When she steps out in the street, she looks her best. Always. This astonishes American women, who "dress up" only in the evening or for a party. An American living in Paris finally got to know a French friend well enough ask her why French women always looked so great, first thing in the morning.

"On est toujours prête," came the response. "One is always ready."

Ready for what?

Ready for The Look. The Look from a stranger, maybe passing her on the street or in a car, of an unmistakable intensity that lets her know that for that man, she's got it.

She can look back, and see what happens... perhaps she will discover what the French call a new "secret garden." Or she can walk on with an extra lilt in her gait, bathed in a caress of wonder and admiration.

Edith Cresson, former minister of Health, was interviewed by the BBC's correspondant in Paris, Philip Short, about what it meant to be a French woman. She said it was about appealing to men, and having that appeal confirmed when one walked down the street.

"When I arrive in London," she said, "I wonder why the men don't look at me. Am I badly dressed, looking terrible or what? – and then I remember. It's just that I'm in London."

The Look works both ways, and can be just as much of a shock to American men as to American women, often misunderstood at first.

Nelson Aldrich, Jr., wrote about it in *Lear's* magazine (January 1992):

"The first months I lived in Paris... I was repeatedly shaken by the way women presented themselves to my attention – all ages of women, in every sort of setting. They seemed to be composing themselves for a performance in my line of vision... the shocking thing was how imperiously each and every one of them insisted on an exchange of looks... For an American, a pale New Englander at that, to be a party to this performance for the first time is to feel acted upon in the most astonishing way. The effect is of being manned, masculated, gendered. The message is not suggestive of an erotic encounter... it says, 'As a woman, I expect your attention as a man.' The experience is stunning... Addressed at this universal, not to say primitive, level, a man feels recognized in all his distinctive selfhood. A wonderful 'you' and therefore an intoxicatingly plausible 'I' emerges from the woman's whispered 'we.'"

An article in *European Travel and Life* (March 1991) by Debbie Seaman opens with the staggering effect of the Look: "My best Parisian romance to date endured the length of a traffic light, but the memory will bring a smile to my lips when I'm a grandmother in a rocking chair."

If Debbie Seaman stays in Paris, she'll find that she's much mistaken. She may be a grandmother one day, but not, as she implies by the rocking chair, beyond the reach of the Look. Age has nothing to do with the "sexual energy measured in megawatts" that she described almost making her swoon at that traffic light.

"I can't get over the feeling of sensuality, of active sexuality that I get from 60- or 70-year-old women in Paris," said Lou Martin, the handsome surgeon from Louisville. "It's as if they feel as seductive as ever – or more so. Their soft, unlifted faces tell you of voluptuous, lived, celebrated love, and that, with experience, everything is better."

Nancy Mitford, the English author who lived in Paris and Versailles for 30 years and knew all about France, makes the agelessness of seduction very clear in her novel *The Blessing*. When the English heroine asks her French husband about the daily meetings of his aged grandmother, and her male visitor, the husband replies, "In such a case you may be sure that there is always love."

Indeed there were few women in the Paris of the 1970's as beautiful and seductive as Countess Nadège de Ganay, then herself in her eighties. She was tall and straight with blond hair and lovely features, and she always wore dark blue with a long strand of pearls, and sandals with *high heels*.

"The trouble with being my age," she told me, "is that there are so few men of the same age. It's no problem for me – I happen to love younger men – but my friends get quite desperate that they must do with other women."

The concept of sexual harassment (*harcèlement sexuel*) only came into the French language a couple of years ago. Much of what Americans interpret as disrespectful is welcome gallantry in Latin countries. French women are pleased to have their femininity confirmed. They not only lean happily into the Look, they are not averse to being spoken to by an attractive stranger. Maybe having dinner with him. Why not? I know three American women in Paris married to Frenchmen, whose romance started like that, on a street corner.

On the other hand, if you're not used to it, it can seem insulting, or even frightening. "A man started talking to me on the street and I was furious! I thought he took me for a hooker," said Deborah Bradley, credit officer at the Credit Lyonnais. "Another man slowed down his car as I was walking on the sidewalk – and I thought he was going to chop me up!"

"It's the most natural thing in the world to talk to a woman you see somewhere and find glorious and marvelous," said Didier Bernardin, my

French businessman-neighbor, who met Eva, his beautiful Swedish wife, in a café. "But it is very disagreeable for a Frenchman to do this in New York! Once when I spoke to a lovely girl on Fifth Avenue, she called the police."

"Suppose a Frenchman asks me out for dinner, does that mean..." asked a pretty American real-estate broker in a seminar. "I mean, what does it *mean*? Does he want something?"

It's a question I've heard a lot. The answer is a hearty *yes*. A Frenchman wants to know if... well, he finds you *séduisante*, appealing, and he wants to know if some good chemistry might start things bubbling... for both of you. What he wants is to be with you and see how you feel, and how he feels, and how you feel together. The concept of "date rape" doesn't exist in France. Women are expected to be able to choose and make their choice clear, like responsible adults. They can take their time. It's important to figure out the codes. If a woman invites a Frenchman to her apartment, it means *yes*. If a girl goes to a Frenchman's apartment, it also means *yes*. Some years after they were married, Hélène R. told me about inviting her future husband, Kevin, an American, to dinner in her apartment. He didn't realize the significance of the invitation, and kept trying to talk her into a love affair over dinner. "I finally had to tell him, 'Look, you don't have to try so hard! You're in my apartment, so you should know that it's already settled!'"

Courting in most western countries has about 30 steps. But the steps are different, and need to be learned by foreigners, as well as the no-no's.

"In Chicago, you talk to people when you pass them on the sidewalk," said Judy C., a blond software programmer visiting Paris from Chicago. "Yesterday I said 'hello' to two men when I was walking by them near my hotel – and they gave me such dirty looks! For heaven's sake! What was the matter?"

The "matter" was that she got the codes wrong. It's one thing for a girl to look back at a stranger, but it's taboo for a French girl to greet an unknown man as she strolls down the street, with or without The Look. The man speaks first. If the woman speaks first, she's looking for business, and gets a glare if the man isn't a client. In France, context counts a lot. In this case, Judy C. may have been on a street for prostitutes, or walking by a seedy hotel.

Getting the codes right has a lot to do with understanding the context of male-female relations in France. *L'amour courtois* of the 12th century is still going strong.

The French weekly *Le Point* recently (February 26, 1994) devoted a long cover article to *Les Françaises*, French women, describing the continuing positive influence of women, with the headline that "French women are *bien dans leur peau* (well in their skin,) attentive to seduction, attached to the idea of equality," yet mindful of their difference. "While the war of the sexes rages in the U.S. and in Germany, Frenchwomen understand how to impose a special harmony in their relations with men." The writer Elisabeth Badinter observes, "I have the feeling that French men are less afraid of women (than British and American men are) and have always wanted to preserve their tenderness." Michèle Sarde, professor of French literature at Georgetown University, tells of being shocked that *Time* magazine would go so far, even ironically, as to propose two separate countries for the sexes. "In France," she says, "the workplace is mixed, the café is mixed (unlike some Mediterranean countries), the restaurant is mixed (unlike Japan), and the street is mixed (unlike Moslem countries)."

The writer Christine Collange, on a BBC radio broadcast, summed it up: "Clubs where women are excluded altogether are unknown in France. French men like to go out with women – their wife, or another woman. French men and women like to be together... they feel better that way."

A French bestseller of 1993, *Les Hommes et Les Femmes* (Men and Women), was written by a man of 44, the philosopher-writer Bernard-Henri Levy, and a woman of 76, Françoise Giroud, writer, editor, and former minister, about what these two *monstres sacrés* (superstars) had to say about love. It sold 80,000 copies the first week after publication. Both agreed that in the U.S., relations between the sexes have been damaged by the feminist movement, and that sexual love holds a singular place in France. According to Lévy, "One cannot love a woman without violently desiring her." According to Giroud, "Love has a special place in our society and literature. Relations here between men and women, while imperfect, are the best in the world."

Indeed, French life marinates in an exquisite bath of love, closely bonded with its language. *Séduction* may be its most significant word. As noted in Chapter 10 about the schoolteacher who wanted to *séduire* (seduce) the children in her class, it's pristine, with none of the underhanded or immoral implications of its leering English cousin. As Yves Saint-Laurent said above, *séduction* is about pleasing. Headlines use it to describe a treaty or an act of Parlement.

"Pleasing" is a close relative of love. Love is implicit in the husky, gravelly male voice-overs of movie and television commercials for everything from cheese to toothpaste and shampoo. Billboards and posters throughout Paris will very often borrow from the pleasing contours of the female anatomy, breasts and buttocks, to make a car, a breakfast cereal or a washing-machine more appealing (*séduisant*).

Avenir, an advertising agency, caused a sensation with an ad in 1981 by correctly gauging the delight of the average Frenchman in the female body. First, a huge billboard was covered with the picture of a gorgeous girl in a topless bathing suit. The caption underneath explained that this was a picture of Myriam... and that next month, on July first, Myriam would take off the bottom of her bathing suit, too. Frontal nudity in ads is still taboo in France. There were traffic jams all over Paris on July first, while the drivers ogled Myriam. Like the agency, she kept her promise, which was the point of the ad – but you only saw her from the back.

Myriam keeps her promise (and stops the traffic)

Female nudity has never been shocking in France, quite the contrary. Marilyn Yalom, writer and professor in charge of Stanford's Institute of Research on Women, says in the Le Point article that Frenchwomen have always felt better about themselves than American or British women because they enjoy their bodies. "It is in France that one has always shown women in the nude. You only have to look at painting throughout the centuries." Agnès Sorel, mistress of Charles VII, was portrayed by Fouquet as the Virgin Mary, with one bare breast, in 1440. Diane de Poitiers, the aristocratic favorite of Henri II, was painted around 1540 with both breasts bared. Even

Delacroix's representation of the more prudish Republic, in the person of Marianne, shows a bare breast. "In England, there has been no visual tradition linked to the woman. And as if by accident, it was the French and Italian women who first dared, several years ago, to go topless on the beach."

If Food be the Language of Love...

Seduction not being confined to the boudoir, and having nothing immoral about it, all of one's encounters are quickened with an erotic sauciness, a spicy glaze.

When the French do talk about making love, then they tend to use the vocabulary of food, thus tossing three French passions, language, love and cuisine, each considered an art and an integral element of French culture, into one great joyous mixed salad. Not even the French can tell where one starts and the other stops. Arte, the French-German TV station, ran a four-hour broadcast October 18, 1992 on *L'Amour et la Table* (Love and Food) analyzing, in another marvelous French mood of logic, the various connections. That the acts of eating and making love were intimately linked was not under discussion. The question was, "Do you like to make love before or after a good meal?"

Thus, one of the tenderest words of endearment is *mon chou* (my cabbage), and a man skillful at love is a *jardinier*, a gardener. Carrots, bananas, turnips, cucumbers and zucchini are phallic symbols and metaphors for *le sexe*, the male member. Figs, oranges and grapefruits are female.

Like seduction, the vocabulary of the cuisine spills over into all of French life and tends to describe things at their most colorful and dramatic. In fact, you can tell a lot about the priorities of a nation by the metaphors they use most. In Britain, it's cricket metaphors. In the U.S.A., it's baseball metaphors. Where an American would say, "he struck out" for he's finished, done for, a Frenchman would say *"les carottes sont cuites!"* ("The carrots are cooked.") *"C'est tout cuit"* means that a project will be a cinch, where an American would say, "It'll be a walk." Someone's dirty tricks, or curve balls, are a *petite cuisine* (small cooking). *Cuisine électorale* (electoral cooking) means electoral scheming.

Beurre en broche (butter on a spit-roast) means, like the butter which quickly melts on a spit, something unobtainable, like catching a fly ball in the bleachers.

A V.I.P. , a "heavy hitter", is a *grosse légume* (big vegetable).

If Americans and French people have trouble understanding each other's metaphors, mixing them can mean total confusion for everyone. In the fall of 1992, during the GATT farm-trade talks, which were causing such anguished battles between the Americans and the French, a French Common Market spokesman, who had heard that "inside baseball" and *cuisine interne* meant roughly the same thing, gamely came up with a compromise pitch to both cultural preferences.

He said, in English, that he was obliged to decline discussing the negotiating tactics because the subject was "inside cooking."

The list is long. Love and food are never far from a Frenchman's heart. And what comes out of his mouth is just as carefully considered as what goes into it. Words are used tenderly, sensitively, sensually, and correctly. His soul is rural, with deep roots. Many Parisians flee to their bit of earth on weekends, and visit relatives there. The land bears them the food and the wine that they delight in.

It hardly need be added that Bernard Pivot, the unofficial Czar of the French language, described in the last chapter, is a self-described *gourmand*. There's another of those *faux amis*. A *gourmand* is not someone who is excessively fond of eating and drinking, someone close to being a glutton, as in English, but someone fond of eating fine things, and a gastronomic connoisseur.

Chapter 14

Two dinner parties

Food, Style and Protocol – Back to Versailles

The French... have surrounded food with so much commentary, learning and connoisseurship as to clothe it in the vestments of civilization itself... Cooking is viewed as a major art form: innovations are celebrated and talked about as though they were phases in the development of a style of painting or poetry... A meal at a truly great restaurant is a sort of theatre you can eat.

Richard Bernstein
The Fragile Glory

An American executive was met at Charles de Gaulle airport by two French executives. He was hoping to persuade them to become distributors for his products throughout Europe. In the car, the two Frenchmen discussed where they would go for lunch.

"We'll take him to a bistro for a sandwich," said one, assuming the American didn't speak French. "Right," said the other. "That's what they prefer. It's a shame they don't know any better."

"Actually, I hate sandwiches," said the American, in French. "I love French cooking."

"Oh, you speak French?" said one of the executives. "You like French food?"

Thereupon, they took him to one of the most expensive restaurants in Paris, for the best meal of his life... and signed the deal.

General de Gaulle, in a moment of exasperation, complained that a nation that produced 350 different kinds of cheese was ungovernable. What he seems not to have appreciated, and what is staggering to a foreigner, is that the French – all of them, all classes and in all the regions – are in extraordinary agreement about one thing: the ceremony surrounding food, and its importance. That is to say, they agree that participating in a meal with friends or the extended family is an almost religious service, with a rigid, demanding, aesthetic ritual, which gives spiritual as well as physical nourishment.

The ritual is the same all over the country, from farmer to nobleman, from factory worker to company president, varying only in details of refinement.

Around the table is where you find French discipline and French morality, giving structure to their other qualities on display: wit, aesthetic taste, style and innovation, not to mention culinary talent. French people may bend the country's laws, for the reasons we've seen, with no stigma attached. They are far from angelically faithful to their wives – this too has no stigma, nor does changing mistresses – or wives. But with matters involving food, there is no fooling around. This game – and everything in France is a game – is the one with the rules that count.

The great chefs of France - Robuchon, Ducasse, Bocuse - are as famous as movie stars and treated with the reverance due the high priests of the country's most important cult. Their restaurants are its cathedrals. No women have yet been elevated to these ranks.

The Duc de Mouchy entertains often at his château in the Oise. The meals are served by two footmen in livery. The Duc, who is a head of one of France's most ancient families, going back to the Crusades, buys the ingredients and does the cooking himself.

"This is too important to trust to anyone else," he says.

The ritual of the feast involves not only the food and its planning, gathering, presentation and consumption, but also everything that takes place around it: how the table is laid and embellished, how people come together, how they look, what they say before, during and after the meal, how they eat, how they drink their wine and how they part.

All this has been given the name of etiquette, which sounds trivial and is sometimes ridiculed in the Anglo-Saxon countries, but which in France is very *sérieux*, another French word that's a distant relative of the English word serious. Something *sérieux* is war about to break out, or a *faux pas* at a dinner party.

A Frenchman's personal worth is constantly being judged according to whether or not he does things *comme il faut* in social gatherings, which always center on food. Breaking the rules of etiquette is absolutely not the thing to do. He risks shame, loss of face and disgrace. All you really need to finish someone in France is to observe that he is *mal élevé* (ill-mannered).

Bernard Tapie started from nowhere, with a working-class Communist background and none of the academic degrees that assure credibility and glory in France, to become one of the country's most successful entrepreneurs – and the most popular. In April, 1992, he was appointed Minister of Urban Affairs.

France reeled. Tapie? A Minister? Tapie in regional politics was one thing, even in the Parlement as a député (member) from Marseille, but up there making decisions with the top people in the government? Helping to run the country? A poll taken after his nomination showed that while 95% of French people thought he was great *(dynamique)*, 60 percent thought he was out of place as a government minister.

Tapie's Problem

So why was it a problem for this self-made tycoon, and owner of a winning soccer team, to be in the Prime Minister's cabinet? Not his lack of class or degrees – the then Prime Minister, Pierre Bérégovoy, also lacked them. No. Tapie had committed a colossal *faux pas*. During the campaign for regional elections, he called Jean-Marie Le Pen, the neo-Fascist leader of the National Front, and furthermore, all the people who voted for him, *salauds*. In my dictionary, *salaud* translates as "filthy beast, son of a bitch."

(1996 update: Tapie, stripped of his parliamentary immunity, faces jail terms for tax fraud and rigging a soccer match, yet is starring in a current movie by Claude Lelouch, *Men and Women, A User's Guide*.)

Edith Cresson's popularity plummeted when she used a vulgar expression – *"J'en ai rien à cirer"* – roughly translated as "I couldn't care a fig" – to show her contempt for the French stock market, and when she publicly insulted two friendly nations. Japan, she said, was a "nation of ants," and as for the English, one in four was homosexual. She lasted just ten-and-a-half months, the shortest term of any prime minister in the history of Fifth Republic. The French don't want to be governed by people who are *mal élevé*.

As with many things in France today, Louis XIV is at the bottom of it. Although the word "etiquette" was coined (by the French, of course) only in 1750, long after his death, one of the most astonishing achievements of the Sun King was that he installed it in the French soul as of the first importance. Knowing who goes through the door first, how many bows, when to rise and for whom, became, along with the use of the French language, a mark of distinction and accomplishment. Europe copied Louis XIV in the 17th century and France in general in the 18th. Many of the rules of French etiquette remain true, in a less rigorous way, for all of Europe today.

The higher you climb the feudal ladder, the more polish is expected of you. No matter how brilliant a manager a Frenchman is, or how many *Grandes Ecoles* degrees he possesses, if he doesn't know the rules of etiquette, he's not going to make it to the top.

"Naturally," said the president of a French company. "You have to be able to respect the high-ranking people you're negotiating business with. If a man doesn't know the rules, how can you trust him?"

If you can cope with social etiquette, office etiquette comes automatically. Most of it is the same.

The French love to laugh. A handy source of merriment is other people's *faux pas*. If you're American, and quite likely also if you're not, you'd probably rather it wasn't you. But don't panic. The rules are not a secret. You can learn them by heart. And if you slip up, foreigners are usually forgiven, after the giggles.

Dinner parties (also luncheons) are what it's all about. They vary, within the parameters of the ritual, according to size, so I'm going to take you first to a large, formal dinner. Then Mark Meigs, a colleague and professor of history married to a Frenchwoman and living in France, will take you to a smaller, more informal one. The hosts and guests are couples plus the odd single. Finally some essential tips about hosting the French yourself. But first a word about an upstart:

The Cocktail Party

A nightmare. As there is no food ritual involved, the French are not interested. As Louis XIV did not have them, there is no etiquette. The only advice I can give you is to go only when you're feeling cheerful and strong, master of the universe, to hold fast to the hand of the person you went with and never, never to go alone.

The first one I went to, soon after coming to France as Ande's bride, was typical. The hostess, an old friend of Ande's, said there would be "just a few people" and "not to dress up." I put on a grey wool dress with a jacket. About 200 people were there when we arrived. All the women were in silky black dresses.

Ande was immediately caught up with all his old friends and disappeared into one of the other rooms. I hung around the hostess. She introduced me to no one. I remembered those first parties in Paris, 20 years before, but by now I was less patient. I went to the bar and started talking to the first man who came looking for a drink. He didn't want to talk. Anyway not to me. He fled. The same thing with the next.

I went back to the hostess and hung around her some more. She ignored me. So I went looking for Ande. He was nowhere to be seen. I asked the hostess if she knew where he was. "Oh, I sent him outside to help someone shovel their car out of the snow," she said, and went on talking to someone else. I spent the next half hour sitting in the vestibule, waiting for Ande to come in from the cold.

Please do not get mistaken ideas about the hostess. We are now firm friends. French cocktail-party hostesses dance to a different drummer, that's all. Other foreigners from all over Europe, Asia, and North and South America have similar Paris cocktail-party horror stories. You should hear the cries of the Italians.

With dinner parties it's different. At least you get introduced.

The Dinner Party – I.

You've actually been invited! Gloat. However dreadful the evening may be, the food will be celestial and you have scored a triumph that few foreigners can emulate. This is owing to four things:

- The difficulty in making French friends.
- The ritual, dictating a Versailles feast taking three agonizing days to prepare, often discourages the French from having dinner parties.
- If they do, family and relatives are invited first, leaving little time left over for anyone else.
- Fear of the foreigner ruining things through ignorance.

But not you! You're going to get it right. Start out by practicing a mindset of the reverence due to your hostess. A French dinner party is an event. It's part theater, part High Mass, part test. (I say "French," but should perhaps say "Parisian"; in the suburbs, or provinces, things may be a little more relaxed.)

The hostess is the stage director and producer of the play, and the priestess presiding over the ritual. She also considers herself to be taking a horrendous exam. You, the diners, are her audience, her congregation and her examiners. Be merciful.

But don't forget the decisive role of the host. He picks the wine and the cheese. Only a man is felt to possess the competence for these choices and it behooves the male guests, especially, to express appreciation of them. If you're in any doubt about the date, or the time, don't hesitate to call and ask. The one really unforgivable sin is not to show up without warning your hosts.

Once there, there are three other *impardonnables* which you must avoid:

- The first is to fail to eat heartily. There will be at least five courses, so fast all day.
- The second is to get up from the table too soon. You'll be sitting there for an average of four hours, even – or particularly – if it's lunch on a weekend. So get your exercise beforehand.
- The third is to deliver monologues.

French dinner-table conversation is like ping-pong. Mark Meigs describes it perfectly later in this chapter. The pace of the French phrases and the rapid change of subjects – smash! slam! – can be hard to catch for a sluggish English ear. The secret is to prepare a few pithy phrases to slip in where you can, on a variety of topical subjects – the latest political scandal, events in Germany, the latest Depardieu film, the current art exhibition, book or play. The pyramid in front of the Louvre bores everyone by now, but the Musée d'Orsay is still good for polemics, and the Very Big Library (la Très Grande Bibliothèque) will induce shrieks of rage for some time.

Dress

In Paris dress matters. Shakespeare got it right in Hamlet four centuries ago. His shrewd verse on the subject is part of the English-speaking world's most famous paternal counsel. The occasion was the trip of Laertes to France, and Polonius, his father, was worried at the *faux pas* his greenhorn son might make. Slipped in among the wise warnings that have weathered centuries —"neither a borrower nor a lender be" and "unto thine own self be true" – is the tip about dressing in the Gallic capital.

> *Costly thy habit as thy purse can buy;*
> *But not expressed in fancy; rich, not gaudy;*
> *For the apparel oft proclaims the man*
> *And they in France of the best rank and station*
> *Are most select and generous, chief in that.*

In other words, shell out every cent you can afford on your clothes when you set foot in France, and then beg, borrow or steal some more. And be sure it has the right touch of elegance, not show.

But that general advice, though still valid today, does not solve the specific problem of exactly what sartorial note to strike at the dinner party you're going to. You know it's going to be fairly formal, because after your hostess invited you she sent you a *pour mémoire* (reminder), a calling card with the date, time and the door code written on it so there would be no mistake. You might be lucky and be given a clue on the card: *smoking*. This does not mean that it's going to be marijuana party. *Smoking* is Eurospeak for black tie; cocktail dress for the ladies.

If *tenue de ville*, or nothing, is on the card, your best bet is to consult your astrologer. The mystery of what to wear lies in answers to questions you can't ask. How big is the apartment and how is it furnished? Rustic or sophisticated? What part of town? How many people are coming? What age group? What social class, what power class? The day of the week is also a clue. On Saturdays and Sundays, the host might receive in a polo shirt.

Of course, you can always ask the hostess what she's going to wear. But my cocktail party fiasco has made me cautious. Even if she says blue jeans, they'll be designer jeans with a Christian Lacroix blouse and delicate shoes. When in doubt, wear dark – dark suit for Monsieur, dark, preferably black dress for Madame.

What a guest finally decides to wear is also a little like passing an exam, particularly for a woman. If you choose a variation on the theme of the black silk dress and arrive to find everyone else dressed similarly, you get high marks and feel great. The woman who showed up one night recently in a red and blue plaid wool dress, when everyone else was in black velvet, failed. The men didn't care – she was a gorgeous redhead and the skirt was ultra-short. But she cared. She was American.

On the other hand, at a big dinner for 50 people at the Chilean Embassy, when everyone was in black tie and silks, a young French woman looked hopelessly out of it in a brown wool suit. She herself, from the television world, didn't seem the slightest bit discomfited. But her hostess told me she felt that Chile was insulted.

I promise you that a foreigner, a man, who shows up in a light blue or grey suit, when all the other men are in dark blue, will – unless he is totally stupid or blind – wish he had stayed home. He might get so nervous he takes his jacket off. In this case, he would've done well to have stayed home.

What to Wear – Where?

What to wear becomes *sérieux* when you've not understood exactly what you've been invited to – you didn't quite catch everything in a cascade of French. Embarrassing to call back. You might not understand the second time either. Just wing it?

Charlotte Coyne, a glamorous redhead from Texas with a great smile, who lives with her family in the Paris suburbs, was delighted when a French neighbor, Madame P., knocked on her door. Her first visit from a French person ! Charlotte was excited. The trouble was that Charlotte didn't speak French and didn't know what Madame P. was saying. It sounded like – well, it was an invitation to do something, Charlotte could tell that much, and she understood the time, 2:00, and the place – *la terrace* – but to do what ? Charlotte asked her to repeat the invitation and still didn't understand. What would Madame P. be inviting her to at that hour ? It was a lovely day, and Madame P. was holding a huge parasol, more like an umbrella. She had seen her sunbathing on her terrace two floors above – she must be inviting Charlotte to sunbathe up there with her.

So at 2 p.m., she showed up at Mrs. P.'s door in a new flowered bikini and a big pink sunhat, with a towel over her arm, and rang the bell.

Madame P. answered the door. She looked dressed for an embassy luncheon. Without a blink, she ushered Charlotte into the living room, where 10 French women, dressed to the nines in their Chanels and Yves Saint-Laurents, drinking a demitasse, looked at her as if she was E.T. It seemed that the invitation that Charlotte had misunderstood was to a Tupperware party.

Flowers? Chocolates?

Mary and Edouard K., a Franco-American couple, invited some French friends and two American couples for dinner. (Small dinner for eight, no *pour mémoire*). The French couple, old friends, arrived first. Edouard fixed the drinks and Mary, exhausted from toiling over the stove, collapsed happily on a sofa to chat.

When the first American couple arrived, it was with a huge bunch of long-stemmed flowers. Very beautiful. Masses of lilies and greens, ingeniously wrapped up, with string entwining them stalk by stalk to confound anyone trying to undo them in a hurry. From the depths of the sofa, Mary rolled her eyes to Edouard to find a vase and arrange them. Edouard, peeved but resigned, fixed his new guests drinks and then disappeared for about 15 minutes. He returned with the lilies in three separate vases – he hadn't been able to find one big enough for all.

He had just sat down with a drink at last, when the second American couple appeared. With a second huge bunch of flowers. Mary looked at Edouard. Edouard couldn't resist saying, "Oh! What beautiful flowers! Just what we longed for!"

The French couple burst into gales of laughter. Edouard disappeared with the second bunch of flowers (for another 15 minutes) while the French couple, now joined by Mary and the first American couple (hesitantly, for they still didn't know what the joke was), went on roaring at the hilarity of the awkward Americans and the miserable, absent host.

The higher up the social or power ladder of your hosts, the more you risk giggles if you bring flowers. Either forget them, or send them. After is nice, before is better. Avoid chrysanthemums (only for graveyards), carnations (bad luck) and yellow flowers (the message to the hostess is that her husband is deceiving her).

No flowers at all is fine, except if it's a big dinner and this is the first time you've been invited. Foreigners often have complexes about showing up empty-handed. Work on this. Chocolates, if you must, but you can't count on their being popular, either, as everyone in Paris is on a diet – when they're not out for dinner.

Never bring a bottle of wine (unless agreed ahead of time). It's an insult to your host, implying:

- that he won't provide any
- that any old wine goes with the undistinguished fare you expect him to be serving.

On the contrary, he will have gone to great lengths to select each wine as the perfect complement to that evening's particular menu. Now he will feel obliged to serve your wine, good or bad, out of courtesy,

The *sérieuse* obligation in accepting a formal French dinner invitation does not consist in playing Santa Claus or in returning the hospitality. It's knowing the rules. It's being *bien élevé*, having *esprit* (zest, pithy conversation), and leaving when the orange juice is served.

Timing

"Americans are always so punctual for dinner parties," groaned a Frenchman. "I'm still in the shower. Thérèse is still at the stove."

Ten minutes late is just right. Fifteen is acceptable. You may have been to parties where half the French guests were anywhere from 30 to 40 minutes late. The traffic... But it doesn't make the hostess happy. She will forgive her *French* friends. The French are quarkochronics, remember?

The safest thing is to ask the hostess when she really wants you to arrive. Point out that you are foreign and you know how careful French people are about food. She'll be pleased, and relieved that you have acquired at least the beginnings of savoir-faire. You can ask her if she means American, French or Arab time, but she might not think it funny.

Arriving

Please, don't look around for a bathroom or W.C. on arrival. Or at any time during the evening. Not after dinner and not before you go home. French people don't. It's *mal élevé*. Therefore the facilities are not tidied up and ready for you (unless your hosts have been living in the U.S.) and your hostess will be squirming.

"So that's why Jérome always stops the car on the way to a dinner party, just before we arrive, and takes a pee in the street!" said Martha F.

Look for Louis XIV, again. The whole court at Versailles had to go to mass every morning. Sometimes the sermons were close to eternal. A priest called Bourdaloue liked to talk for three hours, which meant that the complete service took four hours. No one was allowed to leave before the end. For the elderly courtiers who couldn't hold out, there was always a potted plant near by. But the ladies? They took to hiding a little porcelain pot under their skirts, which came to be known as a *bourdaloue*, in honor of the long-winded preacher. Don't ask me how it operated, but it must have been fairly efficient to be immortalized in French-English dictionaries as "chamber pot."

Nor were ladies who rode to the battlefields in Louis XIV's carriage allowed what are now referred to as "rest stops." (The King, like the French husband Jérome, halted the carriage for his own rest stops whenever he pleased.) The ladies had to bump all the way to Compiègne and back before they could have relief. For one marquise it was too much. As recounted by the Duc de Saint Simon in his memoirs, she got down from the carriage in the palace courtyard of Versailles in desperation, unable to make it across to her quarters. Seeing her brother coming towards her, she asked him to screen her from the King. Then she attended to her needs, as the French say.

W.C. Dilemma

Recently, one of the elderly grandes dames of Paris gave me the honor of coming to tea. She had diarrhea. She was clearly much troubled to have to excuse herself twice in the course of tea. So troubled that she telephoned the next day to excuse herself. She had, she said, been very *mal élevée*.

Preparing an article for *International Management* on which points of etiquette French CEO's thought American CEO's should be informed about before being transferred to Paris, I interviewed Michel François-Poncet, then president of Banque Paribas.

"By now, American CEO's are very sophisticated," he said. "They know everything they need to know. But I 've noticed two curious things about them: they tend to be very tall, and to have a bladder about one third large enough for them."

Jeff Dore, chemical engineer at Elf-Atochem: "I've noticed at meetings that my French colleagues never need to excuse themselves – even if the meetings go on for four or five hours. In the U.S. we're taught that it's unhealthy, but this is clearly bunk."

France isn't the only country that has habits different from the U.S. in this respect. In diplomatic circles, such protocol restraints can lead to international incidents.

The London *Sunday Times* carried this story on January 16, 1994: "James Baker, the former American Secretary of State, dubbed his meetings with the Syrian President 'bladder diplomacy', because tea, lemon juice and coffee were served endlessly, but it was considered bad form to leave the room for the toilet."

Some Other Dinner Party Pointers to Keep in Mind on Arriving:

- Rise, if a man, when your host gives you the pre-dinner drink.
- Rise, if a man, the first time a lady comes into the room, and only the first time. Rise, if a woman, to greet another woman of any age, and your host. It doesn't hurt to get up to greet a man for the first time, either.
- Don't cut the bread; break off a piece with your fingers and eat it before breaking off the next piece.
- Never pour the wine yourself, unless the host asks you to.
- Don't put your bread in the gravy, either with your fork or with your fingers.
- Don't pick up anything but bread and asparagus in your fingers, including chicken legs and all fruit.
- Don't cut your salad with your knife; fold it.
- Don't cut the point off the Brie. The technique with cheese is to cut it so that it retains its shape.

Your Entrance

As you enter the drawing room and see 12 or more unknown faces, try to convert yourself into a piece of furniture, an elegant Louis XV chair, for instance, which moves gracefully on wheels. Then, when no one smiles at you or talks to you before dinner, you won't be surprised. Who talks to a chair? But that doesn't mean you're not much admired, and worth zillions at an auction. As a chair, you don't have to smile, or talk either. You can just be interestingly silent. Think of it as a relief. There are only a few moments when you have to be a handshaking chair, which can say two words, *"Bonsoir, monsieur,"* or *"Bonsoir, madame."* Accompany them with a gentle, firm handshake. No pumping up and down. No macho bone-crunching. Elderly ladies first, then other ladies, then the men.

Introductions

It helps to be an elegant chair when you're introduced to Parisians, because not only do they not waste smiles on strangers, they don't clog up their brains with their names. People who do seem distinctly odd to them.

"I perceive a Freudian connection between Americans and their names," said a French banker. "There is no other explanation for this strange passion. It's as if their name were engraved on a lost umbilical cord that they're forever trying to get back, by repeating their names and other people's names when they meet them. As if both they and the people they're talking to don't exist, if they not only don't know each other's names, but also their spelling. This is very strange, for us."

The banker was being very polite about one of the most reliable occasions for French hilarity.

So the thing to do at a dinner party is to fox them. After removing your smile, wipe out all concern for your own name or any one else's when you walk in the door of the salon. You're a chair. No assistance to the host as he either slurs over your name or blurts out, trying to introduce you to another guest, "Oh – this is – er, gulp – I want you to meet – oh, I just can't remember how to say your name, this is Mr. – ?" but a bland indifference as you say, simply, ignoring his stumbling, *"Bonsoir, monsieur (or madame)"* to the other guest, smugly aware that if the curiosity of that person is later aroused, they are perfectly able to inquire of someone else what your name is and how it's spelled. And that the same applies to you, for theirs.

As the host takes you around to the other guests, introducing you, let him mumble the names of the other guests all he likes – you will not be put out! You don't need to know! You have discovered the joyous freedom of a world without names and you won't fall into the embarrassing trap of asking anyone to repeat it! Much less spell it. As a chair, you will not be tempted to tell anyone you're "glad to meet them" or, just as *mal élevé,* *"enchanté."* Or to break the sacred French rule of never asking personal questions.

I am overdoing it with this chair business, but, believe me, it helps when you've been introduced to the last stranger, the host has rushed back to greet the next arriving guests, and you're left staring into space. For there is nothing to say to that last person. Unless you have something of reliable interest to report, such as having been raped in the elevator or that the hostess has suddenly eloped with her lover, you have to fall back on the weather or the traffic. This does not appeal to the French wit. Therefore, silence is the only policy. Let them deal with it.

If you don't believe me, think of those famous non-smilers, those stone faced cinema icons, Alain Delon and Catherine Deneuve, arriving at a dinner party. Can you imagine either of them smiling and saying *"enchanté"* or inquiring about names – or announcing their own! – or noting that it was raining outside, or embarking on a monologue, with someone they just met, about their problems with the traffic in arriving?

I've been trying to feel, or unfeel, like a chair in Paris for over 20 years, but I still fret at silence. So I ask my hostess if she could possibly send me a list of the other guests ahead of time. Then at least you know who it is you're gawking at and have some hope of coming up with a relevant, non-weather observation. And who knows, you might see on the list that one of them is a member of the same bird-watching group as you are. Then, when you meet, you're off to the races. However, if you see that one of the other guests is a friend of a friend of your great-Aunt Sally, you'd better skip it. Gawking will get you in less trouble.

The main thing to keep in mind, if you resent being a chair, is that you will have to stare into space for at most only 20 or 30 minutes and that glorious food and conversation await you in the dining room.

It also helps to remember that French people moving to another part of the country have exactly the same reception as foreigners. A charming French count from Nice told me of his move with his lovely French wife to Reims, where she had inherited one of the major champagne vineyards. "In six years, we met only four other couples," he said.

Beauty, charm, nobility, brains, riches availed them nothing.

Moving into the Dining Room

La bataille de la porte (the battle at the doorway) can last for 10 minutes, getting a party of 12 from the drawing room to the dining room. Four or five ladies each telling each other to go first through the doorway takes up at least three of these.

The two most obstinate doorway balkers I've experienced firsthand were at a ladies' luncheon. One was an Austrian archduchess in her mid-thirties, a first cousin of the Queen of England and the wife of the nephew of the last Austrian Emperor; the other, a 92-year-old French princess, descendant of a family of non-reigning Russian princes.

Before the *bataille de la porte* took place, the ancient Princesse Galitzine had arisen from a deep sofa in honor of the archduchess and then, to the horror of the other guests, descended in a deep curtsy on one withered, arthritic knee. There was a breathtaking moment waiting for her to work her way up again. At the doorway to the dining room, the much younger woman waited for the much older one to go through.

But the Princess Galitzine, known around Paris for her strong character, was having none of it. Etiquette had regulated her behavior since childhood. An iron rule: royalty precedes aristocracy.

"*Après vous, madame,*" she said firmly, in her deep commanding voice.

"*Non, après vous, madame,*" said the archduchess, politely.

"*Mais non! Après vous, madame!*" said the princess.

This went back and forth at least eight times. The hostess was beginning to get desperate about her soufflé.

Finally the princess boomed forth,"*Voyons voyons, madame! Après vous!* You must go first! You're not only royal, you are imperial!"

The Seating

Don't just plunk yourself down wherever you feel like. The hostess will place you. Not where she thinks you'll have fun. Not next to someone you might share an enthusiasm with, but according to a rigorous study of your profile. French people even place their relatives at a family dinner according to the various nuances of age, number of children, nationality, and rank in the church, government or aristocracy. As a foreigner, you are automatically noble and may well be seated at the right of the host or hostess.

It's called protocol. Watch it, if you're the one doing the inviting. If a French or other foreign grandee feels his rank has been slighted, he may turn over his plate. He will then cross his arms and glower, refusing to be served.

Blame Louis XIV for this too.

Table Manners: Watch Those Hands!

A generation of working mothers has resulted in a national disaster when it comes to the way otherwise well-educated young Americans handle their cutlery. How one eats is one area where there is international agreement between the Americas and Europe except for two things. One is where you're expected to keep your hands when not eating. The United States, Great Britain and the Commonwealth countries are the only ones who think they should rest in your lap. In all the others the imperative is to have them resting on the table, at the wrist, the idea being that, otherwise, lewd things will be going on under the table.

"I couldn't believe it!" said Marilyn N. "In the middle of dinner at the Austrian Embassy, the Frenchman next to me grabbed my hand from my lap and put it on the table! The nerve! I hissed something at him and he explained that it was stronger than he was, he just couldn't bear that his neighbor's hands were not on the table... that he might have trouble keeping his own there!"

A Frenchman enjoying Anglo-Saxon table manners

The other disagreement is whether to park your knife or not after cutting your meat. In England and most of the Continent, no. In the U.S. and France, yes, providing you park it entirely on the plate and not with the handle resting on the table. All agree that, when finished, the knife and fork are parked on the plate neatly together and parallel, with the handles at number 4, clockwise. You'd be surprised how many American executives leave them sloppily on either side of the plate, or even half on, half off the plate. I haven't seen one eating from his knife yet, but there's always a first for everything.

On the other hand, asparagus can be eaten with the fingers. It seems Edward VII, when he was still Prince of Wales and defining what were to be called Edwardians in the Gay Nineties, came to Paris and ate his asparagus with his fingers. The French were delighted and have been doing so ever since.

Conversation Taboos

Expect talk to range over anything – religion, politics, the sex life of squids. Scatological jokes, laxatives, the sky's the limit, except for psychiatry and whom people voted for. For that matter, any personal questions are *mal élevé*, as well as holding forth at length.

"The French are always interrupting me – just before I come to the point!" said Arnold R., a chemical engineer. "It drives me nuts!"

"Americans do go on and on, once they get the ball," said Jacques-Henri H.

French dinner-table conversations are not about information, but wit. A foreigner's criticizing his own government, or the local one, is another taboo – a great way to shut everyone up. One unforgettable moment at a small French dinner party was when the only other American guest, a banker, began haranguing the table about the then President of the U.S., Ronald Reagan. A pall fell over the French, as if they were asphyxiated. There was an eerie silence when he finished. The French have an expression for this: *Un ange passe* (an angel goes by). It generally does when a taboo in the ritual has been broken.

The Food

To refuse any of the dishes, or any of the courses, except the cheese course is another *impardonnable*. If you're a vegetarian, or allergic to smoked salmon or nuts – or anything else – then tell your hostess when she invites you. Moan with joy after the first mouthful of each course, if it's good, but not if it's not, and not necessarily if it's catered. The hostess is hanging on your verdict. Don't keep her waiting.

No matter how delicious, don't, whatever you do, ask her for her recipe. You might as well ask her to hand over her bank account. French people remember every meal they've ever eaten outside of their own home. That recipe is something your hostess has toiled over. It has her signature, it's different from anyone else's and an essential part of her repertoire. If she gives it to you, then it's not hers anymore.

Above all, good or not, catered or not, finish what you put on your plate. This means taking care how much you put on it in the first place.

"You Americans are so wasteful, you always leave food on your plate," is something I hear continually from my French friends. "Wasteful" is the word they use *par politesse*, but what they mean is: Leaving the tiniest morsel on your plate is a personal insult to your hostess as friend, a poor review to her as stage director, a blasphemy to her as priestess, and gives her a failing mark on her exam.

But sometimes you're not in control of what comes on your plate. An IBM executive, Grant K., visiting his son, an engineer at Groupe Bull in Paris, was invited by one of the Bull directors to lunch in the executive dining room. No one thought to warn the host that the IBM father was allergic to chicken. The waiter served directly onto the plates: chicken. Grant left it on his plate, untouched. The host was clearly put out.

I asked several Frenchmen what Grant should have done.

They all agreed that not having communicated his allergy to his boss or the waiter in advance, he was in a mess. Two of the Frenchmen I asked just shook their heads and threw up their hands. Such situations must not happen. If they do, it's because people are *mal élevé*.

The third Frenchman, the president of a bank, was definite: there was only one solution. Extreme, but imperative. Grant should have slid the chicken in his napkin while no one was looking. Well, fine, but – I mean, the gravy? But you can gauge the gravity of the situation by the extremity of the solution.

The Spinach Pudding

Should you harbor any lingering doubts about the long meal-memories of French people, consider this:

Three years after we moved to France, I met a Frenchwoman who right away invited me to a luncheon at her house. I was excited. I still had few French friends and none had ever suggested hospitality until after I'd seen them at least five times. I accepted and went. It soon became clear that we had nothing in common. However, I felt obligated to return the invitation soon after.

It was fully 12 years before I ran into her again. This is what she said:

"*Bonjour, madame.* How nice to see you again... I haven't seen you since that charming luncheon you gave at your house. What a delicious spinach pudding you gave us!"

189

Wait for the Orange Juice!

After dessert, coffee will be served in the drawing room. Then liqueurs. All the different courses, and changing all the plates for all the courses, has had the clock busily advancing. By now it's midnight, unless you've had one of the professional waiters who churn people out fast at the embassies, and at the Elysée Palace for the President, so that their employers can get at least some sleep. (Try one. They are masters at the art of serving, and it is well worth their fee, just to watch them. You get one by phoning the Société des Maîtres d'Hôtel).

But you can't leave yet. Not until the orange juice, or some kind of juice, has appeared. This is the signal that the curtain is down, the play is over and you can go home. *Dormez bien!*

The Next Day

Don't forget to phone the hostess the next day. It doesn't matter how hard you find it to use the telephone in France. The hostess wants feedback and she deserves it, after all that work. She wants to know if you liked Monsieur and Madame D., and what you thought of her mousse au saumon. It's cheating to write a note.

If you did in fact like Monsieur and Madame D., by all means invite them yourself. Strike while the iron is hot. In two weeks they may have forgotten you – Parisians live in a whirl of meeting new people and have short memories about the last ones.

Be sure to invite your host and hostess with them, if you do. This is one of the subtleties of French entertaining relatively unknown to foreigners and an absolutely iron rule. If you break it, you've made two enemies unnecessarily. The idea is to not give your hosts the impression that you are stealing their friends. I think it's a courtesy that we should all adopt.

Dinner Party -II.

This version of a smaller, less formal, younger party was contributed by Mark Meigs, 36, Ph.D., professor of American history, now teaching at the University of Lille. Married to Divina, a French graduate of one of the Grandes Ecoles, as well as of the University of California at Berkeley, Mark is a penetrating observer of the French scene. He is an associate director of Culture Crossings.

You are invited for 8:00. You arrive before 8:30 wearing the dark suit you wore to work, knowing you had a dinner to go to. Upon arrival you are introduced to everyone, that is to say, the other couple or two you are to spend the next five hours with.

You will be seated in low soft chairs and sofas for half an hour or 45 minutes. You wonder if you will be able to extricate yourself from the chair or if you will fall onto your neighbor.

You are left alone with the other guests, strangers, for what seems like long periods of time, while your hostess is in the kitchen and your host arranges wine and pours drinks. The drinks, when they come, are sweet and sticky and not strong enough, and the things you are offered to eat, nuts mixed with dried fruit, and something like salted breakfast cereal, can be neither eaten nor discussed. This is not exactly the harbinger of the great French meal you expected.

Probably this beginning part of a dinner is always awkward, but the French are particularly bad at it. They know things are supposed to be informal at drinks time, but they don't trust informality, so they immobilize you in a chair. They know they should give you something to eat, but they don't want to take the edge off your appetite. They know they should give you something to drink, but if they are about to give you a really good wine, they don't wish to anesthetize your tastebuds with hard liquor. Beer is out of the question. It's German. The result is a slow start to the party.

But the start is the least important part of the dinner. You will be forty-five minutes in that chair. You will not leave the house until after one in the morning.

The Drinks

You'll be asked what you'd like to drink, but in your tireless effort to be part of Us rather than Them, it's wiser to see what other people are drinking and have that.

The French usually have Porto, a sweet red wine, or Martini, a sweet red Vermouth not to be confused with an American gin or vodka martini. (If you want one of those in a bar, you ask for just that, *un martini Américain*.) In the country, you will be offered perhaps some form of anisette – pastis, Pernod or Ricard. These taste of licorice and turn cloudy when you add water. Anisette is very much a man's drink and in some company, to be one of the boys, you'd have some. You may also be offered a kir, which is white wine mixed with a little blackcurrant liqueur; or a kir royal, which has champagne in the place of white wine. If your host is going to the trouble to mix these, you'd better accept, especially if he is opening a bottle of champagne for you. That means this is a special occasion. At formal dinners, champagne is always served, and usually also at less formal ones.

Scotch whiskey is considered stylish among well-traveled French people over 50, and even American bourbon has a following among younger sophisticates. It will be served undiluted, with one small ice cube floating in it. It is for you to decide whether your desire to appear French or your host's desire to appear Americanized is more important at this party. You're playing the game of international manners. But remember, whoever did the cooking will prefer it if you stay away from the whiskey.

Now your hostess reappears. Her face is red, her hair has come a little undone. But no speck of the sauce she has been wrestling with mars her getup. You move to the dining room, leaving your drink on a tray or coaster. There will be wine, and it is rather a relief to leave this part of the evening behind.

Your hostess tells you where to sit. The courses arrive and they are delicious. There may be a different wine with each course, or you may drink the same wine throughout. You do not have to drink very much, but just as the hostess is waiting for some signal about how good the food is, the host would like to hear some lip-smacking over the wine. He will keep filling your glass as you empty it, so at some point it is best to leave it full.

The great thing about eating in France is that it relieves you, the foreigner, of the necessity to contribute much to the conversation, which will probably go by so fast that you only catch a third of it. By eating and drinking, not like a pig, but with attention, you are participating in the social rite without saying a word. Asking for seconds will be taken as a compliment, and prolong your participation (and non-talking). If you are younger than your hosts, they will be overcome with an almost parental love as they watch you putting away the food.

After the *entrée* (the first course in France), there will be various other courses, perhaps fish, game and/or a roast of lamb, or perhaps beef or chicken. Then the cheese and salad arrive, perhaps together. The cheese is the only thing you are allowed to refuse – because it's not made in the house. On the other hand, a liking for smelly, hard cheeses is very masculine and very French, and this is a good moment to show some macho, or some curiosity about France. There are some 350 cheeses in France, without counting the local variations. As with the wine, your host may have chosen the cheese with care, and may have a story about the smelliest of the lot. This is also the course that will not be served twice. So take what you want the first time.

Dessert comes next and then coffee. It is now 11 o'clock and you are still seated at table. Sometimes you move back into the drawing room for coffee and liqueurs, but usually, once planted at the table, no one moves.

Now comes the hardest part of the party. The cocktail moment was grim, but short, and you had dinner to look forward to. Now you have two hours of an empty table between you and your bed. But this is the moment the French have been waiting for.

Frenzy of Talk

They are replete with food, wine, coffee, and probably at least some people will have started smoking. This is when their talk becomes most animated.

Even if there are as many as 10 or 12 people at the table, there will be, now, only one conversation going most of the time. It moves very fast from person to person and from topic to topic. Did you see what Yannick Noah did when his team won? That was just like what the Socialist minister said when they won. Did you hear what the President said to the minister? That is just like what Louis XIV said to his minister. Louis in fact was a poor tennis player. Ah, the great moments of French history seem to take place on the tennis court, you remember that oath...

Anyway, it goes something like that. Silly and witty. It is not unlike the banter one might hear at an Irish bar in the States. It happens at every level of French society. Sometimes, the sport will be soccer, not tennis. The political figure may be the local mayor, but the wit is the same.

It's very hard for any foreigner, particularly an English-speaking one, to follow this kind of conversation in French. The subjects jump. As with any kind of humor, timing is important, so you cannot ask anyone to repeat anything. And probably, worried about tomorrow, you refused that last glass of wine, the strong coffee, the after dinner drink, the cigarettes, all of which have wound up the French into a frenzy of talk, whereby they wring the last ounce of pleasure out of each other's company.

All is not lost if you can keep your head from falling onto the table. They are so pleased with this part of the evening that they will not mind your silence. In fact, most of them are only an audience, contributing just a word or two to the two or three who are really whooping it up. You can be part of the audience too. Look alert, keep your eyes going back and forth as you would at a tennis match, and you will not be letting your side down. It will seem natural to them, as, after all, as with everything, there is a hierarchy. Some people are born to shine in company, others are born to admire.

This is of course frustrating if you are used to being the life of the party some of the time in your own language. So give it a try. Bide your time; there is plenty of it. Think of some topic that is bound to come up – all current cultural and political topics eventually do: the Prime Minister's being kicked out, the new statue in front of the Hôtel de Ville, the new movie with Depardieu. Think of three or four words you might say on this subject and wait. When the conversation comes around to it, you spring your four words. You don't have to say a whole sentence. It's better if you don't. If the conversation is fast enough, if the food, the wine, the sugar in the dessert, the caffeine in the coffee, have all done their work, someone else will finish your sentence, fitting it in with the conversation. Say three words an hour and you have earned the admiration of the whole table for life. You have participated in the highest form of French culture: French conversation. They haven't been fooled, they know you finessed your tricks, but you were in there making the party go, helping sustain their pleasure right to the last hour. You are one of them. Their fears about a bored foreigner bringing their joy to an end too early, who would "curdle the mayonnaise," can be put to rest.

The last Métro leaves each terminal at 10 minutes before 1:00 a.m. This means that by leaving anywhere in Paris by 12:30, you can get home with a change of Métro. Among Métro takers, the party starts to end exactly at 12:30, because when one person leaves, the party cannot be sustained. People with cars will wish to demonstrate their loyalty to the party beyond that last Métro limit. Usually, someone will offer to drive you home. If nobody takes the Métro, everyone will stay until 1:00.

For this kind of small party, you don't need to call your hosts the next day. You were part of things during the party. They saw you enjoying yourself. Those last two hours when they could abandon the kitchen, and where you managed your couple of witty phrases, were their reward. The next morning, you will understand why the French do not eat breakfast.

When Mark and Divina were first engaged, Divina asked some French friends if she could bring him along to dinner. There was a long silence on the phone. "They dreaded it," said Divina. "They saw their party being ruined by this American. But Mark so obviously loved France, he was so obviously delighted with the dinner (despite the sticky beginning) and his six words were so well planned and perfectly timed, that they wanted to know right away when we would all get together again."

Hosting the French at a Formal Dinner

Don't hesitate. French people love to be invited out. But don't be bitter if they don't invite you back – for the reasons given at the beginning of this chapter, plus a couple more: your dwelling, food and friends are too elegant and they can't compete, or they're not elegant enough. Or else they've decided that there just aren't any *atomes crochus* (hooked atoms, or good vibes).

The only obligation they undertake in accepting is to arrive at the right time, dressed properly, to be a lively conversationalist and *bien élevé*, and to leave with the serving of orange juice. If they bring a non-consumable present, it could be a sign that they don't expect to invite you back.

Give the people you're particularly keen on inviting a choice of two or three dates, two weeks in advance. Never plan on receiving on a Monday (fresh produce markets are closed), nor on the weekend (it's reserved for family; anyway they're likely to be away). That leaves Tuesday, Wednesday or Thursday.

If it's the first time, tell them who else is coming when you call back to confirm one of the dates. Then send them a *pour mémoire,* your calling card with the date, time and your door code on it. This reassures them about having understood you correctly, and shows them how to spell your name. They love it if you write the names of the other guests on the back of the card – for the same reason you ask them for their guest list.

If you're not planning a classical French rite, warn them ahead of time that you're serving Mexican, or whatever. French people are extraordinarily adaptable, but by now you've gotten the message that a dinner is not just a jolly excuse to get together. They need to be prepared.

However, why not try a French dinner? Some kind of fish, some kind of roast, salad, cheese and dessert and that's it, if each choice is a "noble" example of its food group. Sardines are not noble, nor is pot roast, nor are turnips and cabbage. No soup! No egg dish as *entrée* (first course) in the evening! If you want to make it easy for yourself, do the classic "noble" menu that French people never tire of: *saumon fumé* (smoked salmon, not the kind done up in plastic); a leg of lamb *(un gigot)* done rare so that it is pink, with thin-thin haricots, the most noble of all vegetables, and roast potatoes; cheese – a Vacherin, if it's the season, makes every Frenchman sigh with joy; salad, dessert. All done at home! (Except the salmon and cheese).

Whatever you choose, watch the colors. Each course must have a different one. Select your palette and enjoy being Monet, with the flowers and tablecloth picking up the tones of the food.

If you want to score extra, have the menu written on standing cards on the table so that people can see what is coming – or what is on their plate. No one likes to ask dumb questions. The French like to know, and it's not always clear.

The American Embassy has one of the best chefs in town. Here is one of their menus:

Dîner

Quenelles de truite de mer
Vert Pré

Emincé de Canard
Périgourdine
Légumes maraîchère

Pithiviers
au foin

Sorbet aux fruits
Elodie

Meursault "Chevalières" 1987
Pommard "Les Platières" 1986
Château Sahuc les Tours 1986

It's a good idea to figure out the seating the day before. You'll be too giddy with the food and table arrangements to make the right decisions at the last minute. The excruciating question of who sits on the right of the host and hostess has to be calculated with care. When in doubt, call the protocol office at the American Embassy or the French Foreign Office. You really do not want one of your guests to turn over his plate and refuse to eat.

Needless to say, you must not only rise but also shake hands with all arrivals. Ladies get up to shake hands with other ladies, and also to greet men. If you notice some French women not doing this, it's because not all French women are *bien élevées*, but it will do wonders for the reputation of your country if you are.

This goes for greeting people anywhere, not just at parties. It can surprise foreigners. A year ago at the France-Amérique, a club in Paris, I saw a friend of mine, then the Austrian ambassadress, across the lobby. I left the New Zealand lawyer I was talking to in order to greet her. The ambassadress, when she recognized me, rose and we embraced, chatted briefly and parted. The New Zealander, a woman, was surprised. "Why would the ambassadress get up for another woman – a friend?" she asked. "And in a public place?"

If you can avoid it, don't seat two men or two women next to each other (unless someone has cancelled at the last minute). This can happen when the host or hostess refuses to vacate her position at the head of the table. Nothing makes French guests grumpier. The hostess should move. Sitting the French way, with the host and hostess in the middle of the table, makes it easier for the host to survey the table.

A seating chart in a frame and propped up for the guests to see on arrival, gives them a helpful clue of whom to avoid during the apéritif, since they'll be sitting next to their dinner partners for about three hours. If you think a drawing looks too tacky, there are elegant devices you can buy, with little cards you stick around a velvet table-shape. Embassies use them. I make a drawing.

"One thing you might tell American men," said one of the French executives I interviewed, "is that in Europe we don't get up the second time a lady comes in the room. Just the first time. American men seem to us like jack-in-the-boxes, always popping up. Apparently it makes the ladies nervous too."

The Fatal Error

Hire someone to come and serve. Your concierge, perhaps, or her sister or cousin. Or one of the waiters I mentioned, who serve at the President's dinners at the Elysée... la Société des Maîtres d'Hôtel.

If you absolutely refuse to hire a serving person, then put the food on serving dishes passed from guest to guest, so that they can help themselves. We've seen that French courtesy demands cleaning up whatever is on their plate. So please don't help the guests yourself from a side table, or in the kitchen. Nothing horrifies a French person more than receiving a plate heaped high with food he may not like. You give him the choice of insulting the hostess... or making himself sick.

They're arriving! Bring out the champagne! "If you can't afford champagne, then you can't afford to give a dinner party," said an American baroness after 30 years of hosting Paris dinners.

Now you can relax. It will be a great success.

Part IV

Office Life

Chapter 15

The Logic of French Management
Why the Thunderbolts are Coming

If corporate life [in France] were generally as formal as it appears on the surface, it would be far more rigid and stifling than it is in practice. Rules and procedures are rarely broken but they are constantly distorted, manipulated and ignored if they do not serve the purpose for which they are intended. The plea for the special case – le cas particulier – is invariably acceded to. Beneath the apparent structure of the organization there is usually an invigorating subculture based on informal networking and characterised by flexibility, scepticism and energy.

John Mole
Mind Your Manners

I asked some American executives about the procedures that landed them in Paris working for a French company.

"I'd had a lot of interviews for the job during a trip to Paris, but for a long time I didn't hear anything. I never did get a notice in the mail, or a formal letter or anything," said Henry Haley, with his soft New Orleans accent. "One day my future boss at Lafarge Coppée in Paris phoned and asked me when I was arriving. So here I am."

The wife of an American now handling the institutional investments at a French bank put it like this: "There were about 15 interviews. They asked about our personal relationship! They studied my husband's handwriting! Then they wanted personal and business references. They sent someone to the States to interview my husband's ex-boss for two hours. We didn't hear from them for months. Then suddenly a contract arrived!"

What happened to Henry Haley and the American banker surprised them because they were confident of being given information at the proper time. So they waited for it.

But for the French nothing is more uncertain than being informed automatically of anything. They have to dig up the information themselves about everything all the time. They build up their networks accordingly. A Frenchman would have known whether a new job was coming through or not, long before the boss's phone call, or the contract arrived. During the interview he would have felt how things were going – whether the questions were becoming general and vague, or more precise. If unsure of the outcome, he would have flogged his network for codes and implicit messages: the boss's secretary and people near the boss. He might have been obliged to find some pretext or other for calling the boss himself, to remind him of his existence. French managers spend a great deal of their evenings after the office on the phone.

"Low Context"-"High Context"

Those of us who live in foreign cultures have the anthropologist Edward T. Hall to thank for making sense out of our crazy lives by showing us what was going on. From observing the cultural use of time and space that we looked at in Chapter 3, monochronic and polychronic, he and his team worked out the ground-breaking concepts of fundamentally different ways of experiencing the world that he calls "high context" and "low context" cultures.

Low context cultures – most of the Germanic and English-speaking cultures, Northern and Protestant – are explicit: direct, clear, linear, verbal. Channels of communication are clear. Working teams share information, cooperate and support each other. If you see some special tubes advertised in a catalogue in the U.S., you can phone the number indicated. Someone somewhere in the United States – it's not even clear where – will answer, "Joe speaking". After taking your order and credit card number, "Joe" (Joe who? who cares?) will say, "Thank you for calling, Susie, have a nice day." End of transaction. End of contact. The context, the who and why of a business transaction, doesn't matter. It's about getting a job done, going forward, making money, not getting to know people before you trade with them.

Low context cultures can generally be classified as achievement cultures, and they're always monochronic. That is, you remember, that people are dominated, not to say tyrannized, by the clock. They are *on time* – not even five minutes late. They schedule their days rigorously. Time is quantified ("wasted", "saved", "killed"). The appointment and the project have priority over everything, including urgent demands on their time by family or friends, and they only do one thing at a time.

High context cultures, which are all the others, – Mediterranean, Slav, Central European, Latin American, African, Arab, Asian, American-Indian – are affiliation cultures. People are more important than schedules and projects. High context people are in permanent touch with other people all day, maybe with swarms of them. They're keeping informed about everything and everyone, soaking up details, news and reports, so that things don't have to be explained to them as they do to low context people. They're insulted and impatient if you do explain it to them (as Germans, who need details, being very low context, tend to do).

Much of the interaction of high context people is implicit: coded, circular, indirect. The message is in the body language, the setting, the relationship between the people involved. They can handle conversations and business with several people at once. They have their own private networks for information, which they keep to themselves, and are constantly updating so that they don't need much background information. They don't do business on the phone, except with people they know. They don't do business at all with people they don't know – and trust. When I learned that there was a company called Thameslink in Windsor, England, that converted word processor disks to compatibility with computers – a specialty I'd been unable to find in France – I phoned up Windsor, talked with the owner, Roger Cullingham, and asked him how long it would take to take to get my Panasonic floppy disk to be acceptable to my Macintosh. "A week or so should do it," he said cheerfully, "send it along." I was totally unknown to him. I got the disk back in 10 days. The bill came later. It 's hard to imagine this happening in a high context country like France.

The relationships of high context people, once established, are for keeps. They don't need contracts, except to set a general direction, which will evolve. And – bottom line – their relationships, honor and face, are more important than business. In many of these cultures, power may also come before business. Many a Frenchman has chosen to lose a deal rather than a portion of his power.

Time Doesn't Fly

High context people have a different sense of time. It's not segmented. They'll be on time, if some greater people-priority doesn't come up in the meantime. Schedules are flexible. But they keep time according to their own system (polychronic), and "on time" for them might be a half hour, an hour or a week or a month "late" for you, depending on the culture and how far east or south you go.

Many cultures are a combination. Australia is low context but polychronic. France has a Germanic monochronic low context culture in Alsace and to a much lesser extent in the North, and otherwise a strong Latin polychronic high context culture. With this richness goes unpredictability. As noted in Chapter 3, I call the French quarkochronics because, like quarks, you can't pin them down. There is no way to tell if they'll be on time, like a monochronic, or late, or how late (though it won't be more than 45 minutes late). It may always be a little different with the same person, unless you happen to be dealing with a totally monochronic Frenchman. There are plenty of them, too.

Logic: What's Logical to You May Not Be to Me

Henry Haley, who was mystified above about the hiring system, is a financial analyst with Lafarge Coppée. Financial officers are numbers people and tend to like precise answers. The French, with their passion for math, are numbers people too – but the similarity ends there.

After six months in France, Henry was beginning to work out a picture.

"The two countries think completely differently," he said. "It's like the difference between football, the national game of the U.S., and soccer, the national game of France.

"In football, you go straight down the field, yard by yard, to your goal. The players are ordered on and off the field, according to whether they're offensive or defensive. It's about teams. It's direct. The strategy has been worked out well ahead. In soccer, you kick the ball around and around until finally you get it in the goal. The same players go up and down the field. They can play both offense and defense. The strategy keeps changing, depending on what's happening. It's more about stars and power plays than teamwork. And it's indirect."

Like football, like mental processes: low context cultures (northern Europe and the U.S.) think in a linear manner, directly. The French are not only high context but Cartesians. They're schooled in theory. They think in a circular, or circuitous manner; going around any given subject or problem until they've exhausted all the possibilities of getting the wrong answer. They approach it indirectly, in nuances, touching on all the complexities.

Or as Elf-Atochem's chemical engineer, Jeff Dore, puts it, "They surround a subject, they taste it, they give everyone the chance to come to the same conclusion. This means a lot of talk, a lot of meetings."

Logic is one of the key words in French. Newspapers drag it into headlines about almost anything. During the Gulf War, there was constant mention of *la logique de guerre* (the logic of war) and *la logique de paix* (the logic of peace). French people, if they want to disagree with you politely, will often say, *"Ce n'est pas logique."* ("It's not logical.")

Their logic, the mode of reasoning of the French mind, is known as deductive. From a given principle, or a theory, they proceed to its illustration in the "real world" with facts. I put quotes around "real" and "world" because for English speakers, "facts" make up the real world, and they can't imagine any other. Americans and Britons are inductive reasoners. Get the facts and then we'll talk. Thus, their logic is to work from the facts (concrete) to the theory (abstract).

For the mathematically trained French executives, the theory is the real world. The world of their imagination is what counts. They "see" things differently. Abstractions are what they like.

For instance, Ray B., a hydrogeologist from Fort Collins, Col., went to Brittany on a project, inspecting some wells with a French hydrogeologist. The French engineer had a blueprint. When he looked at the first well, Ray saw that the diameter of its opening was seven centimeters, or two centimeters wider than on the blueprint. He said so.

"That's not possible," said the Frenchman.

Ray took out his vernier gauge and measured it.

"Look," he said. "Seven centimeters."

"Impossible," repeated the Frenchman. "You can see on the blueprint, it is clearly five centimeters."

This is an extreme example, but believe me, Anglo-Saxons in Paris are full of similar ones. They find it so wacky that they're fond of quoting a joke about a French engineer, who, observing a new invention, comments, "The facts are all right, but it won't work in theory."

What's going on here?

Simply that vision is itself culturally programmed, one of Hall's earliest discoveries. In *An Anthropology of Everyday Life*, he writes:

"Vision is not only highly selective, it is a transaction between the viewer and the world – in effect, we humans put together our own perceptual worlds according to rules and principles which are quite arbitrary. Furthermore, perception is greatly modified not only by the psychological state of the individual but by culture as well."

Hierarchy

Back to Louis XIV and Napoleon – and de Gaulle and Mitterrand. French companies are often run like a monarchy, or like the present government – from top down. The military model (*cadre*, French for manager, means officer) of ranks in a rigorous company hierarchy echoes also the Roman Empire and the feudal structures, which, as we saw earlier with the civil service, only changed criteria, not systems, after the French Revolution.

Jacques-Henri A. : "There is no skipping levels up or down, and each boss is not only careful of his power, but behaves as much like the autocratic CEO (*PDG*, in French) at the top as he can. He passes on every decision on the way down as if it comes from him only – he would lose face if he were seen to be only a mere cog in the machine. Every *cadre* is a Napoleon to himself."

The resulting boss-subordinate relations, wrapped in formality and mystery, are defined by what the cultural anthropologist Geert Hofstede calls a strong "power distance."

Hofstede, who made a study of all the branches of IBM all over the world, also rates France high on "risk avoidance," or the degree to which a culture embraces uncertainty. Caution in the French workplace, like reserve with regard to strangers, is such a staple of French management that venture capital is known as *capital-risque*.

Another high rating for France on one of Hofstede's criteria was a decent quality of life for everyone, stressing social rights extending to all the population, rather than personal, egoistic financial success. Thus the feudal model of the patriarch, now the President taking care of his flocks is updated, with these striking results:

- six weeks vacation for everyone
- first-rate health care and education for everyone
- secure employment. French industry has traditionally been about employment, not profit. Even if not quite unfireable, like civil servants, French employees have been difficult and expensive to fire. At this writing, France is in the throes of a particularly agonizing period of high unemployment. Air France, desperately in the red, has just had a restructuring plan approved by its 40,000 employees which is described as "too little" by analysts. "We're not following the Anglo-Saxon strategy for getting profit at any price," a spokesman told the *International Herald Tribune* (April 15, 1994). "This is a humanistic restructuring plan that respects the employees, because without them, there is nothing."

But what about the battling, bickering anarchistic individualists we're also used to thinking of as French – those truckers holding up vacationers in the summer of '92, the farmers dumping tons of potatoes – or the fishermen dumping fish – in front of the town halls? Well, that hasn't changed either. Clans and corps have been warring since the days of the guilds. Office politics are full of this.

After one year in Paris as editorial director of Groupe Tests, Mike Johnson, former editor of *International Management*, advises foreigners to start out their work life in Paris by "accepting the unpleasant reality of management-labor polarization." This is how he puts it, writing in *Management Today* : "To work effectively in France the foreigner is obliged to unlearn people management methods and to re-learn new ones, to sharpen office skills, to rethink business ethics and to set aside any hope of creating a team effort... Try consensus management, try quality circles, even try acting like a human being. You will be tripped up at every turn. The French business environment is everything they didn't teach you at business school."

While this is especially true for the office of a high-tech magazine, it doesn't hurt to know that it might be like this in your office too.

Here are three charts of some Franco-Anglo-Saxon differences:

	STYLES of MANAGEMENT	
	FRANCE	U.S., U.K.
With subordinates	• gives instructions • answers questions • formal • little brainstorming	• listens • asks for info • informal • brainstorms
Decisions	• suspicious of risk • sends it up to next level	• loves risk • enjoys responsibility
Meetings	• floating agenda • concurrent mini-meetings	• strict agenda • subjects budgeted accordingly
Deadlines	• flexible, unless made absolutely clear	• very serious
Failure	• personal	• impersonal
Bankruptcy	• a stigma	• impersonal

STYLES of THINKING

FRENCH MANAGER

- principle-minded
- thinks circuitously
- distrusts simplicity
- tends to overcomplicate
- feels he never gets full, sophisticated answers from an American
- prefers a priori, logical arguments to reality

U.S., U.K. MANAGER

- fact-oriented
- thinks in a straight line
- distrusts complexity
- tends to oversimplify
- feels he never gets straightforward questions from a Frenchman
- experiments with reality

ORIENTATION

FRANCE	UNITED STATES
theoretical : deductive reasoning oriented	pragmatic : inductive reasoning oriented
Roman Catholic	Protestant
centralized	federal
hierarchical	egalitarian
quality of life oriented	high achievement oriented
power and relationships oriented	profit and task oriented
uncertainty avoiding	bold in risk taking

Perfect set-ups for cross-cultural friction, right? It's all there, in Chapter 16.

Chapter 16

Tricky Wickets

Foreigners' Complaints and French Executives' Suggestions

American managers hold more of an instrumental and functional view of organizations than do most of their European counterparts. An organization is perceived primarily as a set of tasks to be achieved through a problem-solving hierarcy where positions are defined in terms of tasks and functions. Under this model, a manager's superior knowledge about the subordinates' work is not necessarily needed and could even be detrimental to the proper functioning of a decentralized problem-solving hierarchy.

French managers hold more of a social and personal view. They conceive the organization more as a collectivity of people to be managed through a formal hierarchy where positions are clearly defined in terms of level of authority and status. Authority is attached more to individuals than it is to their offices or functions. As a result the authority of managers is enhanced by their superior knowledge. If they are found to know less than their subordinates about the task, their authority could suffer. Thus, managers must pretend to know more than their subordinates, even if they do not.

> André Laurent
> "Managing Across Cultures and National Borders"
> *Single Market Europe*

There is a big American business presence in France. To the over 1,000 American multinationals with branches and, often, European headquarters in Paris, Lyon and Sophia-Antipolis are added the many American companies that have been gobbled up by French companies in the last few years. To name a few, Rorer by Rhône-Poulenc, Pennwalt by Elf-Atochem, American Can and

Triangle by Péchiney, Honeywell and Zenith by Bull, Sterling Drug Winthrop by Sanofi, Square D by Schneider, Equitable Life by AXA.

Such is the international lottery today that many American managers working for these companies have found themselves out in the cold – or, of all places, in France.

From previous chapters, you can probably imagine that many of these managers have been pretty mystified, not to say bewildered, frustrated and possibly furious, about what's going on around them. Managers and executives transferred here by American companies are in the same boat – surrounded by French employees and French culture. Even being aware of the "high context" dimension of French culture; the French love of logic and insistence on hierarchy; their reticience with strangers; their different perceptions of time and space; their delight in the opposite sex, in their language, their food and their art – even keeping all this in mind, the surprises, paradoxes and contradictions of French people are not only endlessly diverting but can also be extremely disorienting when your career is on the line. Just about all of the Franco-American friction at the workplace comes from distress at not recognizing what is really happening, because of expecting something else – due to one's own mental programming. Anger and frustration have a way of sneaking up on people in a new culture.

An American marketing specialist, who was one of these managers transferred unexpectedly to France with a French company, drew up this memo for the benefit of newly-arrived Americans, after six teeth-gnashing months in Paris.

1. No one knows what they're supposed to do, but it doesn't matter, because no one is in charge.
   a) Everyone gets to do what they want.

2. No one is responsible.
   a) It's never absolutely clear who's in control.
   b) It's always someone else's fault.

3. Nothing should ever be decided in a meeting.
   a) The duration of each meeting should be one hour for each person in attendance.
   b) The number of meetings held on a subject should be inversely proportional to its level of importance and urgency.

4. Never ask anyone if they can help you solve a problem.
   a) See rule 1.

5. Never bother writing anything down.
   a) If something has been written down, don't show it to anyone unless
   b) you happen to get something confidential.
   c) If you want everyone to know something, write it down and circulate it with "confidential" on it.

6. However, if you called a meeting, be sure everything is written down, and given to you right away. Lock up these notes quickly, before they get changed.

7. Redundancy is not necessarily a problem.
   a) More is better (e.g. meetings, organizations, paperwork).

8. Never plan where the results can be measured.

9. Any communication should be directed up, not down.

10. Getting promoted depends on how well you know the system and can manipulate the hierarchy.

11. Don't contradict the boss.

12. After satisfying the above, try (but not terribly hard) to find a profit.

It's a bitter, explosive list. It's not surprising that the very bright but abrasive and inflexible young man who wrote it was fired.

But while his arrows are far from the mark in lots of French companies, or French branches of American companies, so many Americans working in France have similar reactions that they bear attention. What the list demonstrates is just how different French management/culture is from Anglo-Saxon management/culture. That there are at least two different management "roads to Rome" (and to making profits) is proven by the global success of French multinationals. Here are a few of them among the top European Union 500 with net profits for 1993, according to *International Management*: Elf Aquitaine, Rhône-Poulenc, Saint Gobain, Total, BSN, Bouygues.

To give you an idea of what that bitter list bubbled up from, and what might be awaiting you, I've collected the problems and frustrations of Anglo-Saxon, German and Scandinavian managers and executives that have been discussed during the last eight years in Culture Crossings seminars, together with comments about them from more experienced foreigners.

For the *French* context of the French working place, two leading French executives, both graduates of the Ecole Polytechnique (X) give their points of view of the main considerations that foreigners, and Americans in particular, should be aware of in handling things here: Claude Bébéar, Président of the Group AXA, one of France's most dynamic entrepreneurs, the mover and shaker behind AXA's acquisition of Equitable Life; and Jean-Claude Guez, a partner of Andersen Consulting*, who works closely with Americans in Paris, where he runs a truly multinational unit of professionals from 14 countries in Europe and the Orient.

Claude Bébéar: The French Spirit

"Our mathematical training gives us intellectual agility and imagination – nothing is more creative than mathematics. We tend to think in concepts.

"We are *séduits* by what is brilliant. French people look for solutions which are the most brilliant and the most elegant, not the most pragmatic or efficient. The Citroën car is a caricature of how we think... it is elegant, but fragile.

"As descendants of the Latins and the Gaulois, we are very individualist, not very disciplined, and quite chauvinistic... the French worker has pride in his honor, and in his *patrie*...he is very *cocorico*. He is vain, *il aime paraître* – he likes to show off – but he has a sense of *équipe* (team)...and he is a *débrouillard*, he gets on with things.

"At the same time, *le patron français* (the head of a French company) has an emotional bond with his employees. In the U.S., if someone makes a mistake, he is thrown out. Here, we don't throw out the people we work with, we try to keep them. If someone makes a mistake, we pardon him. If we have to fire someone, we do it, but with a bad conscience. In the U.S., American employees don't put their heart in their companies; they have a contract. In France, an employee marries his company, his heart is in it.

"French executives have a long-term view. They think in terms of 10 years, while Americans, mindful of their quarterly statements, think in terms of about two years.

"In business, it is the word of two men of good faith that matters, not the written contract drawn up by a team of lawyers, as in the U.S. We have a quite different view of the law, more philosophical, more about what the

* Now named Accenture.

spirit of the law is. Breaking the law here is not a terrible sin, as in the U.S. If a new law is passed, we consider the arguments that were given in Parlement against it. For issues evolve.

"The main thing, if one works in a foreign country, is to try to understand the mentality, to enter into it, and not to be judgmental. Take the question of deadlines, for instance. In a company, there must be discipline – but there must be also liberty for creativity. French people are more complicated to manage than Americans or Germans. What you have to decide is if you want people to be geniuses, or to be on time."

Jean-Claude Guez: French Mental Software

"One of the most important things for Americans to take into consideration is the rigorous training by the state educational system (instituted largely by Napoleon 200 years ago) in pure mathematics and science that most French executives have gone through, finely tuning brains that on the one hand can make swift analyses of situations, and, on the other, insist on 100 percent performance perfection in products.

"Scientific people in France (the business and industry elite) have had 10 years of schooling in demonstrating mathematical theories. Whether in chemistry, physics or pure math, they have never had to understand the reasons the theory works through examples; it is by demonstrating through mathematical equations that they have had to show that the theory sticks together. Therefore, French *ingénieurs* design systems that aim at being 100 percent perfect. If you ask them to design something fast, such as a computerized billing system that is only 80 percent perfect but will have a short time-to-market, they won't be much interested. They will ask themselves, 'Why did I go through these very tough long studies, if people ask me to do something which only partially solves the problem?'

"The Ariane satellite launcher is a good example of how they work best. The *ingénieurs* spent the time necessary to get the blueprint 'just right' before anything was built, designing a long-term modular vehicle which started out with light loads, and didn't have to be modified but simply added onto, like cubes of Lego, those childrens' building blocks, as the loads got heavier.

The Advantage of Thinking French

"Since French people take a much longer time over the blueprint, experimenting with numbers, not material, once the model is perfected, the product doesn't have to be totally reorganized for a larger model, like the different Boeings, for example. The American way is to try to see if you can build 'something' long before it is perfected on the drawing board. If it doesn't work, scrap it and start over.

"This brings up another important Franco-American difference, the battle between form and substance. The French like to discuss substance. They want to dig into the substance and get the whole of it. Only then will they start with the plan.

"Americans start from the opposite direction. Americans are keen on form. They build an empty plan first, or outline. They move subjects and paragraphs around. The French never do. By the time the French start to write, everything is already in its place. The bright guys in France, the ones who address complex problems, this is the way they work.

"One of the consequences of this is that American business reports are about two to three times longer than French reports. The French, already immersed in all the details, write context-dependent reports. American reports drive them nuts. They cry, 'Why do we have to read all this stuff we already know?'

"This different emphasis on form and substance creates major Franco-American clashes."

For French and American movers and shakers, these different modes of reasoning, as noted in the last chapter, produce two fundamentally different ways of perceiving and handling their respective worlds. The resulting Franco-American friction: their cultural vision leads the French to find the Americans superficial, if not sloppy, in their method, while the Americans find the French "wacky" or "endlessly wasting time" over "details."

The Downsides of Thinking French – For Americans

• *The Spirit of NO Compromise*

French analysis is so exhaustive that when they finally get the answer, there is often no budging them. This produces situations like this:

"An important study had been made about an executive-level issue to be decided," said an American executive of a French multinational. "Two executives expressed mutually exclusive opinions about it. Rather than actually listen carefully to what the other one said and try to reach a mutually acceptable compromise, they simply agreed that their positions were irreconcilable, and walked out. So nothing could come of that study – an important one."

J.-.C. *Guez*: "If you have worked something out mathematically to 100 percent perfection, how are you going to compromise? Anything else is simply wrong. Whether *ingénieurs* or diplomats, this is the way the French mind often works, so Americans need to realize it will take a lot of their own energy and time to get their French counterparts to compromise. By the way, the primary meaning of the French word *compromis* is a *faux-ami*, i.e. it does not translate into 'compromise' but rather into something like 'a potentially bad deal that one might be ashamed to make public.' 'Compromising' in French sometimes conveys a taste of 'losing'... or at least 'losing face'..."

• *Lackluster French Efforts at Marketing*

J.-C. Guez: "This is part of the same mindset. They think that if they design the best, if it's technically or aesthetically brilliant, people will buy it. Most French people aren't good at marketing, at selling, because they don't care about it so much as about the process, the creation."

• *Planning Preferred over Executing*

One of the American complaints about this French love of abstractions is that, for the French, the plan is the exciting part of a project, not implementing it.

"They equate writing a beautiful report with executing the project," observed an American director. "Then they delegate someone else to start a new plan, while the whole company has amnesia about the first plan."

Creating the plan is not only more interesting than executing it, it involves much more glory.

• *Meetings*

J.-C. Guez: "This scientific mindset is one of the main reasons that meetings in France seem, to Americans, to go on forever. The French people at the meetings want to go over and over every aspect of the project or projects under discussion."

"We spend up to 15 meetings defining a question," said an American banker.

"Yesterday we had a meeting and went over and over the same points, everyone giving their ideas," groaned an American middle manager in a cosmetics company. "Then after the third or fourth point, after they'd been labored and labored, my boss, who chaired it, lets a guy go back to a previous point.. NO decision was reached. There was no real agenda. My boss had a list. After about half the things discussed, he said, 'Oh, I'll take care of that.' I had a proposal to hurry up getting certain financial information out, to send it in chapters. Everyone said, 'Oh, great idea, thanks!' But the guy who could implement it may or may not. In which case, it was four and a half hours of NOTHING!"

Kevin R., a geologist with Elf Aquitaine, which, as mentioned above, is one of France's most profitable multinationals: "The meetings are so disorganized here. In the U.S., one person speaks, for a certain amount of time; a decision is reached and it's decided who will implement it. In France, there is a free flow of information. Two or three conversations are going simultaneously – while the presenter is presenting! It's difficult for decision making – difficult for Americans."

J.-C. Guez: "Internationally, there are three kinds of meetings for decisions: official meetings, where formal decisions are announced, informal meetings where decisions are reached on the issues to be studied, and small group meetings deciding who will do what. In France, it's rare that formal decisions are reached in meetings. Meetings are to poll opinions and to inform or warn of something. They're for keeping in context, it's part of being polychronic. This is so even at meetings at the cabinet level in government. When they're televised, you can see that the ministers are reading their mail, passing messages or having small mini-meetings, clearly not wracking their brains to make an important decision."

• *French Time*

"What do I have to do so that my French staff gets to meetings on time?" fumed an American director. "I've tried everything but giving a prize – a stuffed toad, for instance to the last arrival."

J.-C..Guez: "French people are strongly polychronic and not obsessed by time. As far as punctuality at meetings is concerned, this is an emotional thing. There is a mental/psychological resistance to the 'military' aspect of companies, the hierarchy and so on. French people are individualists, they want to have a sense of independence, a margin of freedom, and not to be part of a mold. They have fun playing with and by-passing rules (and laws...).

"Another reason is that most of the time, at the hour the meeting is called, they have something else in process and don't want to cut it short. Someone is in their office or they are on the phone. It is very rare that you stop by in an office and someone says, 'Please come back later, I'm supposed to be in a meeting now.' So, bottom line, being 10 to 15 minutes late in a meeting is extremely common, and accepted by most French executives."

• *Deadlines*

A German director: "How can I get my employees to understand that deadlines have the word dead in them – that you're dead if you're late?"

J.-C. *Guez*: "Concerning deadlines, there is a flexible attitude. In France, ASAP (As Soon As Possible) doesn't mean, as in Sweden, 'yesterday', but 'maybe next week'... The French have two kinds of deadlines, hard and soft, a *date cible*, a general target, and a *date butoir*, a critical deadline. A *butoir* is a buffer, the wall that stops trains in railway terminals. If you have an important deadline, you must make it clear that this is a *date butoir*, or they will not try terribly hard, saying, *'La terre continuera à tourner quand même,'* or 'The earth will continue to rotate, nevertheless.'"

• *No Newcomer Orientation*

"I arrive the first day and find Monique," says a newly arrived public relations strategist. "She's my new boss. So Monique shows me my desk. Period. No one tells me when lunch is. No one tells me where the bathroom is."

"The first week I'm meeting about 1,000 new people," says an electronics engineer. "I don't speak French and there's no organization chart. How am I supposed to know who all these people are?"

Jean-Claude Guez: "There is the assumption on the part of the French that people will sense the context and work it out... that they're adults, able to manage alone their own destiny. Remember the joke that the French have about 55 million political parties, i.e. as many as inhabitants. Most Latin people are like this. They don't like check lists, or to be told what to do. They find it very odd in London, for instance, the traffic signs saying 'SLOW' in addition to signaling a curve, or the word 'over' at the bottom of a document. My secretary made this comment about Americans newly arrived in France: 'It's amazing – you have to take care of them almost like kids from the moment they arrive.'"

• *Cold Reception*

"Everything is done so that you'll totally deflate," said *Jeffrey Tarr*, who arrived in Paris with Bain Consultants, straight from Princeton and Harvard Business School. "Maybe you call it *bizutage*, or hazing, but I call it ego-bashing. I was ready to quit after a few months of it. You have to be tough. I guess that's the point."

Bizutage is particularly cruel in French universities and *Grandes Ecoles*, sometimes perverse or obscene, or even fatal. It's been around as long as the University of Paris (founded in 1257). It seems the Knights Templar went in for this sort of initiation in a big way in the 14th century. It's said that, among other things, they were obliged to urinate on a crucifix to demonstrate that they were not under Satan's spell. If they were struck dead, they were. Otherwise, they weren't, and were pure enough to be a member of the Order. Again, *Plus ça change, plus c'est la même chose*. French people will tell you that at every new step in life, the people around you will test you, in a sort of toughening-up *bizutage*.

This is true even for high-level executives.

Larry Waisanen puts it like this: "They want to be sure you're competent before they trust you, before they follow your orders. You have to prove yourself."

There could be other reasons for a cool reception: French reserve with strangers, and an ambiguity about an American in their midst. As in physics, where observing something changes it, so it is in foreign cultures, particularly in the workplace. The fact of an American simply being there changes everything. If he is strong-willed, a *fonceur*, that is, someone with a tremendous drive, then they'll be dreading him telling them what to do.

Whatever the reason, expect a cool reception and don't take it personally.

• Information Retention

After meetings, information retention goes to the top of the foreign managers' hit list.

"They hoard it. It goes with the lack of teamwork," said *Al Langenacker*, part of the senior circle at Groupe Bull. "You're working on a project and in the middle of it, someone will say, 'No, that's not right. Joe told me so last week.' He should have volunteered this a long time before. But he says, 'No one asked me.'"

"Information is not intentionally withheld," said a banker at the Banque Indosuez. "But you have to ask for it."

J. C. Guez: "A newcomer should try to make a blueprint of what I call the Power Map, of who flows information to whom, of who influences whom. Who has the power is usually not at all obvious, but very very important. The social connections between men and women are also very important. He should take female employees to lunch, one by one, to get his bearings... to learn how to navigate. Not just navigating the hierarchy, but often much more.

"As for *organigrammes*, or organization charts, many companies don't have them by design. There is simply a phone book. That is because someone at the executive level doesn't want the Power Map to be known."

Information is power everywhere, but it has imperial status in France. At great expense, a French bank installed a computer system to provide centralized, up-to-date data about its clients. But all the computer spat out was old, limited or irrelevant. After researching the question for a year, the bank discovered that the information was there where it had always been – with the branch managers who knew the clients. They didn't dream of giving up information to a data bank.

If information is power, secrecy is its handmaiden. Secrecy has always been a matter of prudence in France. You don't want the police or the tax people to know too much. In the days when people were taxed on the number of windows they had, they boarded them up. Concierges used to be in the pay of the police, so that you had to be wily indeed to evade their web. The only safe path was never to tell anyone anything, and pull down the shades.

Méfiance (mistrust), another aspect of secrecy, is a gut reaction of the French to everyone they've not known forever. Since they don't know you, how can they know how you will use this information, provided they admit that they have it? Since information is so hard to get, their being so secretive, it takes on a value. That's another reason not to give it out. It might come in useful, some day, when *you* need to know something. You'll have something to barter.

The "high context" dimension of the French, Hall's term for the density of their verbal and non-verbal communication, is the answer to why, as Americans like to complain, they "only give half the answer to a question." This is because they take it for granted that you know the other half. They themselves have a horror of being "treated like babies," therefore don't want to insult you by treating you like one.

• *"They Won't Do One Thing at a Time!"*

An American director: "They're very competent workers at all levels, but not as efficient as they might be. There are too many distractions."

Judy Paynter, American Airlines: "It's very difficult to talk one-on-one to the person you need to talk to when you're being interrupted all the time – by the phone, by other managers. It's bothersome!"

There's nothing you can do about distractions. Part of being "high context" means there is always a lot going on. Something urgent might be happening to change their schedule or their whole approach to something. They can't afford to miss the information. They can handle it. You'll get used to it.

• *Decisions*

"No one wants to take decisions," deplores a Swedish manager in computers. "They're pushed off horizontally, to a committee, with no one responsible. Or they're kicked up level by level to the top, where they sit, because the CEO doesn't have – can't possibly have – the time to make all the decisions in a huge company. In our business, with the life of a product so short, you have to be out in the market fast, with the best you can do. You might have something that really is the best, but if the competition comes out six months before, he's already got 60 percent of the market, and you can forget about your perfect product."

"We are not concerned with being the first with a product in the marketplace, but with being the best," a French executive told me.

An English banker in a Paris bank: "The top dog makes the decisions—but doesn't see fit to tell anyone. So it happened that a leading American professor of economics came over for two weeks of arranged conferences on a bank project – and when he arrived, the *PDG* (CEO) said, 'No! I decided against that project!' The professor's trip, therefore, was for nothing."

The combination of uncertainty-avoidance and the influence of Louis XIV (approving all expenses himself, holding all the reins himself and insisting on the respect of every level of hierarchy) often work effectively to bring everything to the top to decide, or to put off deciding.

Boss-Subordinate

• *Lack of Teamwork, Hesitation to Speak Out*

A J. P. Morgan vice president, desperate to get some opinions from his team, hit on the idea of letting his subordinates tell a computer what they thought. It worked like magic.

"People at functional levels don't dare do anything innovative until they've checked up and down," said the director of an American pharmaceutical multinational in Strasbourg. "The lower echelons resent and despise the *cadres* and all the top management. You can't have any teamwork under those conditions.

"So we took 12 *cadres* and 20 infrastructure people – financial and analytical – and sent them to the head office in Chicago. The first thing we did was take them all to a topless bar down the street, and leave them there. They couldn't believe it. Soon the lower levels began to really believe they could say what they thought and not be punished. Then they refused to go back to France and be humiliated by the *cadres*, now that they'd seen there was another way to work.

"I had to tell them, 'Your mission is to go back and support change — sow the seeds of a new way to survive, with opportunity and challenge.'

"These people have a superb education – they just need to be managed properly."

• *"They Don't Follow Orders"*

"I give an order and explain exactly what I want," said the director of a software company. "But they're individualists. They'll do it as they please, according to some aesthetic idea or something else. It won't be what I ordered. Or they come to me with problems they should have solved themselves. So they 're both sheep and individualists at the same time."

J.-C. Guez: "American managers must be aware of the intensely math-oriented school training in France when they give projects to their French subordinates. As a student here, you can never take anything for granted – a formula, for instance. You must be able to demonstrate why this is so. You must be able to understand why, at the deepest level, something is happening. This continues in your adult life, at work. The key word is context. If you give a Frenchman a task, you must give him the full picture. If not, he won't do it."

The Allensteig Institute in Germany researched the percentage of "yes" answers of managers in various European countries to this statement: "Basically, I carry out instructions from my superior."

France's score was the lowest, down there with Italy. But when asked how likely they were to follow orders if their reason was convinced, France was at the top of the list.

Be sure your French subordinate understands what you want. As the French are high context and communicate in codes and nuances, implicitly, he might not attach the same meanings to your words that you do, particularly if you're not speaking his language.

Above all, convince your subordinate that your project plan *makes sense*.

If it's your colleagues or your boss you need to convince, engineer *George Greene* (Elf Aquitaine) has this advice: "If you have an idea you want to push through, then it is a matter for your personal diplomacy to involve all the individuals who will be affected. You have to see them individually and make sure that all of their possible objections are covered.

Be sure you've won them over. Then, when there's a meeting, it's smooth going."

Advice from a Frenchman to his French team leader in London, before their first meeting with English colleagues working on the same project for their French multinational: "You have to be careful what orders you give to the English – they're likely to follow them."

• *Blame Denial, Again*

"How can you trust people who won't admit they're wrong?" said an exasperated American director.

J.-C. Guez: "French allergy to criticism is probably related to the excess of criticism they had to endure from parents and teachers when they were growing up. As adults, they won't put up with it, or acknowledge error. You have to make it indirect, for it to be effective. For instance, you say, 'It would be nice if, next time, you could do it this way.'"

Larry Waisanen agrees: "If someone has made a mistake you want him to correct, the thing to do is to tell him indirectly. 'I think there is something wrong here,' you say pleasantly. No accusations. No stern tone. Then he'll look it over and be very proud of finding 'an error.' Whereas accusing him of it will bring an explosion of denials, possibly unpleasantness."

Remember that, "One doesn't have the right to make a mistake in France." (Professor *Odile Challe*, Chapter 6)

"In America, admitting error is not only seen as honest, but important," said *Dixon Thayer*, vice president of Scott Europe. "In the U.S., you're not perceived as learning much if you don't make mistakes. Therefore you won't move up, at least not in this company. It's like skiing – you're not going to learn how if you don't take a lot of falls. But in affiliation cultures like France, there is the matter of face involved. If a senior manager makes a mistake, he and everyone below him loses face. If he, or a lower-level manager, admits a mistake, it's perceived as a weakness."

Whereas, in the U.S....

"I've hurt myself a lot by admitting mistakes," said *Cathie Lowney*, strategist for Groupe Bull. "It's hard to remember not to!"

• *Lying by a Subordinate or Colleague*

J.-C. Guez: "Again, the technique must be indirect. Never confrontational. Never say, 'I know you're lying.' Find out the facts from someone else. If you get them, and know he is lying, turn it into a joke – be humoristic, not angry."

• *Unavailability of Boss*

American middle manager: "My boss is never available – I can never get to see him — and then I get chastised because I couldn't read his mind!"

His boss: "I never asked to have this high-paid American working for me. He asks too many questions, he needs too much support, I have had to spend an exorbitant amount of time with him. When I tell him to do something, he should just do it, and not ask all these questions."

American middle manager: "He spent very little time with me ever!"

J.-C. *Guez*: "American management expects to hear about a problem. French management expects not to hear about it – a manager expects his subordinate to use the *Système D*, often leading to comments like*'débrouillez vous'* or – a German version of it, *'démerden Sie Sich'* and get on with it. So in terms of supervision, there is a need for the manager to make spot checks to be sure things are in good shape, because the French subordinate won't tell you spontaneously, unless it is a strategy problem."

Americans are usually used to conferring in detail with their boss about a project, and then given a lot of freedom to carry it out – its success being the basis for the next promotion.

Working for a high-contexted French boss, who is authoritarian, impatient and clearly not keen on having an American around who might try to tell him what to do, is therefore a challenge. French managers tend to mix a concern with details and a general laissez faire ("read my mind") approach. There is more close supervision of certain parts of the process. Often the key is that American leadership is situational, while French leadership usually proceeds from academic degrees – and knowing what is *comme il faut*.

• *Absence of Praise From a French Boss*

Edward T. Hall puts it like this in *Understanding Cultural Differences*:

> *"Because the French are both high-context and polychronic, they expect everyone to know how to do everything properly. They won't tell subordinates or colleagues anything, yet they get irritated if co-workers don't do something right... The French rarely compliment employees on their performance and are critical of any errors."*

An engineer at Du Pont de Nemours: "It's amazing, French bosses don't seem ever to compliment their subordinates on a job well done.

When I did, my subordinate went all red in the face. When he heard that I'd telexed what a great job he'd done to Wilmington, he could hardly handle it."

J.-C. Guez: "It's a question of attitude. We expect people to perform well, so we don't mention it. The French hate to hear *pas mal* – not bad – which is high praise. They're immediately suspicious, thinking, 'What does he want from me?' We rarely use any word meaning 'outstanding.' For us, these words soon lose their value and become fake. It's like selling washing powder —'ultra extra super' which means nothing. In fact, the absence of criticism is itself praise here.

"This difference in attitude of the two countries is very evident in the style of their performance reports. If an American executive saw a French evaluation of someone outstanding, he'd say to himself, 'This guy is no good.' Like everything else, performance reports must be related to the values of the country."

An American multinational with its European headquarters in Paris tried to import an American management-strategy success to France, Performance Management. The result of the effusive compliments to the employees was anger and hostility. "Why are they ridiculing us? They couldn't care less about us. What do they want from us?"

So how do you motivate them? Not with money, not with bonuses. They'll be suspicious of your motives. Appeal to their honor, individually. Make them proud of the company with television spots or full page color ads in major newspapers.

To French people, the absence of criticism is praise, probably also a result of the non-stop criticism they grew up with. All this takes getting used to. When you do, unsuspected new worlds open up for you – abstract ones you hadn't dreamed of.

Employee Relations

• *Sexual Harassment*

French women like compliments and French men like to give them. It's called Latin gallantry.

Sumner Calhoon, a pretty and elegantly dressed young Texas banker, soon got used to this in Paris. "I like the way you get scrutinized here as a woman, the way there's a certain look in dressing you're expected to pick up on, and the men let you know how you're doing with it. I went to a cocktail party last week and was told by a man I'd never seen before that my skirt was too long and very *ringard* ... old-fashioned. At first you mind – but then you realize – they care!"

The attention given by men to women at the office can surprise an Anglo-Saxon. Mike Johnson, after his year in Paris as editorial director for Groupe Tests, wrote in *Management Today*, "In the office, it is always open season, at least verbally. Legs, lips, bottoms, breasts, necks and knees are fair game for the men's respectful consideration. Aside from cheek-pecking, the fooling around rarely becomes physical. Only once did I witness an exception. One of my managers playfully grabbed the left buttock of an art-department mother-of-two... there was a little yelp (more like a yes than a no) from the woman. The man explained to me and to her that he was only expressing his admiration for the roundness of the object, an unavoidable impulse on purely aesthetic grounds."

Sometimes all this gallantry goes too far, and is objectionable, even for French women. Polls show that this is more and more often the case. French law is beginning to catch up, but only just. A new law was passed in 1992, making sexual harassment a crime in France for the first time. A conviction can mean a fine of up to FF 100,000, plus up to a year in prison – but it applies only to "hierarchical superiors" who make known "by a word, gesture, attitude or behavior a view to compel an employee to respond to a solicitation of a sexual nature."

No recourse is suggested for harassment by colleagues.

The comments of Véronique Neiertz, the Socialist state secretary for women's rights and daily life who introduced the bill, are culturally illuminating:

"I do not say there is not sexual harassment between colleagues, but when there is no link of power or economic dependence, the woman or man being harassed can defend themselves," she told a French newspaper, adding: "We must not end up with the excesses of the U.S., where the slightest glance can be misinterpreted."

• *"Tu" or "Vous?"*

The whole subject of *"tu"* for "you" is a can of worms. Don't open it if you can possibly avoid it. Some pointers;

1. *Tu* is for children and dogs – and other relationships that don't apply to you, a foreigner: close family relatives and school friends. Stick to *vous* (the polite, formal form of "you"). Say that, as a foreigner, you can't cope with more than one form of address.

2. In advertising, public relations, high-tech, journalism, all artistic groups (cinema, choral, etc. and some other companies), everyone *"tutoies"* each other. So you'll have to go along with it or be a "snob."

3. In most banks and industries in France, *vous* is correct, elegant and safe.

4. If your boss calls you *"tu"* in a formal *"vous"* company, watch out. Don't be flattered and think he is being friendly. *Tu* does not imply intimacy. He is laying a claim on you. You can demand things of a *tu* person that you would be much more careful and reserved about requesting from a *vous* person. "You (*tu*) can stay late tonight, *n'est-ce pas?"* This is much harder to say to you-*vous*. Above all, don't call your secretary *tu*.

5. If you have already started the *tu* with someone, you're stuck with it. There's no going back, unless you're looking for enemies.

6. It makes hierarchy even harder to figure out. French subordinates are usually comfortable calling their bosses *monsieur*, and the bosses are comfortable being called *monsieur*. It reminds everybody who's who. If you relax to first names, there is still no reason to slip into *tu*. In some other countries yes, but not in France.

7. Things are changing, in that young people out of school may call each other *tu*, but not everywhere. A young French doctor, age 29: "I don't allow anyone to call me *tu* except my family and grade school friends."

• *Secretaries*

In an elite society of *Grandes Ecoles* graduates who have all the command buttons (Chapter 11), guess who are pretty near the bottom rung of the ladder, without expectations of climbing even one rung: secretaries. Nor, usually, do they wish to. Gilberte Beaux, financier Jimmy Goldsmith's top assistant, who is now running Adidas, is the great glorious exception that proves the rule. "Secretary" in French is the only professional noun that has both male and female genders. You can be *un* or *une sécretaire*. There is a message in this.

I don't mean to incite secretaries to insurrection, or to overlook the ones in France who do a splendid professional job, but, if you're lucky enough to have one, don't be surprised if there is a certain lack of motivation.

"Secretaries I had in the U.S. that I thought were incompetent would be great over here," said the audit manager of an American multinational in

Paris. "I have to wheedle and coo to them here to get anything done at all. They won't even make coffee. We have to do our own memos! Because they can't. And I have to give my secretary a good review or she'd sulk, stay home and call in sick."

• *Hygiene*

Most companies in France seem to have at least one employee who makes American noses suffer, even in winter.

"I didn't have to mind that fellow's B.O. too much, not until we had to drive down to Lyon together with some others last January," said the production manager of a soft drinks company. "There we were, squeezed together, three of us in the back seat. I tell you, it was bad. It was maybe the coldest day of the year but never mind, the only way we survived was to open the sun roof. Now whenever we have to take him with us in a car, we say, 'Well, it's going to be a suntop ride!'"

When the employee in question is someone they want to send to the U.S., American management agonizes. Clearly out of the question to send him without a change in habits. But how to achieve it? Strong men quake before the prospect of approaching this taboo. One of the American pharmaceutical multinationals asked my advice about a brilliant and otherwise elegant but particularly malodorous engineer. Houston was screaming for him but the CEO-Europe shrank from this doomed transfer. It was finally decided that only the company doctor could do the job, delicately linking soap and deodorants with health.

You can hardly call French noses less sensitive – after all, who invented perfume? Who produces it? The most sensitive nose in the world probably belongs to a Frenchman.

"But, you see," a French banker told me, "the smell of manly sweat is not perceived as socially unacceptable. In fact, some women say they actually like it."

Some English people appear to have similar noses to the French. Once I invited an English professor of corporate management to be a guest speaker at one of my seminars for American executives. As he stepped into my house, the air reeked so, that I was obliged to hand him some soap, a towel and a deodorant, as my salon doesn't have a suntop. He was less put out than surprised.

"Smells must be a cross-cultural problem," he said.

Indeed.

• *Making Friends*

It helps to remember that the word "friendly" doesn't exist in the French language (Chapter 1). As reserved as French people are with strangers, so with their friends they are extremely close. They "grapple their friends to themselves with hoops of steel" (Shakespeare) and by the time you meet them at the office, they already have as many friends as they can handle.

As for making friends at work, that is, to see people socially that you see at work, by all means try. Maybe you will. But it's not part of the culture, so it is likely to be slow, if at all. The French are famous for compartmentalizing their work and their non-work relationships. Your boss probably won't invite you to dinner, even if he has spent some time in the U.S. – although, if he has, it is somewhat less unlikely.

If your boss asks you out for lunch, fine. He probably won't, and will be embarrassed if you ask him. The same goes for subordinates.

"Socializing out of the office with other office families is dramatically missing in the French environment," said *Robert Elliott*, director of systems information for Groupe Bull. "You don't get a sense that you know your co-workers, and Americans do rely on this. Of course we are part of the problem, until we are no longer incompetent in the French language. Maybe it 's too stressful for them."

"After being in Paris for three years, someone at the office invited me to make a fourth at squash!" said *Kirk Coyne*, in a tone of amazement. "And a week later, someone else asked us to dinner!"

In some French companies, it's against the rules for managers to have lunch with the support staff, or to see them after office hours.

See the Coda for more about making French friends.

Chapter 17

Executive Roundup
What the Multicultural Veterans Say

Getting a group of French people to work together virtually defies the law of dynamics: each of them runs his or her own fiefdom and the operating principle (from the top down, which is the only way French business works) appears to be "management by information retention."

Richard Hill
We Europeans

How fast and how smoothly you take to this new working arena depends first on you – on how open and diligent you are – and how closely you read the last chapter! – and secondly, on how much encouragement and enlightenment you get from the people around you. Six American executives, Larry Waisanen (Lafarge Coppée), Jeff Dore (Atochem), Robert Pingeon (Cigna), Kirk Coyne (Lafarge Fondu), Steve Skoczylas (J. P. Morgan), and Dixon Thayer (Scott) veterans of years in France, reflect on their French experience below.

Larry Waisanen

Larry Waisanen, vice-president and chief controller for Lafarge Coppée in France, now transferred to Istanbul, has been quoted several times in these pages for his astute observations. Coming here straight from Michigan he was at first mystified by the whole scene, and finally, delighted. He arrived totally unprepared for the way French accounts are done. It took him a lot of French lessons and experience to get onto it. When he did, he found the mathematical infrastructure of French minds a revelation. Three years down the road in Paris, he said, "In the beginning here, I thought they were handling the numbers upside down and backwards. I was wrong. They do things with numbers I would never have thought of – I found out how creative mathematics can be.

"Another aspect of working here I find exhilarating is that everything is negotiable. With the auditors here, if you present a sound economic principle for not following an established accounting practice, they're likely to accept it, if you present a good argument. And they'll help you with the reasoning. They love to reason.

"In the U.S., rules are rules. You don't discuss them."

Kirk Coyne

Kirk Coyne, now chief financial officer at Lafarge Fondu International in France, was fresh out of Texas when he arrived in Paris four years ago. He had never been abroad before. He didn't speak much French. France turned out to be a much greater challenge than he had imagined.

"I felt like quitting several times that first year," he said. "I was lost in ambiguities and nuances and the *non-dit* (unsaid), and in the subtleties and the arrogance of the guys from X and ENA and the other *Grandes Ecoles*. I took French lessons initially full-time after arriving in France and later, for half a day twice a week for some time thereafter. After a year and about 500 hours, I felt comfortable. This is an investment you have to make if you want to work in a French environment."

Coyne found that his labors paid off. From being a provincial on the outside looking in, he gradually became a flexible, non-judgmental international, aware that there are several ways of approaching problems, reasoning and doing things, and exhilarated by his new-found versatility.

"First of all, I had to prove myself. I thought the fact that I was hired was proof enough, but that idea was completely false. The French have a skeptical respect for Americans, but think we have a short-sighted way of looking at things. They see Anglo-Saxons (Germans, English and Americans) as more structured and disciplined at work, and want to benefit from the local Americans to help them introduce more structure in their organizations – but not necessarily in themselves. They tend to criticize others more than to admit their own faults.

"They're great on analysis and reflection, much greater than on action and reaction, and they realize this. They have disciplined minds – I never heard anyone explain ideas and analyze problems so well. The way they formulate and articulate arguments is astounding. I often marvel at their clarity and wonder why nothing gets done around here the way you hear it described. Well, I think one reason is that their behavior isn't disciplined – deadlines are flexible, to say the least, and they have a tendency not to follow orders, but to do things the way they think they ought to be done.

"Another is that they're better at developing strategy than implementing it. The mental, creative aspect of any project is more important to them than actually doing it.

"A third reason is that they are simply not efficiency-oriented.

"And certainly less profit-oriented. It's like profit is a fallout of the system – nice to have it, but not the main preoccupation. While in the U.S., of course, profitability is an obsession. The idea here is, if you have a technical advance and an interesting product, maybe someone will want it.

"After a while you understand that the meetings are to bring people together, build rapport and build consensus for the long term, and that the French are able to visualize things for the long perspective and see life as a contextual continuum – a series of actions that lead in a certain direction. Things take so long to be completed, the maturation period from idea to decision to production is so long and so many people have fed ideas into them, that in the end, no one is responsible. Part of the maddening reality is that it is never clear whose fault anything is – so that no one is to blame! They're much less individualistic than Americans, no matter what their reputation is. In the U.S. we tend to compartmentalize actions and results in isolation, without seeing the full consequences.

"The bottom line is that it is a fascinating and exciting place to be – always different, a free sociology lesson going on around you all day. Things are not direct, people behave in ways that merit various interpretations, what you see is not what you get. It is a culture of flexible principles. The rules of right and wrong are circumstantial. For an American used to direct talk and a perceptible action chain, knowing who is doing what, it is an incredible revelation of how different things can be. I'm continually amazed at how I've accepted ambiguity – I even enjoy it sometimes! Because the French are very professional and very concerned about doing a good job, and at the same time, so creative, undisciplined and ambiguous, you never know what will unfold. So there's never a dull moment! It's fun!"

Coyne's advice to newcomers is loud and clear: "Don't come here assuming that you're going to impose your thinking on them. If you're not flexible, if you have a hard and fast idea about how things should be done, then you had better take the first plane back!"

Jeff Dore

No one has pondered Franco-American cultural differences in the workplace more than chemical engineer Jeff Dore, who was transferred to Paris when Elf-Atochem bought Philadelphia's Pennwalt. He contrasts the French way of attacking a problem, the painstaking, thorough critical analysis described above by Kirk Coyne, with the profit-run, time-to-market haste typical of Americans. His theme is that the two approaches are complementary, and that if they each would modify their own slightly, and learn to flexibly apply more of one or less of the other approach, depending on the problem, they'd have the markets sewed up. This is how he puts it:

"Methodology is so important to the French, and they're so cautious about taking risks, that in a crisis, if a compromise has to be made, they'll make it in favor not of shortcuts to save time, but more analysis. Americans are so action-oriented, and so risk-willing, that in a crisis they'll opt for short cuts. Both approaches can be appropriate. You could probably say that Americans are a little too eager to hurry things up, and often make mistakes through lack of thorough analysis, and that the French are a little too slow because of their insistence on totally thorough analysis. The really sharp international manager can handle both styles, and chooses the style according to the problem at hand. He's a rarity – ingrained habits of how things are done come from the culture. Personally, I think the French are moving towards faster action, and the Americans towards more in-depth analysis, and that's what they both need to do."

Robert Pingeon

Directeur Général of Cigna Insurance Company of Europe, Robert Pingeon originally came to Paris in 1989 as Director of Chubb Compagnie d'Assurances. He contributed the following text:

Prior to moving to Europe in 1985, I lived in New York City and for 10 years was a regular commuter on the I.R.T. express subway line. I witnessed screaming matches almost daily, accompanied by verbal and physical abuse of about every kind. In Paris, when I meet newly arrived Americans from smaller towns who, speaking no French, complain about the rudeness and aggressiveness of Parisians, I can only laugh.

Aside from its great beauty and rich cultural heritage, Paris is a clean, efficient and functioning city. After five years here, I am convinced that its inhabitants are no more or less sullen than their counterparts in any of the world's great metropolitan centers. To single out Parisians as particularly disagreeable or unpleasant is nothing less than a bum rap.

The French business scene does have its particularities and special rituals. Americans like myself are struck by the importance of hierarchy and the proliferation of job titles. I recall first reading the collective bargaining agreement of our industry, which listed 28 distinct grades, each one with a clarifying letter coefficient... *"chef"*, *"sous-chef b"*, *"chef adjoint c"* etc. I felt as if I was studying the reorganization chart of an American Indian tribe. Trying to match French titles with our relatively simple numeric grade system ultimately required a special computer program.

Constant handshaking was an equally complex issue, and for me a bit of an ordeal. I was told and observed that this was extensively practiced. When the company was only 32 people, the situation was manageable, but several years later, when our head count had reached 68, I began to feel as if I were running for governor of New York.

Similarly, determining who goes through the door first can generate marathon debates. It would not be altogether an exaggeration to state that this process, including the accompanying sweeping 18th century hand gestures, and the chorus of "no, please, you first!" and "but I insist, *je vous en prie"* can take up to 25 seconds per door. Since I have an uncanny knack of giving up precisely at the same time as my "opponent", I have been involved in some rather spectacular collisions while attempting to exit the confined space of the typical French elevator.

There are, of course, more substantive differences than social habits separating the Anglo-Saxon from the French approach to business. French businessmen are, for example, clearly more rigorous in their analyses of issues, and more intellectual than intuitive in their approach. In the extreme, they view Americans as "cowboys," shooting from the hip and too prepared to change direction radically if things don't immediately work out. Americans, on the other hand, rightly consider trial and error a legitimate strategy in their quest to achieve innovation and customer satisfaction. The clash of these two philosophies is immediately evident to U.S. expatriate executives, particularly those on short-term assignments with specific instructions to get a certain number of things done quickly. They soon learn that the French approach to business and life in general is often less focused on the result than obsessed with how it is attained. To many, the "slam dunk," just-do-it approach is the commercial equivalent of fast food, and its practitioners invariably run up against overt or passive resistance.

In my experience, achieving the business objectives which our group deemed important required patience and consensus building. Because aspects of our commercial mission were extremely sound, i.e. high service standards, rapidity and fairness in dealing with clients, focused marketing, etc., my approach was to base our strategy on certain shared values rather than insisting too much on emotionally charged words such as company "culture". One need only to look at the recent GATT negotiations to appreciate the French view regarding the issue of imposing one culture on another, and my advice to American managers is to avoid mention of this term altogether.

Similarly, I find it helpful to avoid comparisons wherein any one country's business practices are denegrated in relation to another's. This may seem obvious, but I have personally witnessed highly-placed expatriate managers who routinely excoriate local methods and mentalities in front of their most senior staff, and then wonder why they aren't getting the level of cooperation from their people that they would like. Playing the heavy in this way is deeply resented in France by employees and clients, and any business plan not sensitive to this fact is doomed to fail.

Steve Skoczylas

Steve Skoczylas is vice-president in charge of business control at the Paris office of J. P. Morgan, Inc. He came to Paris from New York speaking very little French and not knowing a great deal about France. On the eve of his return to New York, he says he loved the experience. He describes two of the most important things he learned which helped him in the text which follows:

Make an Effort to Learn French

Many of the senior managers in the Paris office impressed upon me the importance of learning French. Skeptical at first – I thought I could probably get by with English – I convinced myself to make the effort. For six months, five days a week, I took two hours of lessons with a tutor in my office, from 6:00 to 8:00 a.m.

Two and half years later, while my French is only average, I can communicate in most one-on-one situations.

What were the benefits?

First of all, I could talk to people at all levels of the bank. Most senior level managers spoke English well. But below senior management, ability in English couldn't be taken for granted. Often the person with the information I needed or the desired perspective was not a senior manager. Speaking French, I was not stuck in an ivory tower, asking questions to the staff reporting directly to me and waiting for the response from the people reporting to them. In addition, personal contact is something I need and enjoy. If you're a people person and your management style requires direct contact, you have to learn French or risk being frustrated!

Secondly, and perhaps as importantly, speaking some French permitted my wife and me to enjoy life outside of the office that much more. We met some very interesting French people, went to dinner parties in French, and traveled to the farthest corners of France on vacations without fear of communication problems. Once, while vacationing in southwest France, we decided to cross over into Spain for the day. I got lost and stopped for directions at a gasoline station. The attendant spoke only Spanish. We couldn't make ourselves understood and were both frustrated. I couldn't wait to get back to France! The experience had an important message for me. France was that much more beautiful and enjoyable because we could communicate. All those hours and effort spent on studying French were abundantly worth it.

Manager/Staff Relations Take Time

I sensed a difference in manager/staff relations in Paris. At first, I thought my staff was too deferential to me. They seemed to be used to an autocratic management style and fearful of making mistakes. However, I wanted their ideas and opinions. I wanted them to challenge my ideas. I wanted them to take initiative, even at the risk of making mistakes.

It took some time for this type of manager/staff relations to evolve, but it did. My staff was brimming with ideas and suggestions. I couldn't handle them all. They seemed to enjoy our consensus building approach. They enjoyed presenting their work to senior management, as opposed to having me take their work and present it for them. The level of trust among my team is as good as any I experienced in New York. I learned that manager/staff relations are different in France, but that over time, people committed to working together will find a way to succeed. Be flexible and find the way that works in your organizational structure. I work differently in Paris than I did in New York. I will probably have to adjust again when I go back.

My family and I return to New York truly enriched by living here. We would certainly do it again. There are so many things to love about France – the beauty of Paris, the countryside, France's history, its cuisine, not to mention the people. There were low points, particularly in the beginning, but for an open-minded, flexible family, it is an unforgettable cultural and professional experience.

Dixon Thayer

Dixon Thayer, a Philadelphian, the vice-president of Scott (Paper) Europe quoted in the last chapter, had spent four and a half years in Mexico, and six months in Brazil, when he arrived in France with a command of Spanish – but no French – to reorganize the French branch in 1991. He successfully developed a strategy which has been very profitable for Scott. With frequents trips to Spain, Italy, Germany, Poland and other ex-Soviet satellite countries, he is a truly multicultural international manager. He contributed the following to *French or Foe?*:

The experience of living and working in France has been wonderful so far. I think my prior experiences in Latin America prepared me well. Living in France is much easier, and the cultural differences from the French are not difficult to assimilate when you understand and respect their history. My only "words to the wise" would be:

1. The great cultural depth of the French is matched (at least emotionally) by each other country culture in the region. It's this diversity that I feel gives Europe such a strong opportunity in the emerging world economy. The challenge is that diversity can be either an advantage (many perspectives on an issue and the possible solutions), or a barrier (unwillingness to subjugate one's own perspective to the good of the whole). I believe that the latter will prevail, but not without significant cultural finesse by international managers. It can't be done by business acumen alone.

2. Don't accept poor management skills as "cultural differences." Once attuned to the idiosyncracies of the French management styles, it became very evident to me that the local resources that hide too much behind the "that's not the way things are done here" cultural defenses are themselves not culturally attuned to the demands of international business. Cultural sensitivity is a two-way street. There are many internationally aware resources in France; you should not accept those who are themselves unwilling to accept different ways of doing things. It's a balance... a very delicate balance.

3. Relax and enjoy the "voyage." Too many people look at their overseas assignment as a necessary but difficult step in their career. They see the "arrival in port" (return to the U.S.) as the key goal of their adventure. What they miss is that an assignment in France is an opportunity to broaden their horizons in ways that will make them much more capable of leading others in the future. It will give them a decisive cutting edge over those who do not get the experience. Besides, it's fun. Soak up the culture, the history, the food, the people. You'll find that life will never be the same again. You will learn that the U.S. is a great country, but it's a little strange, too.

Part V

The Other Side
of the Mirror

Chapter 18

How the French in the United States See the U.S.

L'amour... C'est peut-être notre plus vraie religion, et en même temps, notre plus vraie maladie mentale.

Edgar Morin
Amour, Poésie, Sagesse, 1997

When the sender of a message comes from one culture and the receiver from another, the chances of accurately transmitting the message are low.

Nancy Adler
The Internat'l Dimensions of Organizational Behavior, 1991

"In the U.S., money is beautiful," Stéphane Marchand, *Le Figaro's* Washington correspondent, wrote wonderingly (January 1996). "Money is happiness. 'You look like a million dollars' is high praise that brings a pleased blush to the cheeks of young girls here."

I asked my French daughter-in-law, Emmanuella, what her reaction would be if a man told her she looked like a million dollars.

She stared at me. Not usually at a loss for words, it took her a moment to answer. "Comparing me to money! Why, he would be treating me like a prostitute! What an insult! A high-class prostitute maybe, for the Sultan of Brunei, but a terrible insult!"

In France, money is not beautiful. It doesn't mean happiness. It comes in the same box with theft, extortion, blackmail and fraud. More about this presently.

Meanwhile, here are five more examples of garbled Franco-American communication:

American: We really thought it was terrible, your nuclear blasts in Mururoa. The ecological disaster...
Frenchman: You are quite wrong, *cher ami*. We did extensive tests before and after, and there was no danger of ecological damage.
American: Then why didn't you do the blasts in France?
Frenchman: Mururoa is France!

"There, you see," says the American to himself, hearing this. "The French are totally arrogant."
A German and an Englishman have the same reaction.
I repeated the exchange to another Frenchman and he said, "But he had to dish out a repartee, didn't he?"

American to a French café owner: Do you realize the total debt of the Credit Lyonnais is 170 billion — *billion* — francs?
Café owner shrugs (Gallically).
American: And do you realize that means that every Frenchman will have to pay a tax of 10,000 francs because of that alone?
Café owner (languidly): For how long?

On hearing this exchange, an Englishman who has lived in the Dordogne for 8 years burst out laughing. "How like the French! Selfish egotists! Who cares what the State does! Who cares how much money they throw out the window! All he wants to know is how long is it going to hurt *him* personally — but he'll never try to do anything about it."
But for the French, this isn't what the dialogue was about at all. Simply this: that the French like to make a nimble response which is opposite to the obvious one. Every exchange is a challenge. So instead of exploding in outrage, such as "*Les salauds*! Robbers! Crooks!", the café owner pretended not to care.
"A Frenchman doesn't mind if you think he's selfish or arrogant," said Ernest-Antoine Seillière, chairman and CEO of CGIP, the French holding company which merged Crown Cork with CarnaudMetalbox. "He knows he's not. You can think what you like. But he above all wants to be different — and not have other people really know what he's like. To hide what he really thinks, to have an unexpected reaction is the basis of French repartee, in all the classes. Just as he likes to hide how he really lives behind a

high wall — so he can look out over it and see how you live, but you have no idea how much better (or worse) he lives himself."

American author William Styron addressed a Franco-American group at the American Embassy in Paris as part of a fund-raising campaign for the American Library. Styron spoke of his love for libraries, the vital part they play in a country's cultural life and his fear that with the current passion for political correctness, Americans were in danger of losing their freedom of expression. He mentioned his experiences with censorship as a child in the American thirties.

"When I was 12," he said, "I was longing to learn the facts of life. What better way than from books? But I wasn't allowed to take a book out of the local library because the word 'whore' was in it. When I was 20, I couldn't take a book out of the New York Public Library because the word 'condom' was in it."

Americans afterward discussed his talk warmly, praising it for being so personal and interesting. French people said, "It was *archinul* — zero. All he did was talk about himself!"

An American engineer of about 55, very handsome, was in a hospital in Aix-en-Provence. He was pulling out of a stroke but was still bedridden. He must have presented a moving sight. In any case, to the surprise of his wife, who was sitting in the room, an unknown woman, glancing at him through the open door late at night, slipped into the room and gave him a big kiss full on the lips.

When the wife told this to an American friend, he said, "Was the woman crazy?" When the wife told this to a French man, he said, "Was she pretty?"

A Frenchman, holding up his empty glass to his friend and host, an American: Would you give me some more of that little wine?

The American (upset) shows him the bottle: But — this is a good wine! It's a Château Margaux 1989 *premier cru*!

The American, from a self-conscious culture dedicated to tact, is seriously insulted and never wants to see that Frenchman again, having no idea that he's missing the point — which is the game. A big part of French humor is sparring, the play of wit as they exchange light insults, often saying the opposite of what is the case. Tic tac tic tac gotcha!

For the Frenchman, the American's answer is perplexing, and not a little shocking. He of course knows what he's drinking... and a Frenchman would never produce the bottle. Very difficult to tease an American! If the host had been French, serving the same fine wine, he would have answered something on the order of: "I gave you my worst wine so you wouldn't get so drunk as usual." Then the guest can reply that he wouldn't get drunk in that house if it wasn't so boring.... and so forth.

French people have glowing things to say about living and working in the U.S. when they first arrive. They're almost always *aux anges*, as they say, with the angels — delighted because everyone is so welcoming and nice and seems so eager to make friends. They never tire of the vast open spaces in the U.S., the welcoming smile from strangers — which they generally miss, once back in France, even though they find it weird at first and then "blatantly commercial" in stores and syrupy on the street. They marvel at how fast things get done, how available people are, at the roominess of the dwellings and at the efforts made to accommodate the customer, no matter what wild complaint he makes or unfindable object he is determined to get his hands on.

"You can even get a refund on Christmas presents over here!" said one breathlessly.

They appreciate the American taste for action, for being positive, for moving along and not getting bogged down in negatives, in endless analysis. They praise the practicality of 800 numbers and some of them stumble on delightful customs such as baby showers.

"I got 30 presents for my little baby!" sang Parisian Christiane Morez in Denver. "Do you know how many came from France? Two — and months later."

They are charmed by the lack of intellectual or, it seems, social snobbery.

"In the U.S., whenever I've talked to Americans of a different social background from mine," said Pierre Guerlain, a professor at Sciences Po, "I have felt more at ease than in France, where subtle linguistic and metalinguistic messages always tell you where your place is or should be. (It's even worse in Britain.) I have talked to very rich Americans who didn't make me feel that I was not entitled to open my mouth; and to blue collar people who didn't feel one bit impressed by my university background, and, refreshingly, did not defer to me."

Things seem to be excitingly relaxed — anything goes — both at work and socially, and after the carapace of French life, they feel giddy with fresh air. But then it turns out that behind all the informality are *rules*, invisible at first, but gradually understood to be hung with barbed wire: much, much more rigid than in France.

"People at work — bosses as well as colleagues — laugh and tap you on the back and call you by your first name right away. They exchange information about their salaries — unthinkable in France — and tell you every-thing about their personal life, so you think that the hierarchy and so forth are very supple," said Virginia Boucinha, treasury manager at Rhône-Poulenc Rorer in Pennsylvania.

"And then little by little you find out that everything is different from what it seemed at first. This is very disorienting. At work you begin to notice that the men managers always wear dark suits with a white shirt, and the women managers always wear skirts. Then you perceive that the hierarchy is taken much more seriously than in France. When you hear the phrase 'the boss says,' you notice that everyone snaps to attention. Finally you understand that the rules are in fact much stricter than in France, the importance of conforming much greater. It may *seem* stricter in France, but we French people are impertinent and undisciplined, so we say what we like and do what we like, no matter what the rules are."

They find out that the other side of the lack of intellectual snobbery is that culture and intellect don't rate at all, are maybe even ridiculed.

"In the U.S., if you want to destroy someone politically, you call him an intellectual," said American anthropologist Edward T. Hall.

They find out that action often means not much reflection.

Friendliness, discovered not to mean friendship, leaves many a French person confused.

"Everyone was so nice to me from the very beginning," said Philippe D., a bachelor in Washington with SNECMA. "When I met them just once they were so friendly that I felt very happy with all these new friends. When they said to call them for lunch, I did — and they didn't even know who I was! I got very depressed, for a long time."

Marie-Monique Steckel, president of France Telecom North America, has lived in New York for 33 years with her American husband. She points out that the whole concept of "friendship" is different in America.

"People in the U.S. move around so much that you don't have a circle of friends, as you do in France, but what I call 'association friends' — friends you make at work, or at church or doing a sport together or some other activity. Americans have a terrible shyness of being too intimate, even a fear of it, and they don't want to burden someone else with their woes, so they usually don't have a 'best friend' — they'd rather pay a psychiatrist."

At first, warning notices everywhere seem to indicate that Americans must be idiots or babies.

"You're told to slow down for a curve, to unplug the iron when you're finished ironing, not to suck the pencil because the lead might be harmful, not to dry your pet in the microwave — all this makes a very odd impression," said Ghislain Taschini, assistant commercial delegate at Cegelec in Malvern, Pa. "But after you've been in the U.S. for a while, you realize all this is a cover-your-ass necessity in a country where everyone seems to be suing someone all the time."

This U.S. tendency to sue, indeed the whole legal approach is striking to the French.

"Here in the U.S., if you have a problem with another company, if people don't agree right away on something about a contract, the other company will sue," said Alexandre K., CEO of a French company in Chicago. "In France, you call the representative of the other company, invite him for lunch, have a *long* lunch and discuss the problem. You look at the *spirit* of the contract, and ask each other, 'What did we want to achieve together?' In 80 percent of the cases, you find a solution agreeable to both companies."

Lots of French words that look the same in English actually don't mean the same thing at all: liberty, independence, individualism, humor, for starters. This would be interesting to discuss with Americans, but it is hard for French people to find Americans interested in discussing them. Not only is their concept of repartee (a French word) different, but also, as is probably evident from the foregoing chapters about Americans in France, their conversational themes and patterns, their behavioral taboos, their values, their procedures, their mental processes, their perceptions of good manners, of space and time that have evolved in 2,000 years of Frenchness.

And what about working... and food...

Ah, and love. The way men and women *communicate* — or don't.

They slowly realize that things are different in ways that are important to them. They begin to feel as if they've gone through Alice's Looking Glass. Don't take it any more personally than having the Duchess throw one her of pots at you. But do take a good look at the pot — it contains gold.

And — speaking of gold —

The Money Machine

"Money seems to be the ultimate value in America," said Bernard Azoulay, president and CEO of Elf-Atochem North America, in his airy top-floor office in Philadelphia. "If you've made a lot of money, you become respectable. It doesn't matter how you made it."

A French consultant in Boston added, "Even if you've made it in suspicious ways, even if you have dumped your wife of 30 years and have taken on a trophy wife, you're welcome everywhere. These people would not be invited by respectable people in France."

Sylvie P., an oceanographer with UNESCO, visits the U.S frequently to see her two sons, both married to Americans. "They discuss prices all the time! They ask you how much you paid for your car and your house, they ask you how much a dress cost. They even ask you how much you earn — right away, first question! And they'll tell you whatever you ask. In France, all this is a mystery."

For the last 200 years, travelers to America have been impressed with the American preoccupation with money. They find it so prevalent that sometimes they generalize it to explain other behavior that seems curious. This is where the ground gets shaky. For instance, most Americans don't leave the price label on their wine bottles. But some do. Ghislain Taschini's comment:

"They even leave the price on the wine bottle, so you'll know how much they paid!"

"Ask a young Frenchman why he works, what he wants out of life and he will tell you, 'To earn enough to live nicely,'" said Yvonne D. after two years in San Francisco. "Ask an American and he'll say, 'To make a lot of money.'"

That doesn't necessarily mean that Frenchmen object to making a lot of money. But it's not something they would ever say and they don't dream about it at night. What they say they want, regularly, to all the pollsters is that they want security and if possible, to become a *fonctionnaire* (civil servant).

"Making money is not the goal of Frenchmen — it's not recognized as giving you respect or happiness," said Ernest-Antoine Seillière. "Many French companies do not expand because the owner sees the stress involved in enlarging it as destroying his own happiness in life — he'd rather limit his business success. For an American executive, to be successful is 98 percent of his goal in life. For a French executive, it is 65 percent. That extra 35 percent is for being himself, looking for mushrooms, for instance, in his little forest."

"What the French see in America is a whole society built up on possessions," said Edward T. Hall at his home in Santa Fe, N. Mex., "while French society is built on ideas. The U.S. is the society of conspicuous consumption and rampant individualism. It is winner take all, here. I said all. Nothing must interfere with every American's sacred right to make a buck."

The U.S. Workplace

Finding out just how they work to make those bucks was interesting for Catherine Bacquelin, a Parisian now vice president in charge of marketing at EuroDisney in Paris. As a bachelor girl in New York in the 80's and early

90's, she studied for her MBA at NYU and then she was made product manager for Colgate.

"I loved New York — it has an energy! — but after 10 years I opted out of the rat race," she said in Paris." The New York rush to see everything, be everywhere is exciting when you're very young, particularly when I was there, the era of the Golden Boys. But then it was enough.

"It was interesting to come back to Paris and see how Americans at work are perceived here — that they are so much more efficient and work so much harder. I don't think Americans work harder — here no one ever goes home until 8:00. I'm here until 10 p.m. every night. The process there and here is simply different. Here it is relational — you spend time talking to people. It's important to socialize at lunch, often a long lunch, and find out how people are thinking and feeling. Over there you get a 'Did you do that?' or 'Where is such and such a report?' Never so much as a 'How are you?' At the end of the day I don't think they're more efficient, either.

"What they are is arrogant and U.S.-focused. They think the way everything in the U.S. is done is right, and that non-U.S. people are stupid."

Jean-Marc G., CEO of a French company in Atlanta, is an X who loves math. He has been concerned to create a synergy of French and American working strengths.

"Business people in America use familiar recipes and their gut feeling," he said. "They want to do things very fast, but this often leads to expensive mistakes. It's hard to get them to analyze all the options, study all the issues before making a decision. We have forced our people here to look at the numbers and to operate midway between the French 'analysis paralysis' and the American gut decisions.

"One of the most difficult things for us is the constant praise you have to give subordinates here. You have to pat them on the back, make speeches and tell them how good they are all the time, or they feel they're not liked and they get depressed. We French have to force ourselves to give all this praise; it is a real cultural problem. We feel like hypocrites... particularly when we hear an American praising someone and then later hear him tell someone else that the guy is terrible, we must get rid of him.

"In France the only time your boss calls you is when you've done something wrong. It's the same in education — your teacher never gives you any praise. When a French mother leaves her child at school, she says, 'Work hard.' The American mother says, 'Enjoy yourself.'"

Ernest-Antoine Seillière admires the straightforward, precise American way of doing business. "Americans don't allow sensitivity to mix with business. They say, 'We want this done — how shall we do it?' Their attitude is, 'We discuss this, we decide. You don't like it, you go.' Period. They don't maneuver, they don't have hidden agendas. The British, for instance, never explain what they want, what should be done. You discover only as the plot develops. If you don't do it right, they despise you. You had better make your own maneuvers so that you don't get out-maneuvered."

Time management is the number one thing a French person has to get used to in America, according to Marie-Monique Steckel. "If a chairman here is two minutes late for a meeting, he is full of 'I'm sorrys' and excuses. This is not about politeness but about pride — CEO's here feel, 'If my time is well managed, my company is too.' They structure their schedules months ahead of time."

Steckel feels that the open space concept of American offices is a big plus for working. "It's more efficient, makes for better communication and pushes people to share information. This is very important — Americans don't constantly equate information with power. French managers want privacy — so this can take getting used to."

As for sexual harassment, Steckel finds it a real danger. "Often, men just don't get what it's about."

French culture is Latin, lots of touching of colleagues of both sexes. In America, it can get Frenchmen into serious — and expensive — trouble.

"I was at our Chicago office," said Bruno M., of Air Liquide, "and one of my women colleagues was having trouble with her computer. She asked me for help. I was on her right, and to touch the keyboard and unfreeze it, I had to lean over her. I happened to put my left hand on her right shoulder. This was a woman of about 60 and not at all attractive — and what do you know, she sued me! It cost me a lot! Do you suppose I will ever ask a female associate for advice after that? Much less propose that we go on a business trip together?"

The new CEO of Paribas Bank in New York complimented his secretary on her dress. She told her colleagues about it. They signed a petition demanding that this type of practice be banned from the company. The CEO explained that no harm was meant, this was a *French* bank, and the matter was dropped.

Guidelines at one of the big French multinationals in Philadelphia are very clear: "Our company policy is: Don't comment on a woman's appearance. Don't stare at her. Talk to her as little as possible. Don't touch her."

Love in America

This male-female situation in the U.S. is painful for Frenchmen.

Their first shock is the feeling of being unmanned. They haven't their reputation as Latin lover for nothing. They find it wildly frustrating to have to be constantly decoding all the social padlocks, in public and at the office.

Comments I heard over and over, from coast to coast:

"You're not supposed to look at women on the street!"

"You can't kiss a woman's hand — she'll sue you!"

"You see a girl you think looks as if she stepped out of heaven — and you can't talk to her — or she gets the police!"

"There's no flirting! Flirting is the spice of life — we flirt with everyone from the opposite sex — all day — strangers or not — no matter what the age. Americans have de-sexed life — and taken all the fun away!"

"The relations between men and women in the U.S. are artificial," fumed an executive of a French company in Houston. "You can't look at a woman on the street. You can't flirt at a dinner party. Because of the extraordinary, unbelievable Puritan hypocrisy you can never be yourself, must always be following certain rules. If you don't, you are quickly branded a bad person. All foreigners must learn this. However, once you do learn to live within the rules, you can do what you like."

Said another equally distressed Frenchman: "It's not only that you can't look at a woman in the street, much less talk to her! — but the women dress so badly — except in New York — that you don't want to look at them! They look like sacks of potatoes! How sad this is! Is it because they are afraid of being provocative? Is this also Puritanism?"

Le Figaro's handsome Stéphane Marchand, now back in Paris after 7 years in Washington and author of a brilliant book contrasting the two countries, *French Blues*: "One has the impression that American women tried so hard to imitate men and have equal power that now they resemble men. They walk like men. The essence of French femininity is to *séduire les hommes....* that is, to please men. French women dress to give men pleasure. They walk showing their shapes... Even the voice of American women is a deterrent to any kind of flirting. French couples talk in a tête a tête that no one else can hear, a four or five-layered pattern of communicating, loaded with things not said but implied, gently insinuated."

Bernard Azoulay loves living in America. So much so that he plans to stay there after he retires.

"The quality of life is better here," he said. "I drive to work in 20 minutes without pollution or traffic problems, I have made some real friends among Americans and now there are even adequate restaurants in Philadelphia!"

However, Azoulay regrets the comfortable atmosphere between the sexes in France. "It is very sad. Men here seem to like being with their buddies. Some golf clubs don't allow women to play on Saturdays! This is unthinkable in France. French men like to do things with women. We think it's more fun like that."

A French banker in Dallas says that one of the reasons he no longer accepts charity dinners is that he's always placed next to his wife, and the lady on his other side is next to her husband. "Where is the fun in that?" he says. "In addition, the orchestra is too loud for talking — and I found out I was never invited for myself, for my sparkling conversation, for instance, but because of my position or because they wanted me to contribute to their charity."

French women suffer even more. I talked to dozens and dozens of them on that tour. All of them without exception said they felt non-existent in the U.S.

"We are sensually deprived in America," said Sonia Benjamin, a journalist in San Francisco. "Men don't look at you here. It doesn't matter what trouble I go to, how gorgeously I dress, men — on the street or at a party — don't look at you. They don't compliment you on your dress. An American *woman* might tell you that you look great — but they always say that, and never anything negative, so it doesn't mean anything."

Virginia Boucinha, of Rhône-Poulenc Rorer, puts it bluntly. "The relations between men and women in America are antiseptic."

"I'm hardly off the plane in Paris before I feel the caressing looks," said Marie Juanchich, who lived in Texas for 15 years and was born near Perpignan. "It is wonderful. I can breathe again! And people touch! It makes you feel as if you exist. In America, I am invisible."

"In 3 years in the U.S., the only place I've felt like a woman was in a pizza shop," said Szuzsie G., a nurse in Boston. "The Italian chef flirted with me. No wonder the women here dress so sloppily — and with sneakers! No one ever looks at them or flirts with them."

Lone Taschini, Ghislain Taschini's Parisian wife agreed. "In France, you go shopping because of the flirting and the fun. Here, it's depressing."

Catherine Bacquelin: "American feminists in the 80's screwed up a whole generation of American men, the clean cut Ivy League types. They made femininity a dirty word, so the guys didn't know what the form was, were afraid to flirt and preferred staying with their buddies, which made the women aggressive. French men coming to New York at first thought it was cool that the girls made the first move. But very soon, unless they were out for one-night stands, they couldn't bear the aggressiveness — French men are hunters, Latin. They'd never stay long with one of those types."

Cynthia Strite, an American executive with Aramis (Estee Lauder) in New York, comes often to Paris for her work. She has begun to feel very French in New York — and in Paris. She even dresses French and understands exactly what distresses French women in America.

"Men in New York don't look at women — they have attitudes," she said on a visit to Paris. "It's as if they're too cool to look at women. But in Paris — how different! I feel so feminine. I've been walking for hours and hours today and it's fabulous the way the men give you eye contact here. They don't smile, but they *look*. They make it wonderfully obvious that they *value* you."

The Secret Garden

Getting the *look* from a woman is something that Jack Rostand, a doctor in Alabama, would like to see imported from France.

"It happened to me two years ago while I was doing metabolism research at the Hôpital Necker in Paris," he said, after my talk in Birmingham mentioning the French *look*. "I was standing at a bus stop... and there she was, about 28 years old, lovely, and she just locked into my eyes. It was *something*. The bus came... she got on at the head, I got in at the back and got a seat. She didn't. I saw her coming.... and got up and gave her my seat. That way, she knew that I knew."

Not all American men can handle this sort of devastating glory from a stranger with the finesse of Jack Rostand. Finesse, by the way, is a French word. Odile R., a writer, is a beautiful young Parisian of about 39. She is happily married to a Frenchman and lives in the suburbs in Long Island with their two little children. She told me about riding home a year or so ago on a train with Charlotte, her little girl of 3:

"The guy in the seat next to me, an American, was very handsome. He was reading his newspaper. Then he started playing with Charlotte, and spoke to me. If you have a kid here, everyone talks to you. It's like with dogs in France. We talked about animals and whether they go woof woof or wa wa — he was very funny. We got off at the same station and he said, 'My wife is picking me up.' I was being picked up by my husband. We both went to phone booths to call our spouses and then waited for the cars, chatting. There was something nice between us. I wasn't thinking of an adventure — I felt a current and enjoyed it.

"And then when our cars arrived he said, 'I enjoyed meeting you and I'd like to meet your husband.'

"He really said it. It made me very sad. I didn't want to see him again — that wasn't the point at all. I enjoyed the moment. It was one of those rare intimate things that you don't talk about but keep secretly in your heart. It was sad that he couldn't, that he had to immediately drag in my husband. He must have felt guilty — about what? That was the only way I could explain it, part of this dreadful Puritanism."

French women "of a certain age", as the French say, miss the *look* as much as when they were young. In France, they get it.

"Men never look at us here," said Diane Saltonn, who has lived in Chicago for 30 years. "A few months ago I was walking in Paris and I glanced up and saw a young man who was wonderful looking. Our eyes met. He saw the admiration in mine, and he looked at me as if to say that he had received my look, that he was appreciative, that he didn't take it for granted. It was such a wonderful experience. An American man would have thought, 'What is that old lady doing looking at me like that?'"

Mrs. Saltonn thought for a minute and then added, "We love it here. I don't think I could live in France anymore, but there is something about American men that makes me unhappy in certain social situations."

On Being a French Housewife in America

Josseline Tamers, a French journalist, divorced her American husband. She still lives in Los Angeles but doesn't plan to remarry an American. "He spent the evening watching baseball on television — I gather that's pretty much what a lot of American husbands do. J. C. Penney stays open Christmas Day because the men are watching football — that leaves their wives free to shop all day!

"And, you know, very few American men help around the house. French men, who are supposed to be so macho, do help a lot with the children — and they cook! They like to cook and they're good at it. American men are independent only at college, where they take care of their own laundry, and so forth. They get married and their wife is their mother. So, you can fight — or get a cleaning woman. My husband couldn't afford a cleaning woman. He wouldn't help. And he wouldn't talk either, he couldn't give up his evenings watching baseball on TV. Is that a life? So I left."

Sophie de Quercize is frankly amazed by the life she has been made to feel she's supposed to live as a suburban matron — a young married woman in Chatham, NJ. "Can you believe this, there is a complete separation of the sexes here," she says. "All day I can see only women, no men. In the evening, if we go out to dinner, we are placed next to our husbands.

"The women around here aren't women anymore... their children are more important. They make a profession of being Mother. They spoil their children — they do everything for them. They put all their energy into taking them around to this lesson and that lesson. They're so organized that they have no time to dream, and they neglect themselves. You should see how they look, what they wear. We French women make an effort to be elegant... not to be sexy, not to attract men — though it's all right if we do! — but because it's a pleasure to look well."

For Sylvie P., the U.S. is a country of hypocrites. "All the couples have to pretend to be in perfect harmony," she says, "and then the next year they divorce. And the men are obsessed by work. There are all these taboo subjects — and you can't mention that someone is black or a homosexual. Did you know that Apple has come out with software that automatically corrects political incorrectness in a text?"

It's the "ceaseless medal-giving" to mothers and children that strikes Marie-Christine Whitman, a native of Blois who's been in Mobile, Ala., for 6 years. "At the parent-teachers meetings, half the time is spent thanking everyone and complimenting each other and giving rewards. The children are constantly made to feel good about themselves — about anything. One child got a prize last week for her duck at a pet fair. The prize was for the 'dirtiest bill.'"

Catherine Bacquelin: "This is how American children grow up into adults who are proud of what they're doing, whether it's street-sweeping or running a company. And American managers know how to keep up their feel-good attitudes by giving them special citations — Employee of the Day, that kind of thing."

Bertrand de Boutray moved to Seattle several years ago with his gorgeous blond American wife, Brooke. Brooke is a high-flying stockbroker. Bertrand is a chef at night and takes care of the children during the day.

"I'm lucky," he says. "I get to do what I like — cooking and being with my wife and kids. What's important in life? To spend time with your wife! To look at her! American men.... well, they seem only to care about the next football game at their university."

Le Dîner

After 30 years in France, I have to say that dining out in the U.S. can be sort of an endurance test. Restaurants and hosts often pile your plate with Himalayas of food of an uncertain nature. In restaurants, whatever you order may be swamped in something else, inevitably with mushrooms added (do American chefs have a thing about mushrooms?). The salad is made with iceberg lettuce, and cold as ice. The noise level is deafening, what with the hi-fi competing with shrieks of laughter and booming voices from other diners that get even louder as the evening progresses.

On that nationwide tour last year, I had only two delectable meals gracefully served by politely formal waiters (no "Hi, I'm Tom, your waiter tonight") dressed à la française in black vest and trousers with white shirt. One was at Chez Colette at the Sofitel in Minneapolis and the other at The Highlander in Birmingham, Ala.

But the French, whose most noticeable national characteristic is their critical faculty, are mute on this subject. Considering that for them, dinner at home or anywhere else is close to a sacred rite, that excellence and variety of food are central to their pleasure in life, and that almost none of the accompanying ritual is respected in the U.S. except in the most wildly expensive exceptions, this is pretty interesting. Perhaps it's the reaction you'd have to a teenager peeing on someone's rug. It is so obviously lacking in *savoir vivre*, that is, barbaric, that you abstain from comment. Or perhaps they simply prepare French meals for themselves at home.

But some say that things aren't that bad at all. Michel Besson, president and CEO of Saint Gobain's CertainTeed for 10 years in Valley Forge, Pa.: "In most big U.S. cities, Americans begin to appreciate good food. There are good restaurants in cities all over the country."

A few French people in various parts of the U.S. commented that Americans "*mangent tout le temps, n'importe quoi, toujours la même chose*" ("they eat anything all the time and always the same thing") and others commented on the difficulties they had getting used to strange culinary bedfellows like shrimps with veal, and to dining at 6 or 7 p.m.

And: "They have the most enormous, magnificent kitchens in the world — which they hardly use, nothing but fast food and microwave!" said Sylvie P.

Some made mild comments, like Serge Bokobza, the lively Alliance Française director in Birmingham. Serge is a divorced bachelor. He says a problem with American women is that they always drive with a mug of coffee in the car, which spills. I complained about a turkey sandwich that tasted like oatmeal mush. He had ordered the same thing and professed to be satisfied.

But then he added, "My mother was here last month and said I'd lost my French taste buds."

It's the conversation, the discussions and the slam-bang lightning change of subject at the usual 3-hour French dinner that they miss the most.

Said Ghislain Taschini: "Visitors from France! They rejuvenate us. Then we have discussions at last."

"Here," said Jean-François H., "the moment anyone disagrees with someone else, they change the subject — just when it's getting interesting. Usually all anyone talks about is something very safe like baseball or the latest movie. For us French, passionate discussions are our staff of life... along with French bread. Very often they race through dinner to get to the baseball game on television.

"You know the story: Two Frenchmen meet and one says, 'Ah,' and the other says the contrary and then they have a long and perhaps violent discussion. Two Americans meet and one says, 'Ah,' and the other one says, 'Ah, I see what you mean,' and immediately changes the subject."

French people soon recover from the surprise of frozen sandwiches and the "maintenance function" of food; at the U.S. flags in people's gardens ("one of the people we shared a house with in the Hamptons put the flag up every morning!" marveled Ghislain Taschini); at the public "restrooms" with part-way doors so that you see (and hear) the person in the next cubicle; at the obscenity and lack of elegance at the U.S. Open; at the non-automated grade crossings, now almost non-existent in Europe; at how-to books crowding bookstore shelves (French people are accustomed to figuring things out for themselves) and at American telephone manners. "They're terribly polite — welcoming voices, usually, and they return your calls! — fast! — but they never tell you right off who is calling!"

They come home with rich memories of good people where everything is made easier for couples with children, and where things get done very fast, much faster than in France.

Edward T. Hall gives this advice to French people arriving in America:

"Don't interrupt people. Don't finish their sentences for them. Stick to the rules. Be on time. Let the woman go first into a restaurant. Don't stare. Treat all classes the same. Don't snub the hotel bellhop — he might be your CEO's son."

As for what we can learn from each other...

French people in the U.S. say they learn about the ease of going toward other people and treating each one with respect, regardless of social hierarchy. It's called communication.

And what Americans learn from the French, if they spend long enough in the country, is that ideas matter, that more isn't necessarily better — particularly when it comes to food! — and even more, that the present is the most important... to make this very moment beautiful, and taste good, and sound good, and keep it personal and private, and sit back and enjoy it totally, without worrying what is going to happen 10 minutes from now. Old countries have old sayings, and one of them is, "Nothing better is going to happen than is happening right this moment."

Coda

16 Marvels for 16 Headaches

The French are different from you and me. Theirs is not a puritan country. We speak with an air of detachment, even distrust, of the pursuit of happiness. The French just go ahead with it – and they've organized a country and a great city to make sure they catch what they're chasing.... What I mean is that the French have developed the arts of leisure to a higher degree than we have. Eating, drinking, gossiping, just enjoying – the French do it with unique style.... An American has more of a chance to become the person he or she aspires to be. A Frenchman is more locked in by where he was born, what his father did, how he speaks the language. But, God, the French know how to live.

And thank God the rest of us can share life with them for a while...

Richard Reeves
"An American in Paris"
Travel and Leisure

Winding up

So now you're all set to love France – and the French!

Alert to pick up on a galvanizing Look, you start your day with a lilt in your gait and a smile in your heart – no longer on your face, not missing one on other people's faces because you know you can get them any time – and who's that coming towards you on the sidewalk? Bernard Tapie! You recognized him! You've made it, you're in context, part of the Parisian crowd, and all those hours you spent struggling over *Le Parisien* in the morning and over the 8:00 TV news at night are paying off.

You don't mind if people seem to be bumping you off the sidewalk – you know that they just didn't see you – no body bubble here!

You've gotten so you like the personal contact, actually touching other people, at the office when you shake hands with practically everyone you see except the janitor, every day, on arrival and on going home, adding a "Bonjour, monsieur" (or "madame") or "Bonjour, Marie" or "Bonjour, Didier..."

You get great service from your butcher and baker because you became a regular customer and because you chat with them, at least in sign language. You even manage to get pleasant, efficient service from strangers by chatting with them, taking time to be personal with them (PPO) and putting on all your charm, particularly if you need something special, eternally thankful for the Ten Magic Words. You even thought up some Words of your own. Approaching a stranger (of the opposite sex, of course!) for some information, you say, after the Ten Words, "*Vous, qui savez tout, pourriez-vous me dire...?* ("You who know everything, could you tell me...?") And they love it!

If you're on a sabbatical, or retired, or the "trailing" spouse, you're enjoying yourself more since you made up your mind to take a French-immersion course and then signed up with groups for bridge, bird-watching, and tennis. So you're killing *three* birds at once – doing what you like, making French friends, and learning French. And incidentally learning about French culture – and your own.

Becoming aware of what your own mental programming is.

If you're working here, you don't worry if people are on time... or late. You can wait half an hour for other people to straggle into a meeting – you bring a book, and paper for a letter you've been meaning to write for ages. If you're the boss, you're ready to shut the door, but not too fast. You resist turning on the light right away, you don't really mind the dimness any more.

You know that they're keen on math and deductive reasoners – not inductive and pragmatic. You're ready to see that maybe there's another way to think, and run companies, and are trying to get the two ways to complement each other.

You're aware that their fondness for nuances and indirectness, and circular reasoning (there is no French for "to get to the point") have led them to favor full-blown, elaborately articulated arguments over direct statements. (If you're negotiating with them, you may want to take up Aristotle's *Works*. Seriously. Rhetoric is what it's been about, ever since Abélard.)

You're clued in to the system of protocol at dinner and at long lunches, you've learned all about wine and what wine goes with what, and have been practicing how to chat up French waiters, by asking them their opinion. *Reverently.* You don't talk business until over dessert. You might even wait until you're out on the sidewalk, parting.

If you're a man, you enjoy paying all the chivalric courtesies to the female employees, including compliments, since the recently legislated sexual harassment law in France applies uniquely to promotion or continued employment predicated on sexual favors. If you're a woman, you can lighten up about all this, and enjoy it, too, without fear of delivering (unless you'd like to). It's a good idea to dress like a woman – a female with good taste.

You don't expect teamwork, because of the school system, but you know that you can get it, if you build up your staff's confidence gradually, and empower them. You know all about the power system and forming information networks, to get your projects finished successfully, and recognized.

You know that the family, school and government are built on a system of male hierarchy patterned on the military, and you'll make a point of determining if your CEO is running things in the company today the way Louis XIV did, autocratically, and immersed in details. If so, your boss may be like that, too. Your subordinates may expect it from you. In any case, they'll expect you to know everything. If you're pretty high up in rank, your boss may be an X or an *énarque*, and you know how to deal with that (respectfully). If you're the CEO, and an office chess tournament is organized, you had better win, or not play.

In other words, the hierarchy is strict, the protocol is rigorous, X's and *énarques* tend to be at the top where the decisions are made, whether they have any people and business skills or not; getting power for yourself means working the relationships, information is hoarded – but available if you know how to get it – the tempo is *piano*, and it's the *Système D* all the way.

And after hours you're enjoying the most beautiful city in world, and the best run, with all its pleasures for the sensitive, the aesthetic and the sensual. Why not stop in at 35 rue Picpus for a visit to Lafayette's grave? This champion of both liberty and *liberté* is a great hero in both the U.S. and France...The palaces of the Louvre and Versailles are waiting for you, and the churches and cathedrals – Notre Dame, Chartres, Sainte Chapelle – not to mention the châteaux of the Loire. If you have children, they'll be invited right and left by their French friends, and on vacations – of which you'll have more than ever before – you'll have the whole gorgeous country to explore.

You're in the picture! Things are no longer totally out of control! You sense the dramas and tensions and glories that make France French, there's a zing in the air ...

Until the next time you start to boil over.

There are times when you *will* boil over, no matter how long you've been here. The French! Really! You can handle books without indexes, magazines with pages unnumbered, cartons you can't open, trains coming into the station from the left or right, newspaper photo captions that don't indicate who is where, and news articles that take five paragraphs full of indecipherable acronyms to tell you more or less what they're about, but don't explain the background...

But! People who are so bright and gifted and who can master the subtleties of everything from a Gothic cathedral to the AIDS virus *should* be able to respect lines, drive predictably, be friendlier –

The list of things-infuriating-to-foreigners is long and I offer it herewith, only in order to suggest that all these exasperating features of life in France have another aspect which is a kind of marvel – a special delight, or a special usefulness, or something amazing that you may not be aware of. Calling up the marvels to mind is a great help in soothing exasperation.

Line-jumpers

A well-known and ordinarily calm international lawyer, who loves France and has been here for years, goes into a threatening pugilist crouch just thinking about them. "Sometimes I get so mad I tell the impostor what I think, until he is shamed back to his proper place."

Line-jumping (*resquillage*) jabs a particularly sensitive British and American nerve. French writers have noticed the high pitch of Anglo-Saxon exasperation with *resquillage*. While politely deploring it, they point out that waiting in line is not a matter of morality with them. The French don't hassle the *resquilleur* themselves because they admire his nerve. It's the nerve of the loner: one man or woman facing fearsome odds, alone, daring the elements... or, in this case, the rage of others.

The *marvel* to keep in mind when this happens to you is the French world-class explorers, aviators, mountain climbers, seafarers, deep sea divers and speleologists. Jacques Cartier and Champlain opened up the North American continent. The French, pioneers in aviation, were the first to go up in a hot air balloon in 1782. The most numerous French loners daring the elements are the seafarers alone in a small boat tossed about on the mountainous waves of the Atlantic and the Pacific. Droves of them. They're constantly winning records of solo crossings. One of them, Gérard d'Aboville, *rowed* across the Pacific in 1991. It took him 134 days and he turned over 38 times. In 1986, without a dog, Jean-Louis Etienne, a French doctor, walked 753 kilometers alone to the North Pole from Ward Hunt Island, on foot and on skis, pulling his sled himself. The first person to scale an 8,000-meter Himalayan peak, Annapurna, was a Frenchman, Maurice Herzog, in 1950. (Mount Everest by Hillary was in 1953.)

Waiters

A familiar refrain: "Rude! So arrogant they refuse to serve what I order! One of them told me, *'Vous mangez mal, madame!'* Really! That I eat badly because I ordered two courses of fish! What business is it of his, if I pay for it? Another refused to give me my coffee with dessert!"

Ah, waiters. There are several marvels to keep in mind when waiters annoy you. In the first place, their professionalism: their grace, their consideration for your palate, their high standards of what should and what shouldn't be eaten, and their wit. I know, it's hard to joke with them if you don't speak French, but at least watch the French and how they handle them. What you can do is ask their opinion about what to eat, and you'll find your service is turned into a marvel, itself.

Then there's the food itself, and their pride in it. During a broadcast of *Bouillon de Culture*, Bernard Pivot's television program, one of France's star chefs, Joël Robuchon, discussed with Pivot and his other eminent guests the secrets of... potatoes! For mashed potatoes, he said, it's important that the potatoes be of a sort called *corne de mouton*... and all of the same size. Fried potatoes, he said, had to be *blanchies* (parboiled) first, and salted at certain times with two different kinds of salt.

The discussion lasted for at least 10 minutes and was treated with the gravity any question of food demands in France. That preparing it is one of the things they do superbly well was illustrated by the comment of one of the guests that all the other countries in Europe, even Italy, send their chefs to France to learn how to cook.

Waiters know this. What foreigners perceive as arrogance is often a pride in their profession. And, sometimes, on their part, frustration at the lack of communication with people who don't speak French, and the impossibility of a learned discussion of the various menu delicacies that day.

The third marvel to keep in mind, the next time you feel like kicking a waiter, is the quality of the food he is proud to be serving – not only what has been done with it by his chef, but what his chef has chosen, with great care, at the open markets. Go to one of them at 6 a.m., when the chefs go, and watch them. Check out the produce yourself. Fruit and vegetables have ripened naturally and have been put on display one by one, like jewels, in an aesthetically pleasing order. These markets are all over Paris, some of them in certain places only two days a week. One of the oldest, liveliest and most mysteriously marvelous is open every day right in the center of Paris in the cité Berryer, near the Church of the Madeleine, around the corner from the President's Elysée Palace and Saint-Laurent.

And I promise you one thing. If you're in town for the annual Café Waiters Race, you will learn to love them. The starting gate is at City Hall. Dressed elegantly in their usual black vest, white shirt, black tie and trousers, juggling a tray with three glasses and an open bottle of Perrier for a gallop of eight kilometers, they take off as gracefully as if they were serving you at the Ritz.

Phoning

"No one answers! If they do, they sound cold. Company operators, if you're not 100 percent sure who you need to talk to, treat you like the Grand Inquisitor or hang up! And no one – no one! – ever returns calls! You have to phone at least four times to actually speak to the person you want!"

The French hate the telephone. Until 1974, when the Giscard government revolutionized the whole system, only about 20 percent of French people had one, and as phoning was exasperating - in Paris you had to dial two or three times before you hit the right number - they used it for an average of three calls a month. Emily Borel's neighbors deep in the Normandy countryside still won't answer the phone. She has to go and see them personally. So we have to be grateful when anyone answers, even company switchboard operators who bark at you menacingly with, "Who do you want to speak to? What about? Who are *you*?"

The marvel is that even these Grand Inquisitors become warm and helpful with gentle handling, patience and a joke or two.

Another marvel is the telephone services available. Since the system was totally transformed in 1974, it has been not only one of the most efficient anywhere, but one of the most innovative. Some of those X's (Chapter 11) went to work on it and the result is that the French phone system does everything for you from being an alarm clock in the morning to telling you a story, according to taste – fairy tales or bedtime tales, whatever kind you like.

Most marvelous of all is undoubtedly the Minitel, the computerized telephone network which offers 17,000 different services. The terminal and access to it come almost free with your phone. Aside from consulting its nationwide, up-to-the-minute phone directory for free, for a small charge you can do everything from ordering groceries to reserving plane tickets – and concert tickets, which are delivered to your home. You can order clothes from mail order catalogues, send E-mail, get legal advice and have your texts corrected.

Dogs in Restaurants and Dog Dirt on the Sidewalks

"Please! A dog on the chair next to me in a restaurant! And the owner feeds him – right there!"

Yes, but this is because the French are such passionate animal lovers. Sailors in Brest even had a pet dolphin who showed them the way into the harbor in the fog. Parisians are said to have more cats and dogs per inhabitant than any other city. This means that – the marvel – your dog is welcome almost anywhere. Air France stewardesses lovingly give dogs something to eat and drink instead of swearing at them, as a TWA hostess did to my little Chico. All sorts of professional services are available for them, from *coiffeurs* to hospitals. If worst comes to worst, you can always communicate to a French person through his dog, or your dog.

Customer Service

"I wanted to look at some heavy colored paper for photocopying. It was on an upper shelf. The clerk asked me if I wanted to buy it. I said I wanted to look at it, to find out if I wanted to buy it. He refused to get it down!"

"The salespeople in department stores are always jabbering away at each other at such a rate than you can't interrupt them to ask a question or buy something!"

"Three pairs of shoes – three! – that's all they'd let me try on in the shoe store!" said Madlyn Miller, a real estate developer and mother in a hurry. "They said that was enough!"

Exasperating as it is, there is a marvel about this, and it is French independence of money. For all the avarice celebrated by novelists like Balzac, they really are not out for the next buck. There is practically no fake commercial smile and overly cheerful "Have a nice day" superficiality.

Not only that, they have time – time isn't money here, remember – and they'll give it to you if you're looking for something special (*"J'ai un problème"*). In a bookstore or other specialty shop they'll often spend half the morning helping you find it. Otherwise, PPO (Persistent Personal Operating, Chapter 4) usually overcomes French reluctance to sell you anything. But you have to be in good form for it: rested and full of the energy and good will required for total charm.

Another antidote is to turn your mind to some of the things available in unexpected places. My butcher, for instance, offers several delicious dishes for lunch that his wife has cooked... one portion at 24 francs is always big enough for two.

Or you can think about the changeless 100-year wonder of the tiny ponies in the Tuileries that give children rides... and at the end of the day, seeing these ponies, strung together, crossing the Place de la Concorde, bringing the wild rush-hour traffic to a complete halt behind them, when their masters take them back to their stables at the Ecole Militaire, near the Eiffel Tower... and not a single impatient French driver honks his horn.

Peeing in Public

"The men relieve themselves anywhere! You see mothers pulling down the pants of their little kids in the park and on the sidewalk!"

Yes, well, this is also a part of *liberté* and a marvel in itself, if you think about it. Free to you to do it, too. No shame. No embarrassment. No governesses around to point fingers.

Banking

"It takes forever to get a check cashed in your own bank, you have to stand in at least two lines!"

Not in all banks, and anyway, it really is a marvel, the number of automatic dispensing machines all over Paris, many more than in other countries.

Neighbors

"They rap on our ceiling when we flush the toilet at night!"

"They never greet us in the stairway – and we meet there every day! It's as if we don't exist!"

"I was on a ladder clipping the hedge when my neighbor next door came into his garden," said Jim Nichols, an Apple Computer engineer. "I smiled and said hello. He glared at me and rushed back into his house!"

Here the marvel to remember is French discretion. They've perfected the art of privacy in crowded living. One day I fell against a sharp corner of a stone wall, and soon sported a huge red and purple shiner. The next day, no one in the café where I have breakfast every morning said a word. It was so noticeable that Chantal, my hairdresser, came running out in the street as I walked by to ask me what had happened. When I told her about the silence of the café people, she said, "Well, of course. They were afraid your husband might have hit you." In her village in Normandy, Emily Borel did her daily errands in all the stores while very pregnant. When slimmed down after the birth, no one inquired after the baby. They were afraid something might have gone wrong.

Louise Walker, the English computer engineer at Honda: "I came to work on Friday with brown hair, and on Monday with blond hair. No one said anything."

Not Being Introduced in Public

"I was with a French friend, standing in line waiting for a table at a restaurant, when a friend of his that I'd never met came along. They chatted – for what seemed like ages. My friend never introduced me! I was furious – what's the matter with me? I'm not good enough for his friend?"

I've clocked introductions by Americans in public places. It's almost instantaneous, about five seconds. You can wait till the cows come home in France. This isn't rudeness, it's another marvel of politeness à la française. For French people it's indiscreet to introduce people at an accidental encounter. One of them might not wish to be known to the other.

Driving

French drivers elicit screams for mercy from most Anglo-Saxon drivers. Louise Walker puts it like this: "I'm driving. It is my right of way; why don't they stop? Am I invisible? It is his right of way; I stop, why does everyone toot? If I move forward, I will block the junction for everyone, and if I don't, they'll all toot and try to get round me to block it themselves. Leaving a safe distance between cars confuses them, and they drive round you to squeeze into it. My conclusion is that the French enjoy the confrontation and competition. I think it's just aggressive and rude. So I'm selling my car."

Being from a Common Market country, Louise at least didn't have to go to driving school in France. Americans do, unless they happen to be from the four states with reciprocal driving license agreements. Driving School is not popular.

"I've been driving for 15 years – and now I have to go back to school!" said Jeanine Yates, in Paris from St. Paul with her husband, Ron, head of marketing for 3M Europe. "And it's a complete waste of time – because no one on the road does what the driving instructor teaches us! They do exactly as they please!"

Adds another overwrought American driver: "They turn to the right from the lefthand lane and to the left from the righthand lane! They drive through red lights! They pass on the right! They drive at insane speeds on the expressway – much faster than the speed limit – and it's a crazy 110 miles per hour and they tailgate all the time!"

And they pay for it, with annually about 10,000 people killed on the roads. My theory about French driving recklessness is that they don't have sports in school... only two hours of gymnastics per week. Also, Louis XIV didn't cast any rules in iron about driving, as there were no cars in Versailles. The rules there are have to do with laws, and we've seen that the French like to make up their own minds about whether laws are valid or not. The government is well aware that it is advisable not to push them too far. A six-column headline in *Le Monde* a few years ago was a quote from the then Minister of the Interior: "Don't Bore the French with Seatbelts!"

The police have the same approach. Survival for you lies in imaginatively considering not only what the drivers might do that you don't expect, but also what the police might think about the general situation. This is harder than you might suppose. After 25 years, Paris still had surprises for me when, one evening, I put on my blinker to make a left turn into my house. This happens to be opposite the Prime Minister's official residence, where there is at least one policeman on guard in front of his entrance. That evening there were three. I saw that there was a car behind me, but as I had given him plenty of warning with my blinker, I proceeded to turn left – and almost crashed into him. He had decided to pass me anyway. It was a close shave.

Instantly, while I trembled in shock, the three policemen ran over to us, blowing their whistles. I assumed they were going to reprimand the other driver for his outrageous behavior. Not at all. They went straight for me and demanded my car papers.

"But – but – I had my blinker on!" I stammered. "Didn't you see it?"

"Yes, you had your blinker on – but you didn't wait for the car behind you to pass!" As I stared at him, he added angrily, "It's foreigners like you who cause the accidents in France – you don't know what the French are likely to do!"

The marvel about French drivers is their quick reactions, their impatience and their imaginative escapes from traffic jams in an exuberant application of the *Système D*. They'll back out 50 feet if a street is blocked, or go up on the sidewalk, or down a one-way street the wrong way. Their steely eyes and unflinching courage when inching by a parked truck, only a millimeter away, is equaled only by the Italians.

Smoking

"Crossing the English Channel, it's like hitting a wall of smoke at Calais!" said international management consultant Prabha Guptara. "Smoke in public is much more noticeable and offensive than in the U.K. or the U.S."

Louise Walker: "My boyfriend and I were in a Paris restaurant specifically picked because they had a table in non-smoking. A couple sits down at the next table. The man puts a pack of cigarettes on the table. My boyfriend says politely, '*Excusez-moi, monsieur*... but why don't you ask for a table in the smoking section?'

"So the other diner goes, 'Yes, I know there's a sign saying "No Smoking", but obviously nobody actually minds.' He lights up. My boyfriend gets upset – and the man looks totally shocked!"

Smoking for the French has always been up there with *liberté*... an inalienable right, like wine with dinner, and dogs in restaurants. That someone might really mind it, or that it might lead to a dread disease, has just not sunk in yet.

Here is their side of it:

"It's really too idiotic, the way Americans carry on about smoking," said a French journalist and mother of three, who spent several years in the U.S. "Once when I was stopped at a traffic light, the man in the next car rolled down his window and told me to stop smoking! And here, I went to a party in Chantilly given by an American – and she asked me to go outside if I wanted to smoke!"

When a law went into effect on October 1, 1992 limiting smoking to special sections in public places and offices, another Revolution threatened to break out. But then everyone relaxed when they saw that no one paid much attention to the law.

As the *International Herald Tribune* put it (Jan. 17, 1994), writing about Paris restaurants: "But perhaps the most negative – and predictable – observation is that the non-smoking section has never taken off. Ask to be seated in the non-smoking section of a restaurant and you'll be laughed into the street."

Well, there are some restaurants with non smoking sections. The most encouraging effort is the firm ban on smoking on Air Inter, the domestic French airline.

The marvel is that, in one of the most full-blown of French paradoxes, a profitable government-owned cigarette manufacturing company, SEITA, continues to produce and market these agents of the deaths of so many of its citizens, while the same government, at the same time, spends zillions in anti-smoking campaigns and for medical care for smoking-induced ailments.

Lice in the Schools

Your young children are bound to come home with a head full of them sooner or later. Some American mothers promise categorically that if that happens, they're going home, next day, period. Please, don't.

The marvel is that the French have developed a louse-detecting comb. When it kills one, it squeaks.

Doctors

"No sheet! There I am, in my fourth month, for a medical checkup and the doctor tells me simply to take off my clothes! Like that! No nurse around! So I have to undress – and get up on the examining table – and spread my legs – naked! In front of a stranger!"

English and American women consulting a gynecologist are aghast that no changing room or screen and no sheet are provided for modesty. French women wouldn't know what to do with a sheet. They are just as at home undressing in front of a doctor and chatting with him, as nature made them, as they are changing on a public beach, with or without a towel. It does not imply that they're not modest, only that they have a different relationship with their bodies. This is one of the reasons American visitors in the 19th century wrote such vituperative harangues about France when they got back to the U.S. This is not a Puritan country.

It never was. Have a look at the portraits of queens and aristocratic royal mistresses in the 15th and 16th centuries, naked from the waist up, and you'll see what I mean.

The marvel to remember about doctors in France is that they come to your home – day or night. Without charging a year's salary.

Another is the diagnostic helpfulness of pharmacists, who have passed fearful exams in math and chemistry and very often know what ails you and give good, cheap advice.

Most marvelous of all are the firemen. If you have an accident at night, you phone them and they're there in three minutes with a doctor and emergency equipment. Normal ambulances might take half an hour. The firemen are also there to help you with all sorts of other emergencies besides fires: cleaning out a wasp's nest, for instance. Their number, 18, should be in big red letters on your phone.

Taboos

"Aren't there any more taboos?"

While there are masses and masses of rules you can break, a marvel is how few real taboos there are in France. Two have to do with *mal élevé* manners – asking personal questions.

The first taboo is asking someone whom he voted for.

The other taboo is asking someone who their psychiatrist is, or even bringing up the subject at all. There are plenty of practicing psychiatrists in Paris, but I've never met anyone who has been to see one, or who knew anyone who has been to see one. French people don't have nervous breakdowns, anyway not officially. French people never say they are depressed. They say,

"Je suis un peu fatigué." ("I am a little tired.") When François de Grossouvre, a close friend and associate of President Mitterrand, blew his brains out (April 8, 1994) in his office – at the Elysée Palace, the official residence of French presidents – his doctor said that he had been *"très fatigué"* recently.

Getting Adequate, Accurate Information

An American banker had a crucial meeting in Brussels during a rail strike. He called the SNCF to find out if the trains were running to Belgium next morning.

"The international train service is assured," said the official on the phone.

At the Gare du Nord (North Station), the banker was told that the 7:05 wasn't running. Nothing until the 11:32. "But I was told the trains were running!" he protested.

"Yes, and indeed they are," said the official."But not all of them."

The banker blew up. "Look, this is important! I have to be in Brussels by 1:00!"

He was directed to another information agent, who told him the same thing.

"There must be other lines – if I change somewhere – " said the banker, increasingly desperate.

"Impossible," said the official.

Then a man in the line behind him said, "Ask him about the trains to Tourcoing." He did. Then the same agent magically came up with a train arriving at 10:33 at Brussels, with a change at Tourcoing.

"To get the information you need, you have to ask the right question. But to ask the right question, you have to know the answer already," quips Henry Haley.

The marvel is that sometimes, against all odds, by bidding for time, with judicious use of the Ten Magic Words, you can turn it into a game of Twenty Questions and find out what you need. "I call up to speak to someone staying at Claridge's Hotel," says an Irish journalist. "I'm calling the only Claridge's in the phone book. 'There's no one here by that name,' says the receptionist. I persist. Still nothing. Finally I ask, 'Is there by any chance another Claridge's in Paris?' Yes. Jackpot!"

Now for one of the thorniest and most absorbing of the frustrations of Paris for foreigners:

Making Friends

You can. The best way is to be a charming, gorgeous woman, single and fairly young, who dresses sublimely and speaks perfect French. You'll be asked everywhere. That isn't exactly the same as making a friend, but it's going in the right direction.

For women, the easiest way is having small children and waiting for them after school. It might take a year of standing next to French mothers for 10 minutes or so every day, until they speak to you, but then they start to loosen up. You can hasten the process, if you go gently. One American mother ended up with more French friends than she could handle by volunteering to teach English at the school.

Or you can join a rowing club on the Seine, or a yoga group or one that teaches fencing, or one that tours gardens on weekends. "My German class and tennis class have worked, too," says Julie Winn.

Whatever you would really like to do, do it and you'll meet French people of like spirit.

Steve Hawthorne, a lonely young Cornell graduate in Paris on an internship program, found that he could have fun with French people, if not make actual friendships, at the flea market – through lively bargaining during frequent visits.

But most Americans would like to meet the people they like the look of in their building or on their street.

There are two paths for this. One is to get a dog. Everyone on the block and in your building will adore your dog, coo to it and, finally, include you too in their attention.

If you can't bear dogs, then there is only one way to meet them. Be outrageous.

Some Americans decide to have a block party and invite everyone, all the people in their building, the grocer, the shoemaker, the pharmacist, the florist, the butcher and baker and the candlestick maker, if there is one. It's the first time all these people have been in the same room together. It's usually also the last. But not always!

The most successful of the outrageous Americans was undoubtedly Hal Landers, a movie producer fresh from Hollywood to an apartment on the very short and very prestigious rue Monsieur in the Seventh Arrondissement, otherwise known as Seventh Heaven. The street is named for the brother of Louis XIV (who was always addressed and spoken of simply as "Monsieur") which gives you an idea of the social level of its inhabitants.

Hal lived on the street for several months without ever getting even a responding nod from the French people he saw daily on the staircase and in the street. He complained about this to an American neighbor on the same street, Robert Pingeon.

"I nod to them politely every time I see them," Hal told Robert, "and say, *'Bonjour, monsieur, bonjour, madame'* and all I get is a frown. They seem to have huge hunting dogs on short leashes that drag them into sidewalk gallops every evening at 11:00, just when I'm having an evening stroll or coming back from a restaurant. I say, *'Bonsoir, monsieur'*, and even give their dogs a fast pat – and still they say nothing. What gives with these people?"

"Around here, knowing people for 20 years isn't long enough," said Robert. "Your families have to have known each other for seven generations. You might as well get used to the idea that they will never say hello and never, never ask you for dinner."

Hal's fighting spirit was piqued. "Oh, yeah?" he said.

"Yeah," said Robert. "They take those dogs out to their country places for the weekend, where they go on shoots with each other and only see their families, and then they come back to Paris, where they see other Seventh Arrondissement types, who are quiet and formal like themselves, which is not exactly your style, Hal. You're outgoing, spontaneous and, frankly, outrageous. You don't even speak French, though God knows you try," Robert added with a wink, teasing.

Hal's natural ebullience wasn't suppressed for long. "You know something, Robert?" he said. "I'll make you a bet that I can get asked to dinner by the first one I see on the street right now."

"Fine," said Robert. "$100 says you can't."

"You're on," said Hal, with a mischievous smile.

Spotting an elderly couple emerging from one of the elegant town houses down the street, Hal marched up to them and in a mixture of fractured French, English baby talk and frantic body language told them about his friend Robert's surely ridiculous assumption that he, Hal Landers, would never be invited to dinner by any of his neighbors. As the expression on their faces went from fright to shock to total bewilderment, he managed to convey that his conviction of Robert's error was so strong that he had backed it up with a $100 bet... how would next Tuesday suit them? Slowly they began to show signs of doubtful comprehension.

"Vous voulez être invité chez nous, c'est ça? Au dîner?" ("You want us to invite you to dinner?")

"Yes, oui, oui," said Hal. *"Je bring the dessert, yes, or le vino, vous comprez?"*

Hal won them over. His dinner the next Tuesday was only the first of many. In fact, before too long, he accumulated numerous French friends and became a sort of mascot for the local community. Every year thereafter he invited about 70 people, half of them French, for an American style

Christmas party, at which he donned a top hat and, standing on a chair with a baton in hand, led them in Christmas carols. Although tone deaf, he managed to inspire his formal, elegant French neighbors to belt out the lyrics of "When I saw Mommy Kissing Santa Claus."

In Conclusion...

I hope I've convinced you that France – and the French! – are different and wonderful – wonderfully different. Some Americans and other foreigners don't realize until they get back home that they're carrying France around inside them in a special way.

One of my friends, after moving back to the U.S., tried it for several years and then came back to France to live. "They talk, here. They're involved with each other. They care about *everything* and are never bored," she said.

One of Josephine Baker's hit songs is still a bestseller: *"J'ai Deux Amours: Mon Pays et Paris."* ("I Have Two Loves: My Country and Paris.")

Thomas Jefferson said in his *Autobiography* that his first choice of where to live would always be his own country, where he had his "tenderest recollections." But his second choice was France.

I know what Jefferson meant. I'm "home" when I'm back in the U.S. with my friends and extended family, in the special places of my childhood. At the same time, I'd be at home anywhere Ande was. The specialness of France comes over me with whiffs of familiar smells, and certain street scenes and conversations. I walk along and smell the fresh bread, and the daffodils, and the waffles. I pass the greengrocer and see his perfectly arranged oranges and apples. I watch a policeman helping an old lady cross the street, and then a pedestrian coming to the aid of a blind man whose white cane has bumped into a police-barrier across the sidewalk. A young man rushes up to me and asks if I know the neighborhood, where is there a florist or a baker? Well, which? I ask. "Either — so I can bring something to my *petite amie!*" An imperious old woman dressed in layers of what looks like black rags and a wild black hat demands to know where she will end up if she follows this street. Where, indeed?

Then again it comes when I sit in those sublime spaces, Notre Dame de Paris, and Chartres. Or when a French friend announces a judgment, about almost anything, from a meal she has just had or a political event to a play she has just seen. For instance, *"Ce n'est pas sérieux."* Things must be enjoyed, appraised, discussed and judged; nothing is too great or small to escape a verdict. And then, after the serious discussion, bring out the champagne – which is just as *sérieux!*

It happened again last night. I was invited to the television studio for Jean-Marie Cavada's *La Marche du Siècle.* The subject was serious mistakes (*fautes!*) committed by some French doctors and how to handle and prevent such situations. The studio audience of about 200 people was quiet as a mouse for 10 minutes before the broadcast went on the air. We spent a heartrending hour and a half listening to an adolescent condemned to a wheelchair after an operation, and to a woman who suffered for years from a mysterious and debilitating ailment finally discovered to be caused by a compress left in her body during an operation. We saw a child of seven virtually destroyed at birth and saw, and heard from his mother, what this had done to her life, and her husband's. A writer and a lawyer, doctors and hospital officials gave their views about what must be done and what must not be done about the situation. Filmed interviews with American doctors talking about the number of times they had been sued, and what this had done to their practice and their feelings for their patients, made it clear in which direction France should try not to go. It was wrenching, dignified, provocative, informative and eminently *sérieux.*

And then afterwards all 200 of us went upstairs, where smartly-uniformed waiters were waiting to serve us trays covered with delicious-looking little *amuse-gueules* (literally, "amuse-mouths" – tiny slices of bread decorated with a slice of smoked salmon or prosciutto) – and – champagne!

Robert Daley ended his delightful book, *Portraits of France*, like this:

"Once back in America, I wrote an article for the old *Saturday Evening Post* called 'I Hate Paris in the Springtime.' I got $1,500 for it, and I have never been able to remember it without shame. It mentioned the bad weather, the roaring inflation, the constant one-day strikes... It mentioned a good deal else too, but not what was most important: that Paris – the French – had taught me everything I know about how to live. "

The author then quotes Benjamin Franklin: "Everyman has two countries, his own and France." He adds: "Not every man, certainly. Some. One, anyway."

That makes several of us. I hope you will join us.